Music of Motherhood

Funded by the Government of Canada
Financé par la gouvernement du Canada

Demeter Press
140 Holland Street West
P. O. Box 13022
Bradford, ON L3Z 2Y5
Tel: (905) 775-9089
Email: info@demeterpress.org
Website: www.demeterpress.org

Demeter Press logo based on the sculpture "Demeter" by Maria-Luise
Bodirsky, www.keramik-atelier.bodirsky.de

Printed and Bound in Canada

Front cover photograph: James J. Kriegsmann Jr., "Martha Joy Rose and Zena
Rose Marpet."

Library and Archives Canada Cataloguing in Publication

        Music of motherhood : history, healing, and activism / co-editors,
M. Joy Rose, Lynda Ross, Jennifer Hartmann.

Includes bibliographical references.
ISBN 978-1-77258-134-8 (softcover)

        1. Mothers. 2. Motherhood. 3. Women musicians. 4. Music--Social
aspects. I. Rose, M. Joy, 1957-, editor II. Ross, Lynda Rachelle, 1950-,
editor III. Hartmann, Jennifer, 1984-, editor

HQ759.M97 2017   306.874'3   C2017-906871-7

MIX
Paper from
responsible sources
FSC® C004071

Music of Motherhood
History, Healing, and Activism

EDITED BY

M. Joy Rose, Lynda Ross, and
Jennifer Hartmann

DEMETER
DEMETER PRESS

To the women of Mamapalooza
and all moms who rock!

Table of Contents

Acknowledgements

We would like to thank all of the authors who contributed to this collection; Demeter Press; and each of the anonymous reviewers for their valuable input, work, and commitment to this project.

Overview

In the late nineties, a small group of women in America began writing songs and singing lyrics about what it was like to be a mother. This movement spread to four countries and twenty-five cities before becoming a major contributor to what we now know as mom rock. But in addition to creating branding around mom-made art, music throughout history has been a medium for healing, activism, as well as identity seeking. This book tackles each of these subjects from an academic as well as a personal perspective, and sheds light on not only the power of music, but its ability to transform.

1.
Introducing the Collection

JENNIFER HARTMANN, LYNDA ROSS, AND M. JOY ROSE

Here I am, in a cold, stark public hospital, waiting to meet the child—a child I've carried for forty weeks and four days, but for whom I've really waited twenty-six years. The waiting is not mere sitting around in boredom. It's punctuated by a crippling wave of physical and mental reactions to the profound event happening inside my body. Some reactions are expected, like the oddity of overwhelming excitement combined with blinding waves of pain. Some are not. A fear that I had not previously imagined almost immobilizes me at times; it sometimes feels as if my mind hurts me more than my body. When the pains began at four in the morning, I took a long shower, all the while reminding myself about my plans to deliver this baby as naturally as possible. I would stay home, labouring peacefully and naturally until my body told me it was time to go. Only then would I proceed to the hospital to deliver the baby in what I had considered the safest environment.

But is there such a thing as a peaceful labour? Can the word "natural" even cross a person's lips when her body feels as if it is being ripped from the inside out? At some indistinct point during the day, my plans for a natural birth began to seem ill-advised and naive to my labour-addled brain. My body had other plans, too, or so it would seem. I proceeded to the hospital as soon as my water unexpectedly broke in the early afternoon on my landlord's doorstep. Now, over twelve hours later, I'm only two centimetres dilated, and the fear and pain are starting to get the best of me. I had thought I'd be blissfully holding my newborn daughter by now!

What if I can't handle this? What if something horrible happens to this creature I've never met, but love so much? What if I'm going to be a terrible mother? At this moment, all I want to do is crawl into my own mother's lap and cry. I breathe and try to forget. My husband smiles through the fear in his own eyes and encourages me to take our thousandth walk up and down the maternity ward hall. We talk about mundane things as we walk. As the pain envelops my body again, my end of the conversation ceases. He begins to time my contraction on his iPhone. I relax my knees and vocalize gently, trying with all my mental might to embrace this immobilizing pressure as the mysterious, feminine force that would allow my baby to finally emerge from my body. With my arms thrust around my husband's neck, I recall the rhythmic, meditative music of the bellydance classes I had been taking throughout my pregnancy, and begin to circle my hips slowly; the circles become wider as the pain becomes more intense, then become figure eights. He mimics my motions; I don't know whether he does this to support me or to calm his own mind. The pain tries to seize me, but for now, it reaches a barely tolerable peak and settles. "Is it over?" he asks in a low voice. "Yes," I say, and he continues to hold me as he stops the timer. "One minute long, five minutes apart," he says. "That was a bad one." "I know," I say, "but it hurts less when I dance ... it's like...." I struggle for the appropriate words. "it's like I'm removing myself from the pain enough to let gravity do its work."
—Jennifer Hartmann

HARTMANN'S PERSONAL REFLECTIONS

The passage above is based on my labour experience with my oldest daughter, who came into the world in June 2011. The type of undulating hip movement I describe above had become almost instinctual for me; I had danced through my entire pregnancy, even performing in my studio recital when I was a mere six weeks from delivering. Bellydancing while pregnant and labouring was empowering; for the first time, I felt like my body *should* be on display because of the beautiful thing it was doing. The movement was natural, serene, focused. I found that the music to which I danced—wildly dissimilar from the music I perform as a classically trained violist and liturgical vocalist—encouraged me to engage a different part of my brain. It stirred up the desire, and even the *need*, to keep my knees unlocked and open, my torso and hips moving, and my muscles relaxed. Not only was this instinctual for me (as well as the several mothers I interviewed for this project), but birth professionals often encourage this type of motion and stance because they can promote the normal progression of labour and assist in pain relief. Bellydancing, specifically, is commonly referenced in both vernacular and official holistic birthing literature, and is used often as a means for mentally and physically preparing for birth.[1]

My experience as a mother who bellydanced through pregnancy and labour is only one facet of my own experiences relating to music and motherhood. As a professional musician, music manager, and ethnomusicologist, how motherhood relates to music has consistently struck me as something hugely important to everyday life, but has been left understudied. My own motherhood has been punctuated by musical interludes: I began by singing and dancing through pregnancy and childbirth. I have faced challenges with being a working musician during pregnancy and early motherhood—challenges that range from the very silly (trying to maintain a straight face during a symphony concert while my daughter rolls over in my belly during a soloist's cadenza) to the incredibly taxing (struggling to find last-minute substitutes for gigs when my children become ill). I have invented and sung lullabies for my children. I have taught them to sing in our church choir and to hold and attempt to play 1/16-size violins. I have spent my rehearsal breaks and concert intermissions nursing babies. I have played my instruments to my children's excited preschool classmates. I have spent many late nights scheduling interviews for my research and poring over detailed music scholarship, only to be interrupted by a distressed child crying for a comforting hug after being awoken by a nightmare.

THE MANY INTERSECTIONS OF MUSIC AND MOTHERHOOD

Hartmann's story and reflections, above, shows us how music is so much more than just a performance on a stage; it is shaded with aspects of music business and promotion, writing, research, personal narrative, therapy, and countless other things. As all of the authors in our collection show, motherhood has a unique ability to pull these nuances to the surface, and highlights music as an inextricable part of everyday life.

Christopher Small, author of an oft-cited musicology volume titled *Musicking: The Meanings of Performing and Listening*, describes "musicking" as follows:

> To music is to take part, in any capacity, in a musical performance, whether by performing, by listening, by rehearsing or practicing, by providing material for performances (what is called composing), or by dancing. We might at times even extend its meaning to what the person is doing who takes the tickets at the door or the hefty men who shift the piano and the drums or the roadies who set up the instruments and carry out the sound checks or the cleaners who clean up after everyone else has gone. They, too, are all contributing to the nature of the event that is a musical performance. (9)

Small does not see music as a strict act of performance, but rather as a conglomeration of music-related events happening in a particular place at a particular time. Small broadens the scope of "music" (in its verb form) to encompass everyone in a concert hall, from the concerto soloist to the custodian. He also includes every action, from the tuning of a violin to the conversations held between audience members during intermission. These people and acts inform how the performance is carried out, how it is perceived, and ultimately, how the particular genre of music will develop and grow. The concert hall is only one venue in which "musicking" occurs; it can occur anywhere a person somehow participates in an act of music. This, of course, includes spaces relevant to this collection—such as labour and delivery rooms, commercial spaces, schools, and the home. Since the connections between music and motherhood do not universally occur on a stage (though some certainly do), this book extends the definition of musicking in a similar manner. For example, in chapter ten of this collection,

Jackie Weissman depicts interviewees caring for their homes and families while preparing for shows, and presents these activities as part of that person's life as both a musician and a mother. Talking about this homebased ritual provides valuable insight into how a person can manage a busy schedule as a working musician while being a caregiver.

Meanwhile, *Music in Everyday Life* author Tia DeNora emphasizes the importance of studying the context in which music is couched rather than engaging in fruitless attempts to derive complete understanding from the music itself. In her work, she aims to "conceptualize musical forms as devices for the organization of experience, as referents for action, feeling and knowledge formulation" (24). DeNora suggests that music is a tool for expression and for recreating an experience or emotion. "For while music's semiotic force can be seen to be constructed in and through listener appropriations, a focus on how people interact with music should also be concerned with" (24). Therefore, the intricate meaning of a musical act is ascribed to not only the piece of music but the context and people surrounding it. The perspectives contained in this collection certainly illustrate this idea. They consider music as a job that must exist around caregiving responsibilities—a tool for healing and coping, an interactive space of social resistance, a site for social marginalization, and a stirrer of powerful memories. The meaning of the music and motherhood experience does not exist only in the music but also in the interaction between music and its context (in this case, motherhood).

As the co-editors dove into the many stories told by this collection's authors, it became clear that the relationship between music and motherhood is complicated and remarkably difficult to define. Therefore, while collecting and editing chapters for this book, we, as the editors, maintained flexible boundaries for the authors in terms of subject matter, authorial perspective, and writing style, which has resulted in a rich, nuanced collection from scholars, musicians, filmmakers, songwriters, educators, and human rights advocates. We feel this is reflective of the vast shades of both the musicking and mothering experiences that are possible. Our voices are different and our experiences come from many corners of the world, but the one thing we have in common is that we are or have worked with mothers who "music" in one way or another.

THE CHAPTERS IN THIS COLLECTION

Before proceeding further, we would like to make a few comments about the use of terminology in this edited collection. Andrea O'Reilly, in her book *21st Century Motherhood*, coined the term "motherhood studies" as a way to acknowledge and highlight scholarship on mothering as both a legitimate area of study and one distinctive from other studies. She talks about motherhood studies as grounded in "the theoretical tradition of maternal scholars" (1), a tradition dating back more than half a century. Adrienne Rich has made the critical distinction between the terms "motherhood" and "mothering" to challenge women and the academic discipline of women's studies to take on a new worldview. Specifically, Rich uses the term "motherhood" to refer to a male-defined, male-controlled, patriarchal institution necessarily oppressive to women. She contrasts this term with "mothering," which she identifies as female defined and focused on women's interests. In doing so, "mothering" is a potentially empowering experience for women. Feminists continue to issue "many other challenges that help us to understand the constructions of motherhood as well as how those constructions, past and present, affect women's experiences of mothering and, more generally, women's place in societies" (Ross 5). In other works, including *From Motherhood to Mothering or How Feminism Got Its Mother Back* and *Feminist Mothering*, O'Reilly reiterates the notion that mothering, freed from motherhood, can be a site of empowerment. In our introductory chapter, as well as in all the other chapters in this book, the terms mothering and motherhood are being used interchangeably. Regardless of which term is used, we and other authors contributing to this edited collection use both to imply mothering and motherhood as a positive, optimistic endeavour thought of in ways to promote women's empowerment.

As noted earlier, although mothering and music are complex and universal events, the structure and function of each show remarkable complexity and variability across social domains and different cultures (e.g., Egermann, et al.; Quinn and Mageo). Music's emotive qualities—including its potential to both express and evoke emotions—are commonly believed to underlay humans' attraction to and engagement with music (Pannese et al.). Beyond the enjoyment of listening, as well as levels of participating in the making of music, the therapeutic benefits "to improve health and wellbeing, and increase quality of life have been recognised in both Eastern and Western medical practices for millennia" (McCarthy 1). It is, therefore, not surprising that studies show how music has the power to positively influence not only feelings but also the health and mental and physical wellbeing of pregnant women and their newborn infants (Martin). The literature illustrates, for example, how emotional communication and the bond between mother and infant are enhanced through mutual engagement in play songs and lullabies (Creighton). Although motherhood and music are each recognized as important areas of research, the blending of the two topics is a recent innovation. The chapters in this collection bring together artists and scholars in conversations about the complex and often profound relationships existing between music and mothering. The discussions are varied and exciting. Several of the chapters revolve around the complexities of mothering while having a musical career; others look at what music offers to mothers and children; and some examine the ways in which music inspires social and political change. The topics explored in this collection are approached in different ways. Some are based in empirical research, others in personal experience. Whatever the focus or approach to a topic, each of the chapters in this collection moves the discussion of music and motherhood forward. Although there are overlapping themes in many of the contributions to this collection, we have divided the chapters into three discrete sections. The first interrogates topics surrounding the transmission and meaning of music in the lives of mothers and children; the second explores the therapeutic value of music in pregnancy and postpartum; and the final section looks at the ways in which motherhood combines with music as acts of rebellion.

The first section of this collection opens with Jillian Bracken's chapter, in which she reports on findings from her qualitative study looking at shared discourses in families that surround music and about the kinds of behaviours that shape talk and understandings about the value of music. Based on interviews with five families, the findings are discussed in terms of parents' and children's roles in shaping musical exposure. Bracken articulates these roles for mothers as "filter," "mediator," "companion," "guide," and "model"; and for the child as "heir," "originator," "companion," and "observer." She goes on to connect these various roles with the types of talk that surround mother-child interactions in relation to listening to music. This chapter presents a technical approach to "in-family processes facilitating the intergenerational transmission of information" that help us to understand the hows and whys of the transmission of musical values, and by extension, values, more generally.

Chapter three, by Sally Savage and Clare Hall, provides an insightful discussion about the relationship between "intensive mothering" and music in the lives of children. Savage and Hall open with an overview of intensive mothering theory and discuss the ways in which this ideology imposes on women's lives. Based on a qualitative study of thirteen mothers who had attended early childhood music classes for at least twelve months, the authors reflect on the narratives of "musical mothering" and the costs and benefits of intensive mothering through participation in children's musical lives. Savage and Hall conclude with a brief discussion of the ways in which intensive mothering ideology cannot account for the gains mothers garner through musical mothering.

Continuing with a discussion of the meaning of music in chapter four, Lydia Bringerud presents a compelling personal reflection upon her fieldwork experience when she did a collective ethnography of the St. John's Ukulele Club in St. John's, Newfoundland. Bringerud explores notions of vulnerability in her research journey through her experiences in the club. In the midst of her PhD studies in folklore, Bringerud takes us on a reflective journey exploring her relationships with her mother, also a musician, and with music.

The second section of the collection shifts its focus away from the transmission and meaning of music education toward an understanding of its therapeutic values in pregnancy and postpartum and its healing properties during important moments in the lives of mothers and children. In chapter five, Cara-Leigh Battaglia begins this analysis with a detailed discussion of music therapy as an important therapeutic device. Specifically, she focuses on the properties of music as a healing tool for children who have experienced trauma. Battaglia notes that although music has a positive influence on all children, it can have a particularly beneficial effect on those recovering from trauma. Scientific research, Battaglia suggests, has lagged behind mothers' existing knowledge of the healing properties of music. She calls for more attention to be paid by both mothers and professionals to this important phenomenon.

In chapter six, Amanda Mehl West continues the discussion by looking at the health benefits of music. She assesses the origins and affordances of singing during pregnancy, birth, and the postpartum period. West looks at the ways that singing can be used as a powerful tool to ease a woman's transition into motherhood. She discusses how the act of singing can bring physical calm, connection, and empowerment to both mother and child. West also talks about the ways singing can build trust and understanding between individuals. She draws on the work of music therapists, midwives, doulas, and educators as well as on the stories of women who have used singing successfully during their perinatal experience.

The second section closes with chapter seven, by Elena Skoko, which explores the understudied practice of singing during childbirth. She discusses the ways in which singing, or the modulated voice, is important for the wellbeing of all individuals, and expands upon the ways in which the maternal voice has the potential to affect all humans. Although Skoko's specific focus is on childbirth, as with other chapters in this section, she highlights the importance of understanding the ways singing can be a beneficial and powerful practice for all women.

The final section of this collection focuses on mothers as music makers and on mothers making music in response to untenable social and political contexts. It begins with Rachelle Louise Barlow's work in chapter eight, which offers readers an engaging historic perspective on the life of Welsh musician and mother Clara Novello. Barlow relates Clara's story but also highlights the marginalization of women in musical practice in Wales and how women have been overshadowed by men in this field. She brings Clara's historic contributions to the present day through discussion of a contemporary event created to celebrate Clara's musical achievements. However, by all accounts, her work was overshadowed by her son Ivor's achievements.

In chapter nine, David Eichert provides a timely exposé unpacking what it means to be a mother along the border between Mexico and the United States. He notes the ways in which both Mexican and Mexican American mothers continue to find themselves politically and socially marginalized in societies where violence and poverty are endemic. Eichert examines the music of *Las Cafeteras* and their messages about transborder Chicana motherhood and the ways in which the band and music challenge existing power dynamics of gender-based violence and economic limitations.

In chapter ten, Jackie Weissman interrogates the contradictions between stereotypical images of female rock stars and those portraying motherhood. Her chapter explores the issues encountered by three indie musicians in their efforts to balance musical careers with motherhood. Her chapter draws heavily on her research undertaken for the making of her recent documentary film, *Rock N Roll Mamas*. In challenging universal notions of ideal motherhood, Weissman provides detailed accounts of three mother musicians: up-and-coming hip hop MC, Ms. Suad; Kristin Hersh (Throwing Muses, 50FOOTWAVE, and a solo performer); and Zia McCabe (The Dandy Warhols).

In chapter eleven, Lori Walters-Kramer delves into the music of Michelle Shocked, a musician not normally highlighted as one particularly concerned with maternal issues. Walters-Kramer, however, shows the ways in which motherhood is in fact a topic that Shocked has embedded in her songs in much the same way that her music interrogates other issues related to social oppression. Walters-Kramer argues that through both sound and lyric, and through employing a feminist rhetorical style, Shocked questions cultural assumptions surrounding motherhood.

In chapter twelve, M. Joy Rose discusses the mom rock movement of the late twentieth and early twenty-first century, and traces the efforts of "mom rockers" to effect change. Rose argues that this newly formed community has contributed to changes in the way motherhood is viewed and enacted. She highlights the ways in which the movement empowered women and mothers, and provided them with a sense of connection. Through the lenses of autoethnography and interdisciplinarity, Rose explores not only the ways women's marginalization contributed to the adoption of electric music as a medium for expression, but also the relationships between activism and art within a consumerist society.

In chapter thirteen, the final chapter of the collection, Lynda Ross and Jennifer Hartmann reflect again on the contributions these chapters have made toward advancing the study of music and motherhood as well as toward politicizing the inequities facing mothers in Western societies. As a diverse volume of experience, history, scholarship, and practice, this collection serves to weave multiple threads between motherhood and the creation, performance, and consumption of music. The manner in which music and motherhood are woven together looks different depending on the perspective of the people involved. Because of the collection's broad scope and multitude of angles, we acknowledge the fact that this work is far from being comprehensive, but we trust that what is presented in this volume provides a healthy cross-section of the work being done at the intersection of music and motherhood.

ENDNOTE

[1] It is important to note that the author's experience (as an amateur bellydancer) deals with a remarkably general and Westernized genre of bellydance. This particular research project included interviews with women who were not professional dancers and did not consider themselves associated with any specific style of bellydance, such as American Tribal, Cabaret, or Egyptian. We recognize that there is much more research left to be done on this topic. However, such research is perhaps beyond the scope of this introduction.

WORKS CITED

Creighton, Alison. "Mother-Infant Musical Interaction and Emotional Communication: A Literature Review." *Australian Journal of Music Therapy*, vol. 22, 2011, pp. 37-56.

DeNora, Tia. *Music in Everyday Life.* Cambridge University

Press, 2000.

Egermann, Hauke, et al. "Music Induces Universal Emotion-Related Psychophysiological Responses: Comparing Canadian Listeners to Congolese Pygmies." *Frontiers in Psychology*, vol. 5, 2015, pp. 1-9.

Martin, Caroline. "A Narrative Literature Review of the Therapeutic Effects of Music upon Childbearing Women and Neonates." *Complementary Therapies in Clinical Practice*, vol. 20, 2014, pp. 262-67.

McCarthy, Sarah. "The Therapeutic Power of Music: A Literature Review." *JATMS*, vol. 22, no. 3, 2016, pp. 154-60.

O'Reilly, Andrea, editor. *Feminist Mothering*. State University of New York Press, 2008.

O'Reilly, Andrea, editor. *From Motherhood to Mothering or How Feminism Got Its Mother Back*. State University of New York Press, 2008.

O'Reilly, Andrea, editor. *21st Century Motherhood: Experience, Identity, Policy, Agency*. Columbia University Press, 2010.

Pannese, Alescia, et al. "Metaphor and Music Emotion: Ancient Views and Future Directions." *Consciousness and Cognition*, vol. 44, 2016, pp. 61-71.

Quinn, Naomi, and Jeannette Mageo, editors. *Attachment Reconsidered: Cultural Perspectives on a Western Theory*. Palgrave Macmillan, 2013.

Rich, Adrienne. "Motherhood in Bondage." *On Lies, Secrets and Silence*, editor by Adrienne Rich, W.W. Norton & Company, 1976/1979, pp. 195-97.

Ross, Lynda. *Interrogating Motherhood*. Athabasca University Press, 2016.

Small, Christopher. *Musicking: The Meanings of Performing and Listening*. Wesleyan University Press, 1998.

2.
A Discussion of Mothers' and Children's Roles in the Transmission of Music Listenership Values in Families

JILLIAN BRACKEN

EXPLORING LISTENING ROLES WITHIN FAMILIES

This chapter reports findings from a qualitative, descriptive case study that engaged five families in Miami-Dade County (Miami, FL). Through Internet-facilitated interviews and e-journals, families responded to questions about the music present in their family and the existence of any guidelines governing music listening. The methodological perspective of this descriptive case study examined these five different families in real-life contexts.[1] Kathryn Roulston explains how "the aim of descriptive studies is detailed accounts of events, experiences, activities; new perspectives on familiar phenomena; participants' views of processes, groups, settings; and subjective accounts of phenomena" (156). This study aims to provide one such detailed account, striving to comprehend ways in which families come to establish and share music listening values and guidelines. The goal of the study was to explore the nature of shared discourse within participating families and to examine how this environment created a collective body of talk around music that shaped family members' understandings of music's value. The findings of this study suggest that family members occupy a variety of roles through which they shape and influence one another's music listening. This chapter focuses specifically on roles filled by mothers and children within the study's five case study families.

An exploration of listening roles within families addresses a need for a descriptive level of analysis as identified by ter Bogt and

13

colleagues. Although their quantitative, questionnaire-based study of music listening shared between children and parents found that "music socialization can be proposed as a within-family mechanism for the intergenerational transfer of taste" (313), ter Bogt and colleagues could not identify any specific processes by which intergenerational similarities are established. Their study, which focused on observed similarities in reported genre preferences between children and their parents, reveals the following:

> It is the parents who provide the first musical climate in their households, and this climate is the sum of the fathers' and mothers' tastes. Parents may actively or unconsciously model the tastes of their children; hence, links may be present between parental preferences for particular music styles that were formed earlier in their lives and their children's current preferences for similar types of music. (302)

The question emerging in response to this research is how does intergenerational transmission actually occur in the family, and what specific roles filled by family members facilitate transmission. The study from which this chapter's research is excerpted identifies key discourse processes that facilitate transmission, responding to ter Bogt and colleagues call for future research to "explore the contextualized within-family dynamics that produce such ... pattern[s]" (316).

MEET THE FAMILIES

Each case study family included at least one parent participant and at least one child participant; one of the participating families included two children. The five families are identified throughout this chapter using pseudonyms.

The Alonzo Family (Pamela and Alicia)

The Alonzo family consisted of a mother, Pamela, and daughter, Alicia. Alicia was eleven years old and in grade five. Pamela worked as a coordinator of a community-based program.

The Cruz Family (Lisa and Deborah)

The Cruz family consisted of two daughters and a mother, Lisa. The youngest daughter (age three) did not participate. Lisa's eldest daughter Deborah participated in the study; she was eight years old and in grade two. Lisa worked as an arts administrator.

The Morales Family (Nancy and Liam)

The Morales family consisted of a mother, Nancy, her husband, and two children (a son, Liam, and a fourteen-month-old daughter). Nancy and Liam were the two members who participated in the study. Liam was nine years old and in grade three. Nancy worked in community outreach.

The Santiago Family (Brandy and Laura)

The Santiago family consisted of a mother, Brandy, her husband, and three daughters (four years old, twenty-two months old, and Laura, who was a six-year-old kindergartener). Brandy and Laura participated in the study. Brandy was a former librarian who now stayed at home fulltime with her three daughters.

The West Family (Amy, Kevin, and Kyle)

The West family consisted of a mother, Amy, her husband, and their two sons: Kevin (eleven) and Kyle (thirteen). Amy, Kevin, and Kyle were the only members to participate in the study. Kevin was in grade five; Kyle was in grade seven. Amy worked as a teacher.

The mothers who participated in the study were fairly homogeneous. All were between the ages of thirty and thirty-nine years of age, and all had at least a four-year college or university degree. Net household income across all five families was fairly similar when adjusted for household size—all were middle class.[2] Differences emerged in race, religion, and marital status. The six children participating in the study ranged in age from six to thirteen years old, and included both males and females.

PARENT ROLES

Case study family members described ways in which they fill many

15

different roles that shape their musical exposures and interactions. The following section situates the present discussion in the literature about parental roles, and outlines some of the specific roles case study mothers and children reported filling.

In her study of children's musical landscapes, Patricia Campbell observes that "direct or indirect involvement in music by either parent ... steered these children to many of their musical reckonings" (211). In her observations, she finds that even if the parents were not musical, by virtue of their role in the family, they greatly influenced how their children interacted with and came to value music. In a study of shared family music listening preferences, ter Bogt and colleagues share the following:

> Parents may model their tastes simply by playing music in the environment they share with their children or they may more actively persuade their children of the value of music by listening or singing together, taking them to concerts, or encouraging them to play an instrument. For most people, music is an important medium and it [is] reasonable to assume that parents want to share their enthusiasm for certain artists, bands or composers with their children, resulting in intergenerational similarities. (315)

Similarly, Jane Davidson and Sophia Borthwick show that parents with no musical backgrounds shape their children's musical identities as the children learn to play an instrument: "[the] musical beliefs and experiences of the parents ... shape the way in which the subsequent generation experience and value music for themselves within the family" (76). The data from the current study appear to confirm this previous research.

A large body of research exists on "musical parenting" (Bergeson and Trehub; Custodero and Johnson-Green; Davidson and Borthwick; Ilari; Ilari et al.; Malloch; Papoušek; Parncutt; Trevarthen; Young). In one such study, Lori Custodero and Elissa Johnson-Green observe that the "family context may provide a nurturing environment for a child's innate inclination toward music; however, there are many questions about the role of parents' musical experience in raising their children" (103). Although their study focuses on both music making and music listening exposures in families with very small children (four- to six-months old), their territory of inquiry brings forward questions similar to those posed by this study of music listening values.

The family's transmission of values, which ultimately influences individual identities within the family, is directly shaped by the relationships shared between family members. Perhaps the most impactful relationship within the family is shared between parent and child. In their study of the transmission of musical tastes in Israeli families, Tally Katz-Gerro et al. find that "musical tastes are shaped by parents' rather than respondents' social position" (163). Relationships position family members in relation to one another and involve individuals filling different roles. Of particular interest to the present study is the connection between relational roles and discourse. Roles are ultimately related to discourse—our behaviours shape and are shaped by the way we interact with others. Michael Stubbs observes that "'roles' have to be acted out in social interaction" (8). He goes on to state that "it is principally through conversational interaction, the give-and-take of every-day multi-party discourse, that social 'roles' are recognized and sustained" (8). A role is accompanied by (or sometimes creates) a social orientation providing guidance for interaction. Particular roles, such as that of "parent," can be accompanied by a language register, which is a distinct body of language used by common groups of individuals. In filling the role of "parent," individuals speak a certain way helping to define what it means to be and act as a parent.

The ensuing discussion weaves together sociolinguistic analysis and descriptive excerpts shared by case study participants; it illustrates several ways in which talk and action can work in tandem to create specific categories of discourse with corresponding behaviours. Together discourse and behaviours create social orientations (or roles). Furthermore, analysis speaks to the pivotal, influential place of mothers and the ways in which their actions and words can shape their children's music values. In the case of the present study, it is evident that mother roles happen in relation to child roles (and vice versa), even if not a lot of data to exhaustively detail child roles was captured.[3]

MOTHER AND CHILD LISTENERSHIP ROLES EXPLAINED

Five mother roles are observed in the study: filter, mediator, companion, guide, and model. Four of the five roles are active; the fifth role—model—speaks to the implied, passive role mothers fill by virtue of simply being a parent. Four children roles are also presented here: heir, originator, companion, and observer. These roles are discussed as counterparts to corresponding mother roles.

It should be noted that although the original intent of this study was not to focus exclusively on mothers, the primacy of mothers' involvement in the case study families aligns with trends found in existing literature (Trehub et al.; Fuligni and Brooks-Gunn). Literature looking at the impact of parents' language on children offers further support. Referencing an enormous body of research on parents' language with young children, Catherine Tamis-Le-Monda and Lisa Baumwell find that mothers factor prominently in such studies "because mothers are overwhelmingly the primary caregivers in families" and, citing the work of Janellen Huttenlocher et al., they hypothesize that mothers are "the main providers of verbal input to children" (414).

Table 1 below lists the mother and child roles, identifies the individual in the family who initiates talk or introduces music that results in the mother filling a particular role, describes the role as active or passive, and clarifies who is in control when it comes to introducing music or initiating talk about music. All of these roles involve both listening to and talking about music.

Case study mothers fill different roles in response to a situation or in anticipation of a situation (as is the case with the aforementioned listening guidelines, which parents sometimes preemptively implement). Filter, mediator, and guide represent active processes where the mother takes an active role introducing or talking about music, to which the child responds. The mother role of companion also represents an active process, but the child (acting as guide) introduces or initiates talk about music. The final mother role—model—is a passive, implied role assumed by the mother just by virtue of the parent-child relationship. These roles are not as clearly demarcated as the above table and following discussion may suggest. Family members may switch between roles as a situation

Table 1: Listenership Roles Explained

Mother Role	Child Role	Who Initiates Talk or Music Exposure	Who's in Control	Passive or Active Process
Filter	*Heir**	Both Child and Parent	Parent (in establishing filter); child can also be seen as in control if they accept, understand filtration	Active
Mediator	*Originator*	Child, external source	Negotiated; can fluctuate during mediation	Active
Companion	*Originator*	Child	Child	Active
Guide	*Companion*	Parent	Parent	Active
Model	*Observer*	Parent	Not applicable	Passive

Heir is used here a common gender noun. It is used to describe and include both male and female children.

changes or a new musical exposure is introduced.

Discourse within the family around music listening involves different kinds of talk: expressive (about feeling), directive (influencing behaviour), referential (conveying information), and metalinguistic (focusing on specific words). When mothers occupy roles, the roles are defined by both their actions and the types of talk they put forward. These types of talk are listed below in Table 2.

This next section further examines the mother and children roles outlined above by connecting them to interview and journal excerpts offered by the case study families. These roles are filled by different mothers at different times, but not all of the participating case study mothers talked about all identified roles.

Table 2: Connecting Mother Roles with Types of Talk

Mother Role	Types of Talk Involve	Description of Talk
Filter	Referential, Metalinguistic	Convey information, based on specific words and guidelines, that limit music listening.
Mediator	Expressive, Referential, Metalinguistic	Use feelings and discourse to influence behaviour and convey information.
Companion	Expressive that may become Directive	Share listening experiences that may involve discussing feelings, which can influence values of music.
Guide	Directive, Referential	Purposeful exposures, some of which are accompanied by discourse intended to influence behaviour, convey information.
Model	Passive Role	Passive Role

FILTER (MOTHER), HEIR (CHILD)

In many situations, case study mothers reported acting as a gateway to their children's musical experience. The idea of mother as filter was introduced by Lisa Cruz in her family's first interview:

> *I have to work as a filter. Nowadays, just because it is considered a "cool" song doesn't mean that my daughters will listen to it. For example, Gangnam Style. Just because everyone was dancing.... There are plenty of songs that have a similar beat as Gangnam Style but doesn't have anything to do with, uh, an artist saying a bad word. It doesn't necessarily have to be a cool song.*

Lisa described her role as limiting some music while allowing other kinds. In this role, the mother places limitations on some musical listening—letting certain things pass through—and enforces guidelines restricting some music. Filtering involves both referential and metalinguistic talk through which mothers convey information and guidelines that may limit music listening. Acting as a filter is about establishing guidelines (the size of the filter's holes), which determine what goes through and what impurities are suspended or blocked. How porous the filter is varies from parent to parent and from situation to situation. Differently sized holes in the filter represent differently sized restrictions around the suggestive topics and specific bad words.

Amy West talked about her role as a filter when downloading music for her sons. She discussed how it allows her to make sure she gets the clean versions of songs—those that do not violate her guidelines: "When I download the music for them, I try to get the clean versions. But like, we went to a party and his friends, [Kyle's] friends, they played the dirty versions and I was like, 'Come on! You're going to play the dirty versions?' And then that song has so many curse words that you can't even hear the beat, it was like 'beep, beep,' it doesn't make sense." Filtering works together with the next role to be discussed: mediator. Filtering establishes rules before the fact; mediating is about responding to situations—the process of changing the size of a filter's holes. Although these roles seem quite similar, they are subtly (but importantly) different.

In response to the mother acting as filter, a child acts as an heir. Their listening environment is often preemptively shaped and sometimes limited by the enforcement of music listening guidelines. In the filter-heir dyad, mothers tend to exercise more active control of a listening exposure, and the child is left to inherit the information and music allowed to pass through the parent-created filter.

MEDIATOR (MOTHER), ORIGINATORS (CHILD)

Case study mothers acknowledged in many different ways how they cannot control the entirety of their children's music listening. As a mediator, mothers respond to what permeates or bypasses their filters. Mediation often involves mothers responding to unexpected exposures and music (often unknown to the mother) to which their children have been exposed outside of the family unit. The mother acts as an intervening agent, engages different situations, and responds to music whenever challenges arise. As mediators, mothers engage in expressive, referential, and metalinguistic talk. Oftentimes, mothers talk about how a piece of music "makes them feel" as a way to explain why a restriction is in place. Mediation involves offering clarifying information as part of a responsive negotiation.

Filter and mediator are similar roles but have subtle and important differences. As a filter, a mother sets guidelines in anticipation of exposure. As a mediator, the mother responds to what passes through or challenges an established filter or guideline. The difference between these two roles is the time of implementation. Filters are established prior to an event—in anticipation of an event—whereas mediation happens in response to an exposure and can result in renegotiation or redesign of the filter. The relationship is actually a cyclical one in which mediation results in filtration, as captured in Figure 1.

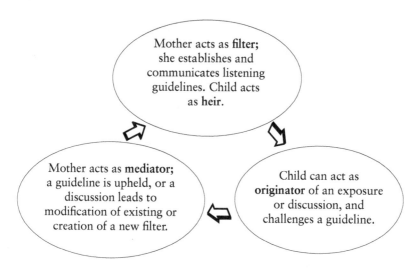

Figure 1: Illustrating the Interplay of Filter and Mediator.

Mediation can be necessary if exposure to an unexpected or unknown song occurs (by way of the radio, for example) while the mother and child are together. The mother is put in a position to mediate the experience for and/or with the child through the lens of their relationship. Changing radio stations is a particular type of active mediation often accompanied by discourse. Instead of restricting a music exposure, mothers put themselves in a position to mediate content by changing the station if a song comes on that violates one of their guidelines. Lisa Cruz described how her process of radio mediation involves both changing the station and conversation:

> *Well, I try to convince them, but it is hard because "my best friend listens to this music" or "my neighbour listens to this music, how come I'm not allowed to?" So basically I speak to them and I tell them exactly why I think it's bad. And when I listen to the radio, I try to change it without them noticing. Since they don't notice, I can literally change it to another station. But when they notice, I tell them that I don't think it's a cool song.*

In this excerpt, Lisa fills the role of not only mediator but also filter. Lisa explained her mediation using expressive language intended to persuade her children. As was the case in this example, the roles of filter and mediator often work in tandem because filtration and mediation are part of a cyclical process through which mediation can result in the establishment of a filter. The situational enforcement is achieved through mediation, resulting in the creation and implementation of filters.

The child role identified in response to parental mediation is that of originator. A child can originate or instigate a musical exposure or discussion about music that requires mediation on the part of the parent. Children, however, are not the only originators of content that may require parental mediation. External music exposures, such as the radio, can also fill the role of originator.

COMPANION (MOTHER), ORIGINATOR (CHILD)

In the role of companion, the mother participates with the child in a child-instigated listening experience or in a music-related discussion. In this interaction, the mother offers support and encouragement, often acting as audience. The mother fills the role of companion when a listening exposure or discussion does not violate or challenge an established guideline, which would then require mediation in response. Companionship involves both listening to music and talking about music, and often puts mothers in a role in which they learn something from their child and/or are exposed to certain music for the first time. Parental talk in this role is directive and referential; the focus is often on conveying information and sometimes on influencing behaviour. In this role, the mother is in a position to accompany the child's discovery and/or sharing of new musical content. In addition to acting as a companion in these situations, the mother may also end up filling the role of mediator should the content challenge any listenership guidelines. The following interaction, taken from the Alonzo family's first interview, is an example of a mother (Pamela Alonzo) filling a companion role:

Alicia: *Like, if I really like a song ... if I really want to hear it then I go on YouTube and hear the song and watch the video. Like "Happy."*

Pamela: *I hadn't heard that one. And that one, you called me over to watch it together.*

Alicia led her mother through a listening experience that Alicia herself initiated. She acted as the guide for this shared experience, and her mother, Pamela, acted as her companion.

The role of companion is one that seems to be more available to mothers when their children are older. Several case study mothers reflected on how the roles they filled would change as their children aged, allowing them to modify or remove listening guidelines. The absence of guidelines would allow them to fill the companion role more often, lessening the time spent actively filtering or mediating. Mothers Laura Santiago and Lisa Cruz both discussed this outlook in several journal entries, and commented on how age played a major part in the roles they filled in their children's lives. Lisa reflected on her relationship with her daughter: "as Deborah grows, and with my guidance, she will be able to make her own judgment calls."

Age transforms not just the child but the relationship between the mother and child and the role the mother plays in guiding music listening, among many other things.

The child role often filled in response to mothers acting as companion is that of originator—the same role discussed as bringing about a mediation response from mothers. Children initiate listening experiences or music-related discussions that elicit parental response. If the child-instigated listening experience or discussion does not violate or challenge an established guideline, then the mother often responds as companion. If the exposure or discussion challenges an established guideline, then the mother fills the role of mediator. In both of these situations, the child acts as originator.

GUIDE (MOTHER), COMPANION (CHILD)

Mothers can also guide their children's listening with directive and referential talk. When acting as a guide, mothers facilitate direct, purposive listening or guide discussion in response to a particular musical exposure or topic. In terms of the nature of the response when acting as a guide, a mother is not focusing on implementing a guideline. Rather, these exposures are more focused on transmitting cultural and/or religious beliefs, family memories, and family values. When acting as a guide, the mother is in control and offers music exposures and discourses that share their experiences, which are often intended to influence and persuade. When the mother acts as a guide, listening and talking about music take place. This is an active process, contrasted with mother as model (the last role to be discussed), which is a passive role.

Nancy Morales commented that sharing music in her family has, at times, been done with a specific goal in mind. She described acting as a guide for her son Liam by sharing what she called "decent" music with him: "We started, like, brainwashing him. We told him about the Beastie Boys. And, uh, and then I overheard him talking to a friend about the Beastie Boys. And it made me feel so proud. Something decent." Nancy described exposing her son to music that she liked and valued. In her role as guide, she purposefully played certain music for Liam with the hopes that he, too, would come to like it as much as she did.

Pamela Alonzo also commented on sharing songs with her daughter Alicia, including searching for her old favorites on the Internet: "So I think that I've shared songs from when I was little, right? And we looked up, um, some of my favorite songs from when I was little online." Pamela described engaging her daughter Alicia in music listening and dialogue whereby she purposefully exposed her to music that held meaning in Pamela's childhood. The Alonzo family spoke, at length, in their journals about songs that Alicia had come to appreciate through ongoing instances of mother-guided musical experiences.

When the mother acts as guide, the child fills the role of companion. This parallels the earlier discussion in which the mother acts as companion to child-instigated discussion and music listening, but the roles are reversed.

MODEL (MOTHER), OBSERVER (CHILD)

Whereas companion is an active role filled by the mother, being a model is a role that all mothers fill simply by having a child and cohabitating with that child. Cohabitation puts mothers under almost constant scrutiny—children see (and hear) how their mothers act, what they do, and how they talk about music and what music they choose to listen to. Mothers model ideas and behaviour, sometimes without even knowing. Just by virtue of the relationship between child and mother, and the common living situation they share, ideas are influenced.

In response to mothers as models, children act as observers. Again, by virtue of the shared living situation and relationship, children are witness to mother actions, conversations, and discussion about the music they like and listen to. Even if they are not actively processing what they witness, children are impacted by that which they observe.

In summary, this study of music listening in five families addressed a gap in the existing literature regarding information around specific in-family processes facilitating the intergenerational transmission of information. The study offered a rich description of ways in which five families engaged with music, and how they formed opinions of what music they listen to, value, and subsequently pass between generations. This chapter has demonstrated how the family serves to socialize and enculturate its members; through shared discourse and experiences, members learn different roles that facilitate interaction. These interactions are first modelled in the family unit by way of listenership role dyads discussed earlier in this chapter. Parents, filling the roles of filter, mediator, companion, guide, and model, and children, filling the roles of heir, originator, companion, and observer, take on different social orientations. Discourse is shaped by and through roles that determine discourse contents and types of interaction.

Although it was not an initial goal of this project, this study did reveal more information about parents, specifically mothers, than it did about children. This is not to say that the information presented about mothers is not important; rather, this limitation illuminates the need for more balanced research focusing equally on mothers and children, or perhaps future research responding to the present study with a similar examination of only children. This study's design and analysis may, unintentionally, be to blame for the unbalanced data gathered by the present study. The way families responded to the study's design—with mothers talking more in interviews and being the ones who administered the journal prompts and typed up responses—resulted in mothers offering more feedback than their children.

The lack of child responses is a limitation of the present findings; the few child-centric findings should be built upon by future research. The lack of child responses may be as a result of the power dynamics characterizing the family talk environment. In addition to this, children's responses to discussed music listening guidelines were mostly positive. A question remains as to whether or not children felt comfortable speaking out if they did not agree with the guidelines. The authority that parents yield, which allows them to enforce guidelines and influence their children's opinions, may also restrict children's ability to voice their opinions. This is not to say that parents are knowingly or purposefully oppressing their children; rather, this may have illuminated a shortcoming of this type of study or, even more specifically, the design of this particular study.

Notwithstanding limitations noted above, in some ways, this

examination of roles facilitating the transmission of music value has provided evidence to suggest that discourse around music as reported by the five case studies is also a way in which families transmit more general family values. Music listening and talk about music are vital components of each family's music value script—the body of information established in the family and, through exposures and discourse, shared within families. It serves as a blueprint or touchstone for evaluating and experiencing music, and provides information about what roles individuals can take when it comes to making sense of music listening exposures. But listening and talking about music also provide information about other family values, relationship, modes of conduct, and roles that may transfer or influence other areas of families' lives. Examining how some of the findings in the present study may apply to other areas of families' lives in future research could provide valuable insights on many different topics.

ENDNOTES

[1]Kathryn Roulston explains how "the aim of descriptive studies is detailed accounts of events, experiences, activities; new perspectives on familiar phenomena; participants' views of processes, groups, settings; and subjective accounts of phenomena" (156). A descriptive case study is one specific type of descriptive approach. It is a "comprehensive research strategy" that guided and defined data collection and overall study design (Yin 14).

[2]The five families participating in the study are representative of a similar socioeconomic status or class—they are all members of the middle class, with the Santiago family belonging more specifically to the upper middle class. This is indicated by similar household incomes and mothers' education level. The case study families represent a fairly homogenous group with similar incomes and education. Four of the mothers work outside of the home; the fifth mother (from the Santiago family) currently stays at home with her young children but has a college education; previous to having her children, she worked outside of the home. Membership in the American middle class is usually indicated by at least a four-year college education, homeownership, and moderate economic secu-

rity, where members are employed but employment is necessary to pay bills (Leondar-Wright). Middle-class people differ in terms of culture, political beliefs, values, and race, but are, for the most part, white. Upper-middle-class people tend to possess more wealth usually from higher incomes, which allows them more luxuries and travel opportunities than middle-class families.

[3]Limited literature exists that examines roles children take in family discourse (see, for example, Barron-Hauwaert; Gillen; Hoff; Hoff-Ginsberg; Hoff and Naigles; King and Fogle; King et al.; Messaris; Yamamoto). The limited relevant literature and limited data gathered in the study speak to the need for more research on children's roles in music listening environments, including that of the family.

WORKS CITED

Barron-Hauwaert, Suzanne. *Language Strategies for Bilingual Families: The One-Parent-One-Language Approach*. Multilingual Matters, 2004.

Bergeson, Tonya R., and Sandra E. Trehub. "Mothers' Singing to Infants and Preschool Children." *Infant Behavior & Development*, vol. 22, no. 1, 1999, pp. 51-64.

Campbell, Patricia S. *Songs in Their Heads: Music and Its Meaning in Children's Lives*. Oxford, 2010.

Custodero, Lori A., and Elissa A. Johnson-Green. "Passing the Cultural Torch: Musical Experience and Musical Parenting of Infants." *Journal of Research in Music Education*, vol. 51, no. 2, 2003, pp. 102-14.

Davidson, Jane W., and Sophia J. Borthwick. "Family Dynamics and Family Scripts: A Case Study of Musical Development." *Psychology of Music*, vol. 30, no. 1, 2002, pp. 121-36.

Fuligni, Allison S., and Jeanne Brooks-Gunn. "Meeting the Challenge of New Parenthood: Responsibilities, Advice, and Perceptions." *Child Rearing in America: Challenges Facing Parents with Young Children*, edited by Neal Halfon et al., Cambridge University Press, 2000, pp. 83-116.

Gillen, Julia. *The Language of Children*. Routledge, 2003.

Hoff, Erika. "The Specificity of Environmental Influence: Socioeconomic Status Affects Early Vocabulary Development via Maternal Speech." *Child Development*, vol. 74, no. 5, 2003, pp. 1368-78.

Hoff-Ginsberg, Erika. "The Relation of Birth Order and Socioeconomic Status to Children's Language Experience and Language Development." *Applied Psycholinguistics*, vol. 19, no. 4, 1998, pp. 603-29.

Hoff, Erika, and Letitia Naigles. "How Children Use Input in Acquiring a Lexicon." *Child Development*, vol. 73, 2002, pp. 418-33.

Huttenlocher, Janellen, et al. "The Varieties of Speech to Young Children." *Developmental Psychology*, vol. 45, 2007, pp. 1062-83.

Ilari, Beatriz. "On Musical Parenting of Young Children: Musical beliefs and Behaviors of Mothers and Infants." *Early Child Development and Care*, vol. 175, no. 7, 2005, pp. 647-60.

Ilari, Beatriz, et al. "Between Interactions and Commodities: Musical Parenting of Infants and Toddlers in Brazil." *Music Education Research*, vol. 13, no. 1, 2011, pp. 51-67.

Katz-Gerro, Tally, et al. "Class, Status, and the Intergenerational Transmission of Musical Tastes in Israel." *Poetics*, vol. 35, 2007, pp. 152-67.

King, Kendall A., and Lyn W. Fogle. "Family Language Policy and Bilingual Parenting." *Language* Teaching, vol. 46, no. 2, 2013, pp. 172-194.

King, Kendall A., et al. "Family Language Policy." *Language and Linguistics Compass*, vol. 2, no. 5, 2008, pp. 907-22.

Leondar-Wright, Betsy. *Class Matters*. New Society Publishers, 2014.

Malloch, Stephen N. "Mothers and Infants and Communicative Musicality." *Musicæ Scientiæ*, vol. 3, no. 1, 2000, pp. 29-57.

Messaris, Paul. "Family Conversations about Television." *Journal of Family Issues*, vol. 4, no. 2, 1983, pp. 293-308.

Papoušek, Mechthild. "Intuitive Parenting: A Hidden Source of Musical Stimulation in Infancy." *Musical Beginnings: Origins and Development of Musical Competence*, edited by Irene Delige and John Sloboda, Oxford University Press, 1996, pp. 88-112.

Parncutt, Richard. "Parent and Infant Conditioning, the Mother Schema, and the Origins of Music and Religion." *Musicæ Scientiæ*, vol. 13, no. 2, 2009, pp. 119-50.

Roulston, Kathryn. "Mapping the Possibilities of Qualitative Research in Music Education: A Primer." *Music Education Research*, vol. 8, no. 2, 2006, pp. 153-73.

Stubbs, Michael. *Discourse Analysis: The Sociolinguistic Analysis of Natural Language.* The University of Chicago Press, 1983.

Tamis-LeMonda, Catherine S., and Lisa Baumwell. "Parent-Child Conversations during Play." *First Language*, vol. 32, no. 4, 2012, pp. 413-38.

ter Bogt, Tom F.M., et al. "Intergenerational Continuity of Taste: Parental and Adolescent Music Preferences." *Social Forces*, vol. 90, no. 1, 2011, pp. 297-320.

Trehub, Sandra E., et al. "Parents' Sung Performances for Infants." *Canadian Journal of Experimental Psychology*, vol. 51, no. 4, 1997, pp. 385-96.

Trevarthen, Colwyn. "The Musical Art of Infant Conversation: Narrating in the Time of Sympathetic Experience, Without Rational Interpretation, Before Words." *Musicæ Scientiæ*, vol. 12, no. 1, 2008, pp. 15-46.

Yamamoto, Masayo. *Bilingual Education and Bilingualism: A Japanese-English Sociolinguistic Study.* Multilingual Matters, 2001.

Yin, Richard K. *Applications of Case Study Research.* 2nd ed. SAGE, 2003.

Young, Susan. "Lullaby Light Shows: Everyday Musical Experience among Under-Two-Year-Olds." *International Journal of Music Education*, vol. 26, no. 1, 2008, pp. 33-46.

3.
Thinking About and Beyond the Cultural Contradictions of Motherhood Through Musical Mothering

SALLY SAVAGE AND CLARE HALL

In this chapter, we discuss intensive mothering and concerted cultivation in relation to mothers' music practices. Based on a small-scale study of a group of Australian mothers and their experiences with their children's formal early music education, we question how and why mothers participate in music with their young children. Early childhood studies have well documented the benefits of young children learning music (McPherson), and sociology has long discussed the intensive labour mothers employ to mobilize their children's social positioning through education (Reay, *Class Work*). But few studies have investigated the particular contributions and experiences of mothers regarding their children's musical lives. This study contributes to growing critical discussions of intensive mothering (Ennis) by bringing into focus mothering and music. We argue that the forms of pedagogy performed by these musical mothers reinforce and complicate the cultural contradiction of intensive mothering.

INTENSIVE MOTHERING THROUGH MUSIC

Researchers have paid greater attention to intensive mothering practices in the past twenty years. The term "intensive mothering," first coined by Sharon Hays, describes the kind of mothering that is "child-centred, expert-guided, emotionally absorbing, labour intensive, and financially expensive" (8). Expanding on this conception, Deborah Golden and Lauren Erdreich explain that "Intensive mothering with its cultural definitions of care and the labour it requires in regards to fostering children's development and education has evolved as a dominant cultural model for women in western middle-class families" (266). Intensive mothering reveals itself in a belief in "'nurture over nature' and an understanding that each decision made would impact on their child in some way, thus raising the pressure to make the right choices" (Shirani et al. 29). Although this pressure is often seen to be detrimental to mothers' wellbeing—creating anxiety and stress for mothers and their families (Golden and Erdreich; Hays; Lareau; Reay, *Class Work*)—this form of mothering has become normative among those seeking mobility in neoliberal societies (Vincent and Maxwell). Neoliberal ideology, which lauds competitive individualism (Reay, "Class Acts"), feeds the deficit paradigm of intensive mothering, and women are deemed inadequate unless they adopt this approach. The "professionalization of parenting" (Holloway and Pimlott-Wilson 94; Perrier 657) makes mothers approach mothering like a project management task in which they are responsible for their children's outcomes. This style of mothering dovetails neatly into neoliberal ideology that diminishes governments' responsibility to provide equitable access to society's resources. Music is an important cultural resource, and the authors' wider interest in musical mothering is to investigate how music education and the ways mothers operate within this field can be "a mechanism through which social inequality is maintained and reproduced" (Bennett et al. 131).

The core work of intensive mothering is the sacrifice of women's own desires whereby the investment in their children's accomplishments becomes central to mothers' aspirations and sense of self; therefore, "the focus is not exactly on the child anymore, but rather on the parenting process" (Paltineau 134). Hays has identified the contradiction between mothers' selfless nurturing and self-interest in "creating a thriving child who is distinguished as unique, more fundamentally, over the many long years to adulthood, set to achieve a similar or better place in the social hierarchy compared with his parents" (Milkie and Warner 68). This ideology does not believe that children may thrive on their own accord; hence, children are often involved in a myriad of organized experiences out of the home in addition to schooling. A form of connoisseurism manifests itself in the search for the best extracurricular activities taught by those with either real or perceived expertise. Much research shows the attraction to group music classes and music instrument tuition as a means of developing academic and social skills—such as creativity, independence, and confidence—that are believed to be a valuable investment for the child's future (Irwin and Elley "Concerted Cultivation"; Lareau; Savage "Understanding"; Vincent and Ball). Furthermore, participation in extracurricular activities is seen as an essential means to "generating their children's biographies" (Vincent and Maxwell 5) in order to develop the child as part of the mother's autobiography as a good mother.

Women and mothers continue to dominate the educational care of children, although shifts in fathering practices are acknowledged as significant (Palladino). It is mothers who predominantly continue to orchestrate and manage children's lives, often in an intensive way. Intensive mothering is the systematic nurturing of children in a concerted fashion to develop certain talents, a process referred to by Annette Lareau as "concerted cultivation." "This parenting logic involves the institutionalization of children's leisure time in order to stimulate children's development, cultivate their cultural and social skills and maximize their potential" (Perrier 664). Involving children in the arts continues to be a popular means by which middle-class parents perform this kind of institutionalisation (Reay, *Class Work*; Vincent and Ball; Wang). Having high levels of knowledge and skill in culturally sanctioned forms of music has long been the domain of the middle class, and we make connections between social class and musical mothering by bringing into focus the mothers' aspirations, values, and practices regarding their children's musical lives and imagined futures (Hall, *Masculinity*; Savage, "Intensive"; Savage, "Understanding"). Although mothers from all social categories seek the best for their child, the capacity to accumulate and exchange capital for the family remains strongly influenced by structural contexts and gendered and classed resources (Bennett et al.; Irwin and Elley, "Parents' Hopes"; Lareau; Vincent and Maxwell). Middle-class mothers can more easily pass on social and cultural capital to their children, and early music education is used as a form of cultural investment for those with higher levels of economic and cultural capital (Irwin and Elley, "Concerted Cultivation").

MUSICAL MOTHERING AS PEDAGOGICAL LABOUR

The participation of young children, aged zero to five years, in organized music activities has increased in Australia, and these musical activities are predominantly the domain of the mother and her children. Although previous studies indicate the importance of music and the arts as a socializing practice in children's early lives (Bourdieu; Hall, *Masculinity*; Irwin and Elley, "Parents' Hopes"; Reay, *Class Work*; Savage, "Understanding"), little empirical research focuses on early-years music making as a site for intensive mothering. This chapter reports on a small-scale investigation of mothering and music by questioning how and why mothers participate in formal music classes with their young children and what costs and benefits are attributed to their musical mothering. Before discussing some of the findings from the study, we introduce our particular conceptualization of musical mothering in order to unpack the relationship between music and intensive mothering.

We look at musical mothering through a sociocultural lens with the aim of extending common conceptions of mothers' music making with their children as an innate form of mother-child intimacy and as an expression of motherhood (Mackinlay). For many mothers, music is an integral part of how they nurture and care for their child, and for some, their dedication toward their child's musical development is extremely time consuming and requires a dedicated application of specific knowledge and skill. Our research focuses on the ways women use music in their mothering as a form of intensive labour, which we suggest is a form of intensive mothering par excellence. The aim is to reveal the role music can play in mothering repertoires for women with young children. What does this look and sound like in relation to intensive mothering? Mothers' musical repertoires include making music with their children, facilitating their children's music making, planning and organizing, and strategizing opportunities to support their children's musical development over the long term. This includes a wide range of musical and extramusical activities: purposefully curating their children's CD collections and concert going; finding spaces and places in the family routine to regularly include music making together, such as singing in the car and at bath time; using their social networks to seek out expert teachers to provide tuition; supervising practice and participating in music classes with their child. The latter is the main focus of analysis in this chapter.

Intensive musical mothering is characterised by a maternal investment in the needs and activities of the child's musical life that takes priority over other things, including the mother's own desires. Intensive musical mothers' aspirations for their children can become so entwined with their personal desires that mothers' own social and cultural lives are lived through their children's musical activities. Intensive musical mothering is also characterized by a focus on using music as a form of pedagogy that is at once educational and pleasurable. Early socialization is the key to later educational success and is consistent with intensive mothering ideology that holds the mother responsible for enriching or supplementing the child's education using the home as a pedagogical space. Informal musical mothering in the home can take many forms, as mentioned, and this is often strategically used in the home for the learning in and through music that is inherent in these exchanges. Music holds a key for some mothers to give her child a head start in dispositions considered valuable for the educational market, such as an ability to sit still, concentrate, and self-regulate—prerequisites for discipline—and to acquire cultural expertise, such as a taste for good music. In this sense, musical mothering can be a significant means by which children are enculturated in society's cultural codes and are taught to play by the rules of school. The mother's self-interest can, therefore, be considered in relation to the sense of achievement in the educational outcomes and social mobility she enables for her child through musical development.

Intensive mothering ideology can also be seen in musical mothering in the vast reserves of emotional labour required to orchestrate musical lives over a long term; managing and coordinating an optimum musical environment takes much care, concern, and forward planning. Sally Savage has highlighted that the cost of the pedagogical labour involved in developing a musical child often includes emotional pressure because of the anxieties and responsibilities to make the right choices for success ("Intensive"). In contrast to discourses of mother-child music making as a psychosocial phenomenon (Barrett; Gerry et al.), we investigate the instrumentality of musical mothering as a form of social action whereby society articulates in mothers' musicking[1] and musical mothering speaks back to society. For instance, our concerns are how gendered and classed practices find expression in musical mothering but also how mothers use music as a form of agency. In other words, musical mothering is about what music does to mothers and also what they do with music. We question whether the cultural contradiction identified by Hays is a useful way to interpret the selfless concerted cultivation involved in musical mothering as being in tension with what mothers gain from this mode of mothering. But first we must look more closely at what intensive musical mothering affords women.

The affordances of intensive mothering through music are not restricted to English-speaking countries. There has, however, been less focus on intensive mothering in the global South and East despite some interesting findings coming from studies of mother's involvement in music education in particular. Hyung Youm shows that mothers' main aims for attending early years music classes in South Korea include learning about child development, how to interact musically with their child, and for their children to develop an appreciation for classical music. Concerted cultivation is most prevalent among middle-class South Korean mothers where music is a means to reinforce and promote their family's social standing and enrichment activities formulate children's extensive resumes in a competitive school market (Cho). Youm's study also illustrates that another key reason for mothers' involvement in early years music education is to develop their musicality for their own sake. Likewise, we further pursue the possibility that intensive mothering through music has personal benefits for the mothers beyond the needs of the child.

METHODOLOGY

The research was undertaken by the first author in a suburban area of a large Australian city. The research participants were thirteen mothers who had attended early childhood music classes with their child for a period of twelve months or more, which was considered a commitment to music rather than a passing interest. These music classes were facilitated by the researcher-educator, which helped to establish a deep relationship with these mothers over time and a level of comfort to discuss their experiences. All participants were women with tertiary qualifications. Three mothers were music teachers, either working in a school, privately, or both. Three of the mothers were born outside of Australia, but have lived there for a substantial time. All mothers were in a heterosexual partnership or marriage, and most were in their thirties when having their first child. The subjects were mostly stay-at-home mothers and mothers working part time, although one of the mothers interviewed worked full time, and one mother studied full time. Eleven of the thirteen mothers studied music as children, often to intermediate or advanced levels, although most were reluctant to say that they are particularly "musical." The names of all the participants in this study have been replaced with pseudonyms.

This small-scale project adopted a narrative case-study methodology. Data generation and analysis pursued themes from the cultural sociology of education. Semistructured interviews, up to one hour's duration, were conducted in the individual participant's home or place of their choosing at a mutually convenient time. This approach made participants feel at ease and accommodated childcare needs and work commitments. The women were asked to share stories about their experiences of music within their family life and why they chose to become involved in early years music classes. The sample used in this research is relatively small, and it represents a localized view of a group of mothers and their experience of early years music education. The researcher acknowledges there are issues concerning being the teacher of the participants' children. As a middle-class, white, educated Australian woman, the researcher's subjectivity attracts people who may identify and value the researcher because of this, which, therefore, presents a limitation on the diversity of possible participants.

The following section discusses the narratives of seven of the women's musical mothering experiences and focuses on their participation in their preschool children's music classes.

NARRATIVES OF MUSICAL MOTHERING

Andrea works diligently to cultivate her children's musicality through intensive mothering. Andrea's musical mothering involves vast amounts of pedagogical labour where she tutors her children in the manner of the specialists: actively sitting in on lessons, creating a home conducive to practising music, setting aside time to practice with her child, and attending a range of musical activities provided in the community. Participating in her children's music classes provides Andrea opportunities to learn how she can optimize learning in the home:

> *I learn ... just talking to the other mothers ... what do they do; you exchange ideas ... I see what you're doing in the group and now we sort of do the same style at home, so that I know what to do. I think if I didn't actually go to your classes or any of the other ones for that matter really, I wouldn't really know how to promote music at home ... I kind of know what to do [laughs].*

The professionalization of Andrea's mothering is illustrated in how she manages the family's schedule with calculated efficiency. Andrea uses participation in early childhood music classes as a learning tool for herself through which she becomes the expert tutor for her children to replicate aspects of formal learning in the home. For instance, she tells how she adopts the use of soothing classical music for calming her children. She sings instructions rather than speaking to pique her children's listening for transitioning from play time to dinner time and uses other musical techniques for behaviour modification similar to those used in our classes. "Dinner time it's not songs; it's [classical] music ... it's our way of calming them down I suppose ... Sometimes we play [a] game where ... you sing 'sit down on the ground,' [we sing] 'everyone to the table" [sung in same notes], and they sing back to me 'okay, mummy' [laughs]. So it comes through in so many ways at home." Andrea uses music as part of her domestic mothering work and as a way of combining the skills learned in class to meet her parenting goals. Much of mothers' work in fostering the desired skills in children is subtly embedded into family practices early in a child's life; the routine of such activities becomes an accepted practice and what Beatriz Ilari describes as "aesthetic conditioning" (181).

Ruby, a mother of three young children, also fosters an appreciation for music as part of her children's aesthetic conditioning. Unable herself to learn music as a child, Ruby has resolved to make music part of her life and that of her family:

> *I would like them [her children] to grow up and have music in their lives ... go to concerts ... cause that's another thing we do a lot too. I take them to playschool concerts, the symphony orchestra ... cause I enjoy it but I want them to also have that ... I want them to, when they're grown, go "ah I'd like to go to a concert" and enjoy it; it is a lovely part of life, and I'd like them to sort of appreciate [it], yeah.*

The development of aesthetic conditioning, as seen through Ruby's and Andrea's practices, highlights how "the home becomes a site of pedagogy ... through trips to the theatre, art galleries or concerts, 'exposure' to high status cultural activities ... in an organised, interventionist approach to child-rearing" (Vincent et al. 430). Such pedagogies give the appearance of incidental acquisition; they adhere to gender-based assumptions that mothers are natural carers and children's talents are innate rather than nurtured through their mothers' "domestic cultural training" (Bourdieu 46).

Ruby's pedagogical care of her children uses her own educational capital to introduce her children to the right kind of music in which her children learn to participate in high-status music activities requiring embodied capital in the form of etiquette and behaviour in order to appreciate. She converts this know-how into cultural capital for her children, which reinforces the family's affiliation with middle-class dispositions. The mother's role is critical in the family's accumulation of cultural capital, as Pierre Bourdieu suggests, and the role of music in these processes, particularly as a resource for social agency in children's early years, is an underresearched field. The researcher is complicit in these women's cultivation of their children by making mothers aware of these concerts and activities through our classes. As Ruby alludes, there is a shared understanding of what is meant by "going to concerts"; it implies an appreciation for Western art music and an attendance at concert halls and prestigious theatres with others "like us."

Exposure to a vast array of cultural activities may appear a less concerted form of cultivation; however, high amounts of cultural and economic capital are required to orchestrate this approach successfully. Early years music classes, in their customary child-centred, play-based approach, do more than help mothers and children pass time in an enjoyable way; they can assist in introducing children to the structures of Western music education and teach mothers how to continue this education in the home as shown above. This is a critical difference between other popular early years activities such as ballet or gymnastics, where the adults' participation either is not required or permitted, or is secondary to the children's involvement and is not expected to occur outside the context of the class. Early years music classes, however, will usually promote parent-child interaction through music as fundamental to the experience, and home practice is often encouraged, if not expected. Making the learning visible through strategies, such as student performances and "homework" activities, is part of the appeal of formal music classes to intensive mothering. However, it is the mothers' "hidden curriculum" that is perhaps far more complex. The mothers not only are preparing their children with prerequisite skills for musical futures but are using music as a means of shaping their personhood. Julie stated the following: "I'd like him to learn how to dance and be involved in music a bit ... we're not putting pressure on him. I'm not wanting him ever to be on X Factor or anything like that—I just want him to have music in his life and dancing too just to have some fun, you know, and it's quite nice for a boy to be able to dance."

Such a statement shows how early in their children's lives these mothers are fashioning their futures without wanting to appear as intervening.

Julie, like the other mothers, narrates her children's choices as "free"; however, the mothers' work to encourage and expose their children to particular opportunities is how they regulate the choices their children have access to. Julie's comments also reveal how her son's projected future personhood includes his imagined gender identity, clearly something more than "just fun." His mother's comments show her desire for her son to become a dancing boy, which in Australia is an extremely counterhegemonic form of masculinity.[2] By exposing him to music and dance early in life, she hopes they will become desires throughout his life. This kind of investment in the symbolic gendered meanings of participation in the arts is consistent with other research on masculinity and music, which shows the significance of singing as an important means of shaping gendered subjectivity in early childhood and the influence of the family (Hall, "Gender"; Hall, *Masculinity*).

Monique's comments also show how the sociality of music is perceived to afford an aesthetic conditioning of superior moral standards, which is emphasized in her frequent use of the word "good":

> *I thought it would be a good way to meet new people, for the children to meet new people, and I believe, just from my experience at school and seeing kids at school, that if they learn an instrument at school that gives them a lot of confidence; it gives them a lot of social skills and a good group of friends. I thought down the track that that's something I'd like them to be involved in ... if they're interested in ... I wouldn't push it ... so this might be a good grounding ... and it has been. My ultimate goal is so that they will not be tempted to mix with the wrong people or do anything that's you know, not safe. If you're in a band when you're older, it gives you a whole social group that have similar interests and requires some kind of commitment so you don't have loose, random time that you're going to try and fill with anything.*

Monique—who did not have any formal music education as a child and is a stay-at-home mother working occasionally as a primary school teacher—constructs a binary between right-wrong people, good-bad friends, much-little aptitude, safe-unsafe, and productiveness-unproductiveness. For her, music represents everything to do with the positive side of these binaries, which is a pattern among the other mothers' narratives. Monique desires to produce good children through music, and she is relieved that music classes are giving her children so much so-called goodness; here, music conflates with the social. An image is produced of the engaged, committed musician as an embodiment of this imaginary exemplary person. The use of music to productively fill up time is constructed as a meaningful way to develop a work ethic similar to the study by Carol Vincent and colleagues, whose participants saw spare time negatively because children could potentially get up to no good. We suggest that this indicates a middle-class orientation to time because working-class parents are less likely to perceive the arts as the most valuable way of instilling a productive work ethic in their children.

Musical mothering through concerted cultivation and intensive mothering practices is a seemingly selfless pursuit invested in advantaging the child; however, we argue that it is also an investment in mothers' own emotional futures, which the next section explores.

AFFORDANCES OF MUSICAL MOTHERING

Intensive mothering is known to generate serious costs to mothers in terms of emotion, time, and energy (Hays). Intensive mothering can produce "an extensive range of emotions in relation to their children ... guilt, anxiety and frustration as well as empathy and encouragement" throughout their involvement in their children's activities (Reay, "Extension" 572). There are "constant worries about getting things wrong, about failing the child, about mistaking priorities, about not finding the perfect school or right university" (Ball 171). For the mothers in this study, they endure the costs because of the potential benefits music offers their children, which is consistent with the self-sacrificing aspect of intensive mothering. Hannah weighs up the benefits against the costs of going to music classes with her child: "If you could see the benefits that were happening for your child, you'd maybe go ... For me, I think it would be more outweighed by what was happening for the kids, so if they were getting benefit and they were happy, I would probably put aside whatever thing I was having."

As mentioned, these women devote much of their resources to their children's pursuits at their own personal expense. All had successful careers prior to motherhood, and many suggest that they are ambivalent about the transition to motherhood; several have difficulty coping with the drudgery of stay-at-home domestic life and the relentless demands and guilt of mothering. Music class is a space to escape this temporarily, as Penny described: "I got to spend dedicated one-on-one time with them for that time without feeling like I still had the washing and the ironing and everything else that was dragging out and had to be done ... music was on and we were there." Although participating in music classes with their children can be viewed as an extension of intensive mothering and therefore another potential cost to these mothers, it also represents positive affordances that go beyond Hays's conceptualization of mothers' self-interest as ultimately child centred. What is important to highlight is the benefits musical mothering has also brought for the women themselves outside their mother subjectivities. Andrea, for instance, finds being a co-learner with her child in music class satisfies an element of her unrealized dreams of being more musical herself, which she connects with a strong sense of self-contentment: "I think it's your responsibility to develop your talents ... and flourish with them 'cause that's what will make you happy."

One recurring theme in the women's stories is how music classes helps to replenish depleted emotional resources. For example, Olivia had weeks where she could not even face leaving the house, but coming to class to make music with her child helped her to cope with her difficulties at the time: "I hope you understand how important us coming to your classes is. Like there's been so many times when I've been about to lose the plot ... I don't have to go to music and then I think, 'I do, I do! I have to go to music,' like that's the best day of the week! Like it's so important. Maybe it's for me as well." An important dimension of the emotionality of this musical context is the relationships the mothers form with the other adults. The mothers discuss being "enriched" by the class beyond music itself, which is consistent with research showing the impact music making, particularly singing, has on personal growth, a sense of belonging, and wellness through enjoyment, self-realization, and positive relationships (Hurst). Hannah shared the following: "As a stay-at-home mum, you need to have some other stimulation apart from playing Barbies and reading books all day; you've got to be able to get out and do those things to feel enriched." In a sense, another form of musical mothering is the mother-to-mother sharing of knowledge and reassurance about their mothering through musical interactions. Although this could be regarded as another way intensive mothering manifests itself in a project of self-improvement through music in order to become an even better mother, we argue this music class is an important space the women seek out to cultivate themselves alongside their children for their own benefit. This pedagogy of the self affords these women self-knowledge, new musical capacities, confidence, and reassurance in their mothering in a supportive environment.

The teacher facilitates this environment by addressing mothers' concerns and promoting empathetic interaction through music. Singing is the main mode of interaction in these classes, which is encouraged to promote wellbeing and life enhancement (Judd and Pooley) and to create a "relational consciousness—a deep sense of connectedness with others and within oneself" (Mellor 194). The effects singing can have on health, wellbeing, and a "shared sense of belonging" (Mellor 192) are important findings that may explain why some mothers, like Penny, find leaving their child's music class so difficult: "It's actually quite sad for me because this is the last day of music ... it impacted me far more than it impacted him because I said, you know, this is my ritual. This is what I've been doing until the kids went to school ... that was sad that I didn't get to go anymore. What am I going to do with my Mondays now?" Not only does mothers' participation in their children's early years music classes advantage the children educationally, it contributes to the women's wellbeing as individuals, which complicates the construction of intensive mothering as allowing little space for the mother's best interests.

In summary, this chapter has discussed how the collective narrative of these mothers show music is an important resource in their conceptualization and practice of good mothering. We have argued that the musical mothering of these women is a form of pedagogical labour that has multiple purposes requiring elaborating on past theorizations of intensive mothering. Consistent with previous discussions of concerted cultivation, these women deploy musical mothering as a means of maximizing their children's educational potential in and through music. We illustrate how the mothers use music learning and music making to shape their children's lives as well as their own. Participating in their children's early music education imbibes the mothers with pedagogical know-how that they use in the home as a space to further cultivate their family. Here the cultural contradiction of intensive mothering is highly apparent in the ways these mothers attempt to construct their musical mothering as disinterested, which they do by narrating the freedom of their children's musical choices and emphasizing the many benefits of musical mothering for the child as opposed to themselves and their family's social position. This position is in tension with the significant interventions the mothers make for the child to have a good life through music at the cost of her time, energy, and money. Consequently, intensive mothering ideology does not account for the intrinsic personal affordances of music making, as distinct from the costs and benefits that this pedagogical labour represents to "professional" mothers. We have argued that these women strategically use their children's music learning as a pedagogy of the self, whereby they concertedly cultivate their own musical capacities, emotional reserves, support networks, and wellbeing through music for their own betterment. Finding such counternarratives of musical mothers' agency within intensive mothering may help to locate and advocate change in mothering ideology and promote the power of music to compose motherhood in a different key.

ENDNOTES

[1]"Musicking" is a term coined by musician and philosopher Christopher Small as a verb to describe any musical activity including composing, performing, and listening (Small).
[2]In 2012, the Australian Bureau of Statistics figures on children's participation in cultural and leisure activities indicated that 3.5 percent of boys and 27.1 percent girls aged five to fourteen years were involved in organized dance. This compares to 16 percent of boys who were learning an instrument and 2.5 percent who were involved in singing, as well as 19.3 percent of girls who were learning an instrument and 7.9 percent who were involved in singing.

WORKS CITED

Australian Bureau of Statistics. "Children's Participation in Cultural and Leisure Activities." 2012, www.abs.gov.au/AUSSTATS/abs@.nsf/DetailsPage/4901.0Apr%202012?OpenDocument. Accessed 13 Nov. 2017.

Ball, Stephen, J. "The Risks of Social Reproduction: The Middle Class and Educational Markets." *London Review of Education*, vol. 1, no. 3, 2003, pp. 163-75.

Barrett, Margaret, S. "Sounding Lives in and through Music: A Narrative Inquiry of the 'Everyday' Musical Engagement of a Young Child." *Journal of Early Childhood Research*, vol. 7, no. 2, 2009, pp. 115-34.

Bennett, Pamela, et al. "Beyond the Schoolyard: The Role of Parenting Logics, Financial Resources, and Social Institutions in the Social Class Gap in Structured Activity Participation." *Sociology of Education*, vol. 85, no. 2, 2012, pp. 131-57.

Bourdieu, Pierre. *Distinction: A Social Critique of the Judgement of Taste.* Routledge and Kegan Paul, 1984.

Cho, Eun. "What Do Mothers Say? Korean Mothers' Perceptions of Children's Participation in Extracurricular Musical Activities." *Music Education Research*, vol. 17, no. 2, 2015, pp. 162-78.

Ennis, Linda Rose, editor. *Intensive Mothering: The Cultural Contradictions of Modern Motherhood.* Demeter Press, 2014.

Gerry, David, et al. "Active Music Classes in Infancy Enhance Musical, Communicative and Social Development." *Developmental Science*, vol. 15, no. 3, 2012, pp. 398-407.

Golden, Deborah, and Lauren Erdreich. "Mothering and the Work of Educational Care—An Integrative Approach." *British Journal of Sociology of Education*, vol. 35, no. 2, 2014, pp. 263-77.

Hall, Clare. "Gender and Boys' Singing in Early Childhood." *British Journal of Music Education*, vol. 22, no.1, 2005, pp. 5-20.

Hall, Clare. *Masculinity, Class and Music Education.* Palgrave. (Forthcoming).

Hays, Sharon. *The Cultural Contradictions of Motherhood.* Yale, 1996.

Holloway, Sarah L., and Helena Pimlott-Wilson. "Enriching Children, Institutionalizing Childhood? Geographies of Play,

Extracurricular Activities, and Parenting in England." *Annuls of the Association of American Geographers*, vol. 104, no. 3, 2014, pp. 613-27.

Hurst, Katryn. "Singing Is Good for You: An Examination of the Relationship between Singing, Health and Well-being." *The Canadian Music Teacher*, vol. 55, no. 4, 2014, pp. 18-22.

Ilari, Beatriz. "Concerted Cultivation and Music Learning: Global Issues and Local Variations." *Research Studies in Music Education*, vol. 35, no. 2, 2013, pp. 179-96.

Irwin, Sarah, and Sharon Elley. "Concerted Cultivation? Parenting Values, Education and Class Diversity." *Sociology*, vol. 45, no. 3, 2011, pp. 480-95.

Irwin, Sarah, and Sharon Elley. "Parents' Hopes and Expectations for their Children's Future Occupations." *The Sociological Review*, vol. 61, no.1, 2013, 111-30.

Judd, Marianne, and Julie Ann Pooley. "The Psychological Benefits of Participating in Group Singing for Members of the General Public." *Psychology in Music*, vol. 42, no. 2, 2014, pp. 269-83.

Lareau, Annette. *Unequal Childhoods: Class, Race and Family Life*. University of California, 2003.

Mackinlay, Elizabeth. "Singing Maternity through Autoethnography: Making Visible the Musical World of Myself as a Mother." *Early Child Development and Care*, vol. 179, no. 6, 2009, pp. 717-31.

McPherson, Gary, editor. *The Child as Musician: A Handbook of Musical Development*. Oxford: Oxford University Press, 2006.

Mellor, Liz. "An Investigation of Singing, Health and Well-being as a Group Process." *British Journal of Music Education*, vol. 30, no. 2, 2013, pp. 177-205.

Milkie, Melissa, A., and Catharine H. Warner. "Status Safeguarding: Mothers' Work to Secure Children's Place in the Social Hierarchy." *Intensive Mothering: The Cultural Contradictions of Modern Motherhood*, edited by Linda Rose Ennis, Demeter, 2014, pp. 66-85.

Palladino, Hallie. "The Cultural Contradictions of Fatherhood." *Intensive Mothering: The Cultural Contradictions of Modern Motherhood*, edited by Linda Rose Ennis, Demeter, 2014, pp. 280-98.

Paltineau, Maya-Merida. "From Intensive Mothering to Identity Parenting." *Intensive Mothering: The Cultural Contradictions of Modern Motherhood*, edited by Linda Rose Ennis, Demeter, 2014, pp. 120-41.

Perrier, Maud. "Middle-Class Mothers' Moralities and 'Concerted Cultivation': Class Others, Ambivalence and Excess." *Sociology*, vol. 47, no. 4, 2013, pp. 655-70.

Reay, Diane. *Class Work: Mothers' Involvement in their Children's Primary Schooling*.: Routledge, 1998.

Reay, Diane. "A Useful Extension of Bourdieu's Conceptual Framework?: Emotional Capital as a Way of Understanding Mothers' Involvement in Their Children's Education?" *The Sociological Review*, vol. 48, no. 4, 2000, pp. 568-85.

Reay, Diane. "Class Acts: Parental Involvement in Schooling." *Is Parenting a Class Issue?* edited by Martina Klett-Davies, Family and Parenting Institute, 2010, pp. 31-43.

Savage, Sally. "Understanding Mothers' Perspectives on Early Childhood Music Programmes." *Australian Journal of Music Education*, vol. 2, 2015, pp. 127-139.

Savage, Sally. "Intensive Mothering Through Music in Early Childhood Education." MEd Thesis, Monash University, 2015.

Shirani, Fiona, et al. "Meeting the Challenges of Intensive Parenting Culture: Gender, Risk Management and the Moral Parent." *Sociology*, vol. 46, no. 1, 2012, pp. 25–40.

Small, Christopher. *Musicking: The Meanings of Performing and Listening*. University Press of New England, 1998.

Vincent, Carol, and Stephen J. Ball. "'Making Up' the Middle-Class Child: Families, Activities and Class Dispositions." *Sociology*, vol. 41, no 6, 2007, pp. 1061-77.

Vincent, Carol, and Claire Maxwell. "Parenting Priorities and Pressures: Furthering Understanding of 'Concerted Cultivation.'" *Discourse: Studies in the Cultural Politics of Education*, vol. 37, no. 2, 2015, pp. 1-13.

Vincent, Carol, et al. "Raising Middle-Class Black Children: Parenting Priorities, Actions and Strategies." *Sociology* vol. 47, no. 3, 2013, pp. 427-42.

Wang, Grace. "On Tiger Mothers and Music Moms." *Amerasia Journal*, vol. 37, no. 2, 2011, pp. 130-36.

Youm, Hyung Kyung. "South Korean Parents' Goals, Knowledge, Practices, and Needs Regarding Music Education for Young Children." Dissertation, University of Missouri, 2008.

4.
A Vulnerable Observer and a Circular Gift
Personal Reflections on St. John's Ukulele Club

LYDIA BRINGERUD

Mary's Ukulele (Lydia Bringerud, 2014)

When was the last time someone said to you, "I don't want to study that topic because I won't enjoy it anymore?" Often as academics, when we spend time in the deep analysis of a topic, its initial mystery dissipates, and we are left with yet another paper neatly explaining a facet of someone else's life. What are the topics that we choose *not* to study, and what anxieties keep us from studying them? Furthermore, how do our choices not to study a certain topic (or to examine what it means to us) affect our complex subjectivities as ethnographers?

Historically in the ethnographic social sciences, a spectrum of options for authorial voices has existed. We have at one extreme the removed, authoritative academic who pretends to have perfect objectivity, and at the other extreme, the fieldworker who has "gone native"—so deeply involved in a culture that he or she can no longer be objectively extricated from that experience (Pratt; Tedlock). I see both of these extremes as motivated by anxiety: the anxiety over getting too close and not being taken seriously and the

51

anxiety over how to reconcile deeply meaningful experience with study. Today, we try to mediate these anxieties with reflexivity—the efforts to respect our collaborators and to be aware of how our presence affects them (Hufford; Lawless, "I Was Afraid"). What is less frequently discussed, however, is how collaborators affect us as ethnographers (some exceptions include Behar; Meyerhoff; Narayan). Sometimes all the reflexivity in the world cannot prepare us for deeply emotional experiences in fieldwork. Anthropologist Ruth Behar asks, "How do you write subjectivity into ethnography in such a way that you can continue to call what you are doing ethnography?" (6-7). I offer here a personal reflection on a fieldwork experience that I had recently that made me anxious.

In the winter semester of 2014, I attended a course called "Advanced Ethnography" as a requirement for my PhD at Memorial University of Newfoundland (MUN). There were three other students in the course, and we were instructed to do a collective ethnography on the St. John's Ukulele Club. One of our graduate students was an ethnomusicologist, but the rest of us were folklorists, unaccustomed to approaching music academically. This discomfort, however, made me aware of just how complex my own subjectivity was in relation to music as a research topic, and I became, in the words of Behar, a "vulnerable observer" (1). Behar uses this expression to refer to certain ethical dilemmas faced by ethnographers. She writes:

> Loss, mourning, the longing for memory, the desire to enter into the world around you and having no idea how to do it, the fear of observing too coldly or too distractedly or too raggedly, the rage of cowardice, the insight that is always arriving late, as defiant hindsight, a sense of the utter uselessness of writing anything and yet the burning desire to write something. (3)

For me, studying music became an emotional topic because of the legacy of musicianship in my family. My experiences coloured my subjectivity in documenting the St. John's Ukulele Club such that the only way I felt I could write about this group was through autoethnography. Patrick Mullen writes that it is much easier for a scholar to admit subjectivity than to be aware of the "hidden assumptions" (133) he or she might have. This was certainly the case for me; I knew my gaze affected my conclusions in fieldwork, but my unexamined assumptions were the ones that caused my deepest reactions. Renato Rosaldo writes that ethnographers, as positioned subjects, are "prepared to know certain things and not others" (170). In the false sense of security this creates, it is the unexpected that can undermine our preparatory measures. On the other hand, these slippages reposition our gaze and can serve to make us awake to some of our hidden assumptions.

Folklorist David J. Hufford has suggested that in ethnographic writing, the scholar is always the subject of his or her own text, and those being studied are passive objects of that text; oftentimes, we learn more about the author's worldview than the topic of study. By choosing autoethnography as my medium, I can demonstrate how my own positionality affects my fieldwork conclusions. In terms of writing about music performance in particular, ethnomusicologist Timothy Rice points out that "experience is not an inner phenomenon accessible only via introspection to the one having the experience. Rather, experience begins with interaction with a world and with others" (157). This is especially true considering the nature of participation in performance. A key aspect of my vulnerability in studying the St. John's Ukulele Club was just that—the dissolving of the line between observing and participating.

Behar writes that "The exposure of the self who is also a spectator has to take us somewhere we couldn't otherwise get to" (14). Using my own fieldwork experience as a case study, I ask, why do we study the particular topics and groups that we study (and not other topics)? How are our own subjectivities quietly embedded in the questions we ask? This becomes pertinent for ethnography in the twenty-first century when social scientists increasingly turn to their own backyards for fieldwork. In my case, I study North American converts to Eastern Orthodox Christianity because my own family became part of this community when I was in my early teens. As an apostate, I use my "insider-outsider" status to delve into why people choose this faith in the twenty-first century and the personal experiences that keep them there. I believe that my personal relationship to my research, however, is complicated both by my relationship to my mother and my relationship to music. Unexpectedly, my feelings about my mother, music, and Orthodoxy cropped up in my observation of the St. John's Ukulele Club, forcing me to reexamine my limitations as an ethnographer and a human being. The following chapter alternates between my fieldwork in the Ukulele Club and my memories of music growing up. In this way, the reader can begin to see how my subjectivity is constructed, both in terms of the conclusions I draw and my presentation of self as a narrator.

TWO UKULELE OBSERVATIONS AT HAVA JAVA

The first time I attended a meeting of the St. John's Ukulele Club, there were only four members present, and one did not play the ukulele at all. The presence of four graduate student ethnographers was a glaring one in this context, and I think it made the ukulele players (and their one groupie) a bit self-conscious. I told Sam, a gangly high school student with a bleach-blond coif, "We're some weird people from MUN who are observing," to which he said, "I'm observing also ... I'm not particularly musical, but I like to listen." He first heard the ukulele in his junior high school when Mr. Grant, the math teacher, coached a ukulele club. Sam liked to hang around them too, because, as he put it, "I like the people, and I like the music." Sam had been coming to the club meetings at the Hava Java, a downtown coffee shop, only a few times, but he intended to pick up a ukulele at some point. For the moment, he sang. In fact, the first time my classmates and I visited, he did all the vocals for the group's rendition of "Toxic" by Britney Spears. The others present were Maryanna, a friend of Sam's from school; Lauren, an undergraduate who came for the first time; and Matt (aka Mr. Grant), the club's leader. I think part of the subdued quality of this particular meeting was related to the fact that Lauren was new, and although she had been playing the ukulele for a few years, she was unfamiliar with the group's songbook, and time had to be taken in between songs for Matt and Maryanna to explain chord progressions to her.

The second meeting I attended was completely different. Our little group of ethnographers was easily in the minority, surrounded by ten players (one of whom brought her two grandchildren); Sam, knitting a hat this time; and a few sundry passersby. As with the meeting I attended a month earlier, this one opened with a Britney Spears song, "Oops! ... I Did It Again." I got the impression that Sam was a fan because he not only sang the words to the song but when the ukuleles petered out in the middle, he continued to sing even when the rest of the club showed no signs of continuing their accompaniment. Matt leaned forward and said to him, "Hey, we're done," to which Sam replied, "Well *I'm* not!" which was met with laughter all around.

Second meeting I attended of the St. John's Ukulele Cluib above Hava Java.
(Lydia Bringerud, 2014)

One of the first words that comes to my mind in trying to describe the group meeting is warmth. It might have been the space—a bright yellow room above the Hava Java coffee shop, hung with original portraits of musical legends. Lauryn Hill, Outkast, Jimi Hendrix, the Beatles, the Doors, Bob Dylan, and others presided over us benevolently as some of their songs were reproduced on comically small string instruments. Beneath these portraits, I romantically imagined this informal group participating in a musical lineage of people who just did it for the love of sound. There was a sonic brightness in the hum of ten ukuleles being strummed in unison. The colour of the space, its cozy size, and the cushy bench with pillows along the wall gave the room a kind of intimacy, as though we were in someone's living room. Perhaps most importantly, I perceived warmth in the interactions among players. Laughter shuttled between players, weaving together tones from ukulele strings and vocal cords. The meeting appeared to be easy and comfortable. The group's art was a patchwork quilt of singing, ukulele, laughter, play, nonverbal interaction, and above all, music making, none of which were mutually exclusive.

Ethnomusicologist Thomas Turino would describe this musical event as participatory performance. According to him, in these events, "one's primary attention is on the activity, on *the doing* and on the other participants, rather than an end product that results from the activity" (emphasis in original, 28). Furthermore, the quality of the event, or the music, has less to do with this end product and more to do with how many people participate and how those participants feel. It almost does not make sense in this context to observe detachedly. Turino writes that "in fully participatory occasions there are no artist-audience distinctions, only participants and potential participants. Attention is on the sonic and kinesic interaction among participants" (28). This kind of interaction can be described as bonding. Building relationships through the music seemed more important than how beautiful or technically correct it was. This, in many ways, is the opposite of what we are trained to do in academe. It was certainly the opposite of what I was trained to do with music.

MY FAMILY, MUSIC, AND CHURCH

This was fieldwork for which I felt unprepared. I knew very little about ethnomusicological observation or ethnography, and even less about the ukulele. I do, however, come from a musical family. My mother and grandmother both have graduate degrees in music, concentrating in piano performance, and my grandfather (the same grandmother's ex-husband, about whom she says, "Two pianists cannot ever be married.") has a double master's degree in piano and violin. I minored in vocal performance in my undergraduate studies; however this, too, was mostly restricted to Western classical music, and in my case, art song and operatic repertoire. My musical background gives me an understanding of harmony, timbre, and artistic collaboration. What it does not prepare me for is an appreciation of informal musical settings. In many ways, this is what the St. John's Ukulele Club seemed to be all about.

Reflection: I can't recall how many times, before I started college, people asked me if I was going to major in music, like my mother. They were mostly church people who asked. After all, my mother was our church choir director, being by far the most qualified individual for the job, and both my father and I were valuable singers in the ensemble (being music literate and able to match a pitch were all it took). Some people at church knew that I was taking voice lessons privately, and I did sing for a year in my high school choir. For at least six years, I had taken piano lessons, in the past, and I dabbled in violin as well. When people asked me if I would major in music, I told them, "I don't want to because then it won't be fun anymore."

What the people at church didn't seem to know was how much pressure there was in my family to perform music perfectly. As a child taking piano lessons, I would get up early before school to practice for at least half an hour. I always tried to be as quiet as possible so that my mother wouldn't wake up and tell me what was wrong with my playing. My hand position might not have been curved enough, or I might have missed a note or, more likely, I misread the rhythm in a phrase. If I was bored or exasperated enough, I would try to stop practising sooner, and I was rarely let off the hook for that either.

Outside our home, there were other musical pressures. When I played the piano, I was asked to play for family members at gatherings, for church Christmas events, and once or twice at school. My piano teacher held mandatory recitals for her students. Thankfully, this teacher was not my mother because as we later learned, the pair of us was a disastrous combination on the same instrument. In high school, when I took voice lessons, I was asked to sing in similar capacities. By this point, however, we had converted to Orthodox Christianity, and as all Orthodox liturgical music is *a capella*, choral participation was essential (read: *my* participation was essential—or at least I was led to believe that).

Before my family became Orthodox, we had been part of a self-contained charismatic[1] Christian group, one that composed its own music (the group formed in the 1970s, and there was a lot of hippie energy in there) (Bringerud). Singing was unstructured: there were written scores, but no one adhered to them seriously because so few people read music. Harmonies were frequently improvised, and it was common for people to get "lost" in song: eyes closed, hands raised, swaying sometimes. A family friend of ours used to call it "singing in the spirit." When I remember being a child in those moments, I remember the air feeling thick with music. I was little, no higher than anyone's waist, and it was as though I were swimming in an ocean of sound, the harmonies like currents swirling. Few people in the congregation were formally trained musicians, but many had nice voices all the same, and they blended well. On top of that, there was intense emotion poured into the singing: it was wild and alive, and I believed at the time that God became present among us. J.R.R. Tolkien described an angelic race of beings, the Valar, in his book *The Silmarillion*, and in his mythology, these creatures sang the world into being. It seemed so much like we were doing that in the charismatic church days—singing God, or something filled with him, into existence.

A SENSE OF COMMUNITY

Matt, the leader of the Ukulele Club, pointed out to the newcomer Lauren that there were many ways to play chords. He emphasized, "There's no wrong way to play chords, as long as you can get it out." A theme that came back again and again throughout the ukulele observations was the concern for accessibility. Both the first and second Ukulele Club meetings I attended involved participants playing song introductions for as long as necessary to make sure everyone was on the same page. In waiting for Sam to sing, Matt instructed the group, "Just strum until Sam is ready to come in," no matter how long it might be. In addition, if Sam could not sing a song in its written key, group members were often willing to transpose it so that he could participate. Matt, by contrast, sang pretty unselfconsciously, regardless of his key or whether he could hit pitches. The group's accessibility seemed dependent in some sense on its informality—you didn't have to be a great singer, you just had to be able to contribute your part to the greater whole. Players, likewise, were willing to help one another become better contributors to this greater whole.

In the second meeting in particular, I observed mentoring between ukulele players, discussing chord variations or helping one another through difficult passages of songs, usually in preparation for the next one to be played. These supportive interactions created a sonic atmosphere in between songs that was not unlike the expectant sounds of an orchestra tuning. There seemed to be a kind of otherworldly ambience to tinkering ukuleles accompanying mundane conversation about the Winter Olympics and *Star Trek*.

Sam speculated that people were drawn to play the ukulele in the first place because it could be learned relatively easily. As he put it, "It's fun … it's not, like, serious … you can casually play it." He conceded that some people took it "really seriously … taking lessons and stuff," but he believed that the St. John's Ukulele Club was more laidback than that.[2] Members did practice, but they didn't come together to make something polished. Maryanna, Sam's friend and classmate, said the club "forces you to practice playing the ukulele," and that was its primary purpose for her. Matt recounted the following: "That's originally how the group started. Just a bunch of random people…if we peer-pressure each other, then we're forced to learn! And [back] then, none of us knew any chords, but between all of us we knew all of the chords. So we carried on until we could jump back in." In this way, the club was less about producing a clean, professional sound, and more about creating community. In the beginning, no single person could play an entire song, but with group effort, they eventually could. Matt said that in the club's early days, "People used to come in and ask to play a certain song, and we'd be like, 'I don't know that song,' and then they'd start singing it, and we'd be like, 'Oh!' and then we'd just play it [by ear]." By belonging to the club, members challenged one another to get better and to expand their repertoires. The second time I attended the meeting, I was sitting by two people who were maybe in their sixties. Mary, nearest to me, joked once or twice, "Play some songs the old people know!" However, she told me later that she had learned a number of new songs by contemporary bands as a result of being a member. Exchanging songs in the Ukulele Club context was also a means of exchanging cultural capital. There was a shared group context, but there was also the exchange of pop culture references.

Maryanna explained to me that in her experience, "A lot of nerds play the ukulele." When I asked her to expand on this, she said, for example, that people who are drawn to the ukulele are into "comic books [and] comic book culture" and also identify as "science nerds." I wondered if this might not be connected with Matt, being Sam's and Maryanna's high school science teacher as well as the one who introduced them to the ukulele. Maryanna said that any club she was ever a part of was "full of nerds," such as "chess club and the *Settlers of Catan* Club." Beyond familiarity with specific interests like comics and chess, I took Maryanna's use of the word "nerd" to have another meaning: being willing to be quirky or silly. For me, somehow, the act of being silly contributed to my vulnerability as an observer, and I found that I was unprepared for what that meant.

BECOMING VULNERABLE WITH UKULELES

I know that when I was documenting the Ukulele Club, I started singing both times. The first time I attended, I was quiet, and tried not to be intrusive. The second time, when I heard songs I knew, I didn't hold back. It was the Simon & Garfunkel that did it. The last line of my notes read, "It's 7:39, and I've completely gone native." I wrote this jokingly in reference to the taboos of early anthropological literature, which praised distant removal from the subjects being studied (Pratt 38; Georges and Jones 81; Briggs 293). Indeed, there was at one time a fear that becoming overly empathetic with those being studied would lead anthropologists to "behave as native," thereby erasing the class line between "us" and "them" (Tedlock 70). Of course, this term is no longer used by serious social scientists; it is not only pejorative terminology but a pejorative way of thinking about those whom we study. In writing this joke in my field notes, I recognized my own anxiety;

I had crossed a line from observation to wholehearted participant observation. Indeed, I began to participate with enthusiasm, starting with "The Boxer," during which I felt the need to create canon sound effects in imitation of the album recording. After that, I was simply looking for opportunities to sing, improvise a harmony, and turn digital pages for Mary, struggling with an iPad beside me. If I had not been as familiar with the songs, I know I would not have become involved in this way. However, even when I listen back to some of the video recordings I made that second time, I can feel something deeply emotional welling up inside of me. I don't like knowing that I can become vulnerable in the most unexpected circumstances.

Reflection: Looking back, I wonder at what point I succumbed to my maternal family's musical perfectionism. I know that music was something that attracted my parents to the charismatic Christian movement, but I cannot imagine how it was that my mother could set aside her professional musicianship long enough to embrace something so unstructured. When we became Orthodox, everything about it became rigorously structured, from the liturgy to the formation of a choir (with rehearsal times) to the singing style. My musical participation at church became more of a job than a spiritual experience.

Still, the free kind of singing expression I had enjoyed previously did not end completely with our conversion. Every summer from the time I was eleven, I attended church camp. There were at least three singing times a day and other opportunities for musical expression. During singing times, everyone had books with the charismatic music, and we would sing, with unselfconscious abandon, to the accompaniment of three or four guitars. The church camp had gone on for years during the church's charismatic period, but even after the church's conversion to Orthodoxy, the daily structure of the camp changed very little, and we continued to sing almost all of the same music. As with many other kinds of charismatic Christian contexts (Lawless, *Handmaidens of the Lord*; Titon), the music was an integral part of experiencing God, and I saw many people (both long-time and new campers) have emotional and spiritual experiences connected to this music.

I have plenty of memories of camp that were not enjoyable, like not fitting in socially or struggling with messages I heard about God and morality. The most powerful memories I have of that time, however, are those that involve music. I struggle with this because I am suspicious that the music was a means of manipulating my emotions. (I don't think this was conscious on the part of the campers or counsellors—I think it is inherent in the tradition of charismatic Christianity.) What I cannot ignore is that when I hear that music today, or more pertinently, music that reminds me of it, I become emotional. Just listening to my field recordings of the Ukulele Club cause me to weep. I often wonder how I (or someone else) would hear this music differently if I did not have these particular emotional memories. All I can think is that there are layers to this experience—there is a layer of music itself and what music might mean to me in terms of the act of singing, which I seldom do these days. There is a deeper layer here, though. This is the layer that disturbs me, as Bonnie Sunstein and Elizabeth Chiseri-Strater might say. The very experience of singing in an informal group context, most especially with strummed instruments that resemble guitars, touches something in me that I identify as spiritual.

Sitting above a coffee shop, surrounded by ukuleles, I felt as though I were in the midst of something more than warmth. It sounds cheesy to say it, but all I can articulate is that I heard what I identified as the sound of love. The group of ukulele players takes people as they are. If Sam is not ready to play the ukulele, but wants to sing, he can, even if his pitch flounders. People build each other up, and they wait for one another to be on the same page before starting a song. What I saw in the St. John's Ukulele Club was the love people had for their instruments, for playing together; they had a genuine fondness for one another. I felt joy in that room, and I believe I was not alone in that. I can analyze this and connect it to my religious background and the role that music played in it. I recognize this as significant in my experience and to ignore that would be foolish; however, I do not think that this discounts my experience of something that I felt was profound.

No one asked me to sing, but when I responded to the singing around me in kind, I felt welcomed into it for whatever I had to give. I wasn't being judged on the quality of my contribution (at least,

I don't think so). This, more than anything, was what connected me back to those experiences of charismatic singing at church and church camp. In those times, I felt like my musical contribution was valued unconditionally just because it was mine. My conflation of musical experience and emotional experience made me feel that God loved me unconditionally for offering something that was imperfect, but uniquely mine. When my family became Orthodox, and singing became a job, I think I lost that window, feeling as though I could be loved for my imperfection. This scenario is not cut and dry because I started participating more professionally in classical music around the same time as the conversion, and I was applying that new lens to all musical experiences. I was very proud of my musical training, and I did like the music we sang in the Orthodox Church. My teenaged and young twenty-something selves were, however, far more likely to judge my neighbour for his or her untrained singing and become completely consumed by that. I thought of worship as presentational performance, defined by Turino as "situations where one group of people, the artists, prepare and provide music for another group, the audience, who do not participate in making the music" (26). I may have even thought of God himself as part of this audience, silently judging me on the accuracy of my pitch and breath support as I judged my neighbours. Much of our music had been composed by such accomplished artists as Sergei Rachmaninoff and Nikolai Rimsky-Korsakov, and it was impossible for me not to constantly compare our humble, musically untrained church choir with majestic recordings I had heard of the same repertoire by professional choirs. When I felt the overwhelming beauty of those professional recordings, I was full of awe, and I think I was (completely unfairly) resentful that our church choir could not reproduce this awe for me. The lack of awe (and my irascible frustration with musical performance) was probably what led me to leave the choir, and then, the church altogether—but that is a different story.

In the charismatic days, by contrast, the music we made was different in style. I did not yet have my elitist classical standards, and I could appreciate the communal, egalitarian genre; no single voice could be extracted from it, and sour notes were covered up by a small instrumental ensemble. It seemed as though there was no wrong way to sing the music. We were just expressing what we had to express, and no one was there to measure its quality or authenticity. My memories of this kind of singing connected me to the Ukulele Club in that the accessibility of participation through singing was, for me, an invitation to participate in joy. This is a circular gift. It gave me joy to participate, but I felt as though I was contributing to the creation of joy by adding to the musical body. I felt like I was sharing a life-giving, creative experience with others around me.

I wonder whether or not ethnography can be a kind of circular gift in this way or whether it is more one-sided than that. Elaine Lawless has coined the term "reciprocal ethnography" ("I Was Afraid," 311) to refer to her own process of giving her research back to her interviewees, dialoguing about representation and interpretation, and then including that dialogue in the final scholarly product. This is an ideal scenario, however, as many scholars know; it does not completely erase the power dynamics between the authorial voice and subjects' voices (Hufford). Perhaps this is why I gravitate toward autoethnography. Scholarly analysis is still involved, but the personal remains as a great equalizer between author and reader; a relationship is built on shared human experience. I wish for ethnography to achieve what a ukulele club can—empathy, not taking oneself too seriously, and relationship building. Writing about ethnographies of music, Turino discusses "sonic bonding" that occurs between people who make music together, as they experience "a feeling of oneness with others" (3). Sometimes "in-group solidarity supports the dehumanizing of other groups—that is, overvaluing difference and undervaluing the basic sameness of people" (3). Turino cites this human tendency as a reason to study expressive forms from cultures outside our own. Even in ethnographic scholarship, however, there can be anxiety in seeing ourselves in those whom we study. Ethnography is often a presentational performance rather than a participatory one. Indeed, ethnographers even build a sense of self-worth on the distance between ourselves and those whom we study.

There have been very few times in my life where I was not afraid of rejection and failure: for being "weird," awkward, not pious enough, technically skilled enough, competent enough, or smart enough. I chose to become an academic, which in some ways can be a giant competition for intelligence, creativity, and networking. I am energized by this environment, but it does create a sense of insecurity—I must keep moving so that the others don't get ahead or so that the others don't find out that I'm not as smart as they are. It is no secret that ours is a culture of criticism, where a good portion of our academic prestige is based upon how well we can find the flaws in others' work. How often do any of us hear "*You are enough*," or "Your gift is beautiful because it's *yours*"? How often does anyone say to you, "Take your time. I will play an intro chord for as long as necessary until you are ready to come in, however you are ready to come in?" It does not have to be the place of our jobs to give us this kind of affirmation. I do hope that my meditation here shows how important it is to have sources of affirmation and meaning outside of our respective disciplines. We do meaningful work as ethnographers, but one of the most direct uses of those ethnographies is to further us in the game of career success. As in all games, we win some, we lose some. For me personally, the most meaningful part of ethnography has not been a professional end goal; it has been human connection. In my experience, personal interviews are a platform like none other to delve into other people's perspectives, values, and even, sometimes, their hearts. When I teach Introduction to Folklore, I find, increasingly, that students struggle with making these kinds of connections with other people, especially in person, as opposed to a digital medium. I tell students that I do not expect that any of them will become folklorists after taking Folklore 101, but I do hope to give each of them a tool kit to take with them in other career paths and life in general. This is a tool kit for deep listening, asking questions, and paying attention in the world. Some students surprise themselves; they thought they really knew their grandmothers or their friends, or what leatherworking is all about before doing their first interview projects. They begin the interview process for a class project, and they learn entirely new stories about people and topics they thought they knew.

Not unlike my students, I thought I had a good grasp on ethnography. I thought I could separate my scholarly and personal voices—to be authoritative with my analysis yet reflexively human in my subjectivity. Hufford writes how tempting it can be for a scholar to pretend that his or her opinion is authoritative simply because he or she happens to be an academic (74). After all, we certainly have our biases. He goes on to write that "in addition to the pursuit of truth we are in pursuit of tenure, promotion, prestige, reassurance, personal affirmation, empowerment, and so forth" (64). To be truly honest about our scholarly and personal voices, we must admit our limitations and become comfortable with uncertainty. My experience documenting the St. John's Ukulele Club brought me right to the edge of that uncertainty. How could I document this group with any authority even as it revealed to me my own wounds? How could I be a scholar at all if I could not write objective ethnography?

We must find places where we are loved in the midst of honest imperfection. The St. John's Ukulele Club taught me that if there is not a place we can go, a thing we can do, where being ourselves is enough, we will go mad trying to feel good about ourselves by performance alone. I do not mean to essentialize the St. John's Ukulele Club as a utopia of unconditional acceptance. I am certain that it is many things for many people. I know that if I were a professional musician, a ukulele player, an ethnomusicologist, or even a regular member of the club, my experience would have been different. I would have become a perfectionist about musical quality or more analytical about social interaction. Paradoxically, I think it is *because* I did not become a musician like so many others in my family that I was *able* to have the kind of meaningful experience I did at the St. John's Ukulele Club. The option of valued, imperfect participation was available to me, and I took it.

I do not believe that all music is joyful. Certainly not all music invites participation. The St. John's Ukulele Club, however, offers both. I have no doubt that different people will experience the group and its music differently. Some might strongly dislike the ukulele or the particular genres they play. These too, I recognize, may play a role in my perceptions of accessibility or what is meaningful. I still think that there is something valuable—perhaps profoundly so—about people getting together to make music and share it with others in love. Maryanna told me, "I think all people should learn to play the ukulele." If playing the ukulele, or at least becoming involved with a group that does, means sharing laughter and bringing light into the world, then I agree with her. Maybe I should buy a ukulele too.

In closing this chapter, I want to say that I made a conscious decision not to pursue music professionally because of my emotional baggage involving my family. When I study my family's faith, I avoid (some) potential emotional baggage by avoiding a discussion of music. Not all fieldwork is of our choosing, and being assigned to observe the St. John's Ukulele Club brought me face-to-face with some of my deepest discomfort. I could not have predicted the emotions that it would spark in me, or the way in which it would connect with my other research. Sunstein and Chisari-Strater ask fieldworkers to address what surprises, intrigues, and disturbs them when they write ethnography. In my case, it was disturbance that made me a more vulnerable observer than I have ever been.

ENDNOTES

[1] I use this word to refer to Christian traditions that believe in gifts granted by the Holy Spirit. In the case of this particular community, this might mean speaking in tongues, or it might mean gifts of prophecy or spiritual knowledge. Music facilitated heightened emotions in these services, which contributed to the expression of these gifts and, thus, proof of the presence of the Holy Spirit.
[2] This was in contrast to the St. John's Ukulele Orchestra, which Marianna laughingly described as "a cult." This was the group that did public performances, in contrast to this group that met for informal practices.

WORKS CITED

Behar, Ruth. *The Vulnerable Observer: Anthropology That Breaks Your Heart*. Beacon Press, 1996.
Briggs, Jean. *Never in Anger: Portrait of an Eskimo Family*. Harvard University Press, 1970.
Bringerud, Lydia. "Converts' Cradle: An American Orthodox

Church's Search for Authenticity." MA thesis, Indiana University, 2012.

Georges, Robert, and Michael Owen Jones. *People Studying People: The Human Element in Fieldwork*. University of California Press, 1980.

Hufford, David. "The Scholarly Voice and the Personal Voice: Reflexivity in Belief Studies." *Western Folklore*, vol. 54, no. 1, 1995, pp. 57-76.

Lawless, Elaine. *Handmaidens of the Lord: Pentecostal Women Preachers and Traditional Religion*. University of Pennsylvania Press, 1988.

Lawless, Elaine. "I Was Afraid Someone Like You ... an Outsider ... Would Misunderstand": Negotiating Interpretive Differences between Ethnographers and Subjects." *Journal of American Folklore*, vol. 105, no. 417, 1992, pp. 302-14.

Mullen, Patrick. "Belief and the American Folk." *Journal of American Folklore* 113.448 (2000): 119-43.

Narayan, Kirin. *Mondays on the Dark Night of the Moon: Himalayan Foothill Folktales*. Oxford University Press, 1997.

Pratt, Mary Louise. "Fieldwork in Common Places." *Writing Culture: The Poetics and Politics of Ethnography*, edited by James Clifford and George E. Marcus, University of California Press, 1986, pp. 27-50.

Rice, Timothy. "Time, Place, and Metaphor in Musical Experience and Ethnography." *Ethnomusicology*, vol. 47, no. 2, 2003, pp. 151-79.

Rosaldo, Renato. "Grief and a Headhunter's Rage." *Death, Mourning, and Burial: A Cross-Cultural Reader*, edited by Antonius C.G.M. Robben, Blackwell Publishing, 2004, pp. 167-78.

Sunstein, Bonnie Stone, and Elizabeth Chiseri-Strater. *Fieldworking: Reading and Writing Research*. 4th ed. Bedford/St. Martin's University Press, 2011.

Tedlock, Barbara. "From Participant Observation to the Observation of Participation: The Emergence of Narrative Ethnography." *Journal of Anthropological Research*, vol. 47, no. 1, 1991, pp. 69-94.

Titon, Jeff Todd. *Powerhouse for God: Speech, Chant and Song in an Appalachian Baptist Church*. University of Texas Press, 1988.

Tolkien, J.R.R. *The Silmarillion*, edited by Christopher Tolkien. Ballantine Books, 1999.

Turino, Thomas. *Music as Social Life: The Politics of Participation*. University of Chicago Press, 2008.

5.
Healing Music, Healing Mothers

An Autoethnographic Journey of a Foster Parent Using Music for Therapeutic Care Children

CARA-LEIGH BATTAGLIA

Remember that iconic image of Mom holding a baby in a rocking chair and singing? That image embodied safety, security, comfort, healing, love, and a sense of home for several generations. Lullabies were a common part of soothing children at bedtime or during illness. Those women were just being moms. Yet perhaps they were doing much more than soothing those babies. Now, science and technology are validating what moms already knew: music affects the brain and the heart, both literally and metaphorically. Music can be a positive influence for all children, but it can be an especially healing influence on those recovering from trauma. It can be an educational, psychological, and healing tool. Although science has begun to verify music's healing effect on medical and emotional damage to body, mind, and heart, mothers have instinctively been using it to foster social and emotional healing. There are many (too many) damaged and broken children in America today. They silently slip between the cracks in a system defined by stressed budgets and broken legislation. Such children have experienced abuse and neglect that has fractured their minds, bodies, and spirits. Mothering with music effectively changes and heals children who have experienced trauma.

MOTHERING AS A HEALING ART

Mothering is more than giving birth to a child or raising a child with love and protection; it is more than the legal responsibility of caretaking. It has also been called an art. The word "mother" is used as an adjective, noun, and verb, and embodies the characteristics of affection. As Sara Ruddick proclaims in "Maternal Thinking," mothering need not refer to a female. Or as Martha Joy Rose states in her thesis on mothering and motherness, "mothering has historically been enacted by women, but in the twenty-first century, *birth* via a man (a male-mother as in the case of a trans man) is not unheard of, and perhaps in the future things like artificial wombs will continue to blur the boundaries" (emphasis in original 29). Mothering, in other words, can be defined beyond gendered limitations. For the purposes of this chapter, I am including an expansive definition of mothering, including but not limited to othermothers, adoptive parents, and primary caregivers.

Mothering can be a very different experience for people living in different situations and societies. Regardless of the context in which mothers and children live, the power of mothering has been undervalued as a healing strategy. In America, there are the folk remedies of Mother's chicken soup healing colds, or the belief of a kiss healing a "boo-boo," perhaps because mothering is also a form of healing. As Anne Boykin and Savina Schoenhofer state, "Nursing has long been associated with the idea of mothering, when mothering is understood as nurturing the personhood of another" (15). Mothers have long been healing children, not just by nurturing and nursing, but by engaging with music. Lullabies were and still are a common way to soothe children at bedtime, and a way for mothers to engage with music, using it to comfort and teach. While what mothers sing may or may not matter (a nonsense piece, an ABC song, or an operatic solo), the close proximity, the sound, and the repetition all play a role in creating an atmosphere of wellbeing.

History tells us that sound is an important part of the prenatal experience; sound also has educational and medical uses. People worldwide—from Native Americans to Tibetan monks—use drums, rattles, and chants for healing purposes. Premature babies thrive when relaxing music is played. In a study from the Utah Bally Regional Medical Center, two twenty-minute doses of vocal lullaby tapes each day slowed premature infants' heart rates and increased the amount of formula and oxygen they took in. Rosalie Pratt, a music professor at Brigham Young University who oversaw the research, has noted how "any song with a soothing melody and steady rhythm can calm a colicky or teething baby ... Instrumental music is soothing, but a human voice will make babies feel more secure." "A parent's voice is best," says Pratt, "even if you can't carry a tune or ... make up the lyrics" (Cordes). In southwestern Virginia, I studied the private journals of pregnant mothers in a Lamaze class. Every woman independently recognized that sound was important. All commented that their fetuses reacted to sound and music, and they spoke to and sang to them in utero, played music, and documented reactions. The women assumed their unborn children could hear them. Research suggests that "as early as the second trimester of human development, children can hear ... their mother's heartbeat, digestive system, and voice vibrations. Even the sounds outside the womb entered into an unborn child's ears— human laughter, dogs barking, traffic, conversations" (Shenfield).

In fact, music has been identified as a healing phenomenon throughout history. "In the Middle Ages, the study of music be- came a mandatory part of a physician's education. ... In his book *Awakenings*, neurologist Oliver Sacks writes of patients who went from being catatonic to fully functional when music was added to their environment" (Janis). Although the medicinal and neurological treatment "awakened" them, it was music that helped patients to move. Using music for healing has been explored by physicians, philosophers, music therapists, and psychologists. Today, we see music therapy and the acts of creating, performing, moving to, or listening to music as educational, psychological, and physical tools for trauma recovery. Science has been verifying music's healing effect on medical and emotional damage, yet mothers have long been using it to foster social and emotional healing.

I am a mother. I am not a psychologist, social worker, music therapist, or musician. My work using music in mothering-to-heal is anecdotal and not officially therapeutic from a scientific point of view. I use music simply because music soothed me through a long, painful recovery from a spinal injury. Since the 1990s, I have been adapting that tool in my roles as a teacher, administrator, and therapeutic level foster parent working in Central New York. I have worked for a national children's charity in a residential therapeutic centre for severely abused children. I fostered traumatized children in my home and adopted one.

Fostering and adopting neglected or abused children is an often misunderstood path to motherhood. In the U.S., foster mothers and the children they foster may be constrained by social, educational, cultural, governmental, religious, and cultural expectations. Women must often negotiate their understandings of mothering in coming to terms with, for example, relationships with the foster child's birth parents, the financial implications of fostering, and understanding the varied needs of children placed in foster care. Many of the therapeutic-level children in foster care suffer from physical, emotional, and mental problems requiring medical, psychological, or spiritual support. They are not easy children to mother. In this situation, motherhood often means advocacy, education, healing, and building societal bridges. It may also mean constant conflict with family, peers, and authority figures; dealing with academic and social failure; or handling children's socially inappropriate behaviours. It may mean a bankrupting stream of medical professionals, evaluations, and therapies. It may include postadoption visits with the very birth parents that traumatized the children.

Mothering children with medical and emotional damage requires more than mainstream beliefs. It requires another level of personal soul searching. Mothering foster children who require social and emotional healing from posttraumatic stress disorder (PTSD), starvation, effects of poverty, and prenatal abuse is a different commitment than simply loving, feeding, clothing, and raising a child who has not gone through these traumatic experiences. Oftentimes, adoptive mothers hear from others that "No child comes with a guarantee at birth." Truly, any child may fall into societal traps or face medical challenges. But children adopted from long-term therapeutic foster care are guaranteed to have deep wounds, which may or may not heal over time. In America, there are many children who have suffered horrible abuse and neglect, which has fractured their minds, bodies, and spirits. These children are often misdiagnosed or overmedicated. Schools are quick to label them, but youth suffering from PTSD or anxiety often demonstrate physical, emotional, or social behaviours that mimic other disorders or are triggered by sounds, smells, words, sights, or actions. The symptoms associated with childhood trauma even mimic those of attention deficit hyperactivity disorder (ADHD), autism, and Asperger syndrome. The difference between a disorder like ADHD and children suffering from trauma is that the former tends to be environmentally specific. Someone with medical conditions, such as ADHD, cannot turn the disorder off. Schools and other institutions and professional environments have yet to catch up with trauma-informed care, and, therefore, they do not recognize or respond to it. Children living in situations defined by multigenerational poverty or abuse often do not respond to typical treatments that help other disorders. They silently slip between the cracks in a system typified by stressed budgets and broken legislation and by an inconsistency in responding to children's needs and rights. As therapeutic foster parents, my partner and I have worked with multiple agencies and facilities, and children have improved in our home. We adopted one of the children we fostered. As a mother, I loved them all and provided food, clothing, safety, and security. I met their needs. But the biggest differences emerged in the children's behaviour when I used music and meditation as strategic tools.

Music evokes memories, emotions, and energy. In the preface to his book *Musicophilia*, Oliver Sacks highlights Schopenhauer's idea that the "inexpressible depth of music [is] so easy to understand and yet so inexplicable ... due to the fact that it reproduces all the emotions of our inner most being" (xii). Sacks goes on to explore how "listening to music is not just auditory and emotional, it is motoric as well: 'We listen to music with our muscles' as Nietzsche wrote" (xii). As any mother who has used the "clean up" song with a two-year-old knows, a singsong tune can motivate kids to participate. Preschool teachers use such methods daily with kids who find it difficult to follow directions by adding rhythm, making up simple tunes, or singing directions to the tune of another song. I have always found certain music to be soothing, and other music effective for studying or writing. As a teacher, I have explored the effect of music on journal writing and the effect musical components have had on student writing. Music focuses students and allows them to explore ideas and express themselves. In fact, we have used all kinds of music—from classical to punk, heavy metal to New Age, and jazz to Broadway. Students often relate different feelings to different music. In my classroom, I have used warning bells, chimes, and music to signal transition, and to calm and re-focus after high-energy events. For example, when students enter my classroom, I often play music, and they take their seats and respond to a journal prompt on the board. Sometimes they just listen to the music. Five minutes before the end of class, I ring a bell, signaling the time to finish up and prepare to leave. Children enjoy the quiet time, particularly following recess or lunch. Such transitions and warnings are equally important in mothering foster children.

As an educational speaker, I am often asked about student challenges. Often it is the foster mother, not the educator, who identifies chronic trauma affecting students as an unrecognized factor from the educational perspective. Few schools train teachers to recognize the impact of chronic trauma on children's behaviour; educators often do not know how to respond to these students. Joyce Dorado has worked with San Francisco Unified School District through her "Healthy Environments and Response to Trauma in Schools" program, and states the following: "While educators sometimes see a misbehaving child as a 'bad' or 'mean' or 'oppositional' kid, Joyce helps them to see a scared kid [whose] behavior is the result of chronic exposure to traumatic events" (Dorado and Zakrzewski). In addition to impacting behaviour, trauma can wreak havoc on a student's ability to learn. Scientists have found that children "subjected repeatedly to trauma suffer from other social, psychological, cognitive, and biological issues, including difficulty regulating emotions, paying attention, and forming relationships" (Dorado and Zakrzewski).

For Dorado, trauma is like a "vinyl record":

When a song is played again and again, a groove is worn into the record. If, when playing a different song, some-one knocks the record player, the needle will skip across the record and land in the deepest groove, playing that song again. Even when you reach the end...sometimes the groove is so deep the needle skips back. Like a needle on a record player, complex trauma wears a groove in the brain. So when something non-threatening happens that reminds us of a traumatic incident, our bodies replay the traumatic reaction—mobilizing us to either run from or fight the threat, while shutting down other systems that help us think and reason. If this happens over and over, we become more easily triggered into that fear response mode, never giving our bodies time to recover. After a while, as we adapt to this chronic triggering, our behavior can seem crazy or rude when taken out of the context of trauma.... In a classroom, something as simple as the teacher raising his or her voice to get everyone's attention or accidentally getting bumped by another classmate can steer that child into this groove. When triggered, the child's out-of-proportion emotional and sometimes physical reaction often makes no sense whatsoever to the teacher, making it difficult for the teacher to respond appropriately. (Dorado and Zakrzewski)

Educators can mitigate the effects of trauma. Dorado recommends that teachers create calm, predictable transitions between activities:

That feeling of "uh oh, what's going to happen next: can be highly associated with a situation at home where a child's happy, loving daddy can, without warning, turn into a monster. Some teachers will play music or ring a meditation bell or blow a harmonica to signal transition. The important thing is to build a routine around transitions so that children know: a) what the transition is going to look like, b) what they're supposed to be doing, and c) what's next.

Though traumatized, these children are neither weak nor victims. They are survivors, with strength and resilience. They size up adults quickly and lash out first before others can hurt them. They are smart, strong, and resourceful. What they lack are resources. When music becomes a resource, it brings educational, social, psychological, emotional, and physical benefits to their lives.

At one facility, I met Kim Draheim, a male, who has had a twenty-five-year residential care career; the act of mothering is not gender specific. Single fathers and male caregivers also mother these children by nurturing, healing, and elevating them to a place where they can find their voice and move forward. Teachers, nurses, daycare providers, and other caregiving professionals (male or female) mother children daily. Draheim is also a rock musician. At the centre's school, as part of an extracurricular attempt to reach youth, he turned to his own passion: rock music. Now labelled a recreation specialist, music making is 40 percent of his job, but 100 percent of his success in empowering youth. Draheim chokes up telling stories about his kids, and about how his Youth Voice Band performs throughout New York.

Originally Draheim taught kids to play well-known songs on instruments, but that changed when he listened to one boy's criticism: "You're doing it wrong. Instruments are great, but help us make our own music that expresses our thoughts and feelings." He followed the boy's advice:

The way youth engage with music varies; some are never going to play again, but while in therapy or care, they found respite, escape or a way to express themselves and gained experience. Some will be musicians the rest of their lives. Some are finding their voice, literally and figuratively, by expressing themselves artistically and expressing emotions in a healthy way.

Although Draheim is not a music therapist, he uses music as a therapeutic aid to healing and nurturing.

Songwriting with kids from traumatic backgrounds "is about the real stuff," says Draheim. "Sometimes lyrics are a gifted poet's contribution; sometimes multiple kids contribute, but all songs are kid generated." The titles on their recent CD are not preteen pop in nature. "Christmas in a Place That Isn't Home," written by a child in care for eight years, is poignant and sobering. "I'm Gonna Be Me" expresses the frustration of a young man forced to be someone he is not. Such song titles as "Can You See Who We Are?," "The Misunderstood," and "Monster" reflect their reality. As these children find their voice through music and lyrics, they heal and learn in a way that allows them to embody their strengths and vent their frustrations. The less formal aspect of the experience presents them with a new level of freedom and empowerment conducive to healing.

As with Draheim, my partner and I found lyrics were an important breakthrough while fostering "Lizzie," a child with deep-rooted anger who felt unsafe and angry at adults. We began using all types of music to decompress her after school and home visits and as an option when people got on her nerves. She gravitated to different styles depending on mood and emotional upset. Eventually instrumental music combined with nature sounds soothed her, along with movie soundtracks that told a story. The lyrics resonated with Lizzie's experiences. Initially, she could not stop escalating her behaviour, but once I realized she needed control, I made quiet time and choice of music her decision. Lizzie's behaviours escalated when she perceived control was in adult hands, and she became a master manipulator.

Eventually, she began to value her control and decided when to meditate. In doing so, she regained balance, self-control, emotional control (or release), and privacy. Lizzie could not invoke a decision to meditate in order to escape a reprimand or consequence, but she could recognize and avoid a situation heading in that direction. Respect, privacy, empowerment, control, decision making, and praise were all new to Lizzie. We also shared stories set to her choice of quiet, soothing music (she could neither fall nor stay asleep), which eventually eliminated the need for sleep medications. But it was words and lyrics that broke through to her. After school, transition time helped her to calm down from social stresses; she would colour, write and draw to music, and would select lyrics about strength, control, survival, and family. Supervised family visits were an emotional vortex for her, and postvisit readjustments were an emotional tightrope; for these transitions, we chose music with reassuring lyrics. Often though, music was a mirror of her own emotions. If she was angry, she chose loud, raw music about fighting. If she was hurt, Lizzie chose gentle and peaceful sounds with no lyrics. But she literally found her voice through singing. She first began by copying lyrics, then writing her own words; she finally used her voice to talk through problems, to confess information, and to talk about what had hurt or confused her. It was ultimately lyrics that led to her greatest breakthroughs.

Draheim discovered, as did I, that lyrics were a positive tool. Michael Friedman suggests that "exposure to pro-social lyrics increases positive thought, empathy, and helping behavior. The message in a lyric ... may be able to reach more people than all of the psychotherapists in the world combined." Whether in a band or a family, music is a connecting experience that builds relationships and communication. Research clearly demonstrates that improved social connection and support can improve mental health outcomes. Thus, any music that helps connect people can have a profound impact on an individual's mental health. Our anecdotal mothering experiences indicate music evokes, induces or controls mood and emotion. Indeed, music may be used "to retrain emotional and psychosocial competence—not in the traditional music therapy sense of improving well-being, but rather as a functional goal in cognitive ability" (Thaut and McIntosh).

Music also brings a social benefit, which Draheim calls "the cool factor." As he explains, "when they go from being nobody to lead guitar in a rock band ... these kids are suddenly faced with their first chance to be 'cool' when others notice their talent; they finally feel they have something to offer." Listening to music is also tied to identity; children's likes, dislikes, trends, and way of dressing can be tied to music preferences. So beyond that so-cial status, Draheim notes the following: "there's also a sense of camaraderie in working together as part of a band and belonging to the team. Kids learn to respect musical talents and each other. They begin to relate to each other. They discover a new, improved identity through the creative act of making music, and the pride of 'I created this.' It's real." As one boy told Draheim, "I can hold on to this for the rest of my life."

In my experience, music always affects behaviour. We found it worked with every child placed with us. Draheim found it worked in residential care. Children learn that to participate in his music program is a privilege and responsibility. Behaviour simply improves because they're happy and can express themselves. Oliver Sacks identifies this and suggests that "much of what is heard during one's early years may be 'engraved on the brain for the rest of one's life" (xii). The acts of creating, performing, moving to, or listening to music can be considered paths for healing if only for the reason that it is a resource given to children who have previously had none. Whether listening to or creating music, children do not need talent; they need an emotional outlet tailored to their specific needs.

However, music is not a miracle cure but rather a step forward on a healing path. Oftentimes, children's behaviours will regress. Draheim tells of a drummer who had been doing well until he went on rampage leaving the classroom and its furniture and computers demolished. When asked why he became violent, the boy said he chose to hit computers instead of people. However, he took responsibility, made restitution, and continued to attend rehearsals. He believed he would not be allowed to perform, but he knew the band needed a drummer for practice. Draheim asked him, "Six months ago this wouldn't have happened. What's changed?" The boy answered: "I have." Although he had been unable to control his emotional reaction, he had grown enough to take responsibility for his actions, and he did not want to let his bandmates down.

Music makes you feel good. Period music from our youth makes us nostalgic. Memories are associated with songs. In my experience, teens and angry youth initially prefer harsher, more discordant music. They have told me it mirrors their internal feelings of anger and resentment. Just because it is not meditative music does not mean it is not soothing. Music is perceived and reacted to differently by different individuals.

The act of making music can be nurturing because the act of making music is self-soothing. Draheim says "music can be a path to change a proclivity from a negative choice, such as resorting to violence, to a positive source of soothing." When children feel bad, they often turn to destructive or socially unacceptable options. Learning to turn to something that feels good—like playing a guitar—is a new, powerful lesson. In a situation where the fight or flight response has been triggered but cannot be acted upon, music can provide an appropriate release. It puts us in touch with our emotions. According to Draheim, "Learning to run toward something that feels good or to pull out of that bad feeling is a new internal emotional resource for these troubled youth." It is also a defense or escape mechanism that is socially acceptable. Draheim wants his students to learn to play music when they feel down rather than turn to violence.

In her 1981 article *"The Therapeutic Use of Music: A Literature Review,"* Janet Cook identifies the ways in which music has been used as a healing tool throughout history. Other studies have identified the ways in which the brain is impacted by music. One Stanford medicine study has found that "Music moves the brain to pay attention." For example, findings from this study suggest that "music engages the areas of the brain involved with paying attention, making predictions, and updating the event in memory" (qtd. in Baker). Studies have also demonstrated that infants in utero are affected by auditory signals (Skwarecki). However, much more work remains to be done to quantify the neurological and psychological effects of music on foster youth.

Informal programs, like Draheim's, continue to show success. One 2012 online article in *Parenting Magazine* explores an Austin, Texas, program called "Kids in a New Groove," which connects foster children with music. Founded by Karyn Scott, the program provides music lessons to foster children. Nicole Villalpando notes how the children in this program learn skills, develop focus, and "a sense of self-worth." Mentors have a different relationship with children than do teachers. Mentors nurture their students in a one-on-one way: "Music is a nonverbal positive influence for kids in foster care. It can help break through barriers and help them trust an adult ... kids who have behavior problems at school or in foster homes, music motivates them" (Villalpando).

Like music, religion and spirituality also have healing properties. Foster motherhood often means advocacy and education as well as healing and building societal and cultural bridges—for example, accommodating ethnic differences in food, language, or ways of living. Healing help for these children, when their spirits have been broken, can be a difficult and painful journey. Mothering children with medical and emotional damage to body, mind, and heart requires more than mainstream religious beliefs; it requires personal soul searching, which often challenges and can force a foster parent to put aside previously held beliefs and tenets. As a parent, I expect a baby to cry when they wake from their nap. But an infant who was neglected does not cry when they wake. The infant does not cry because there is no expectation—no faith—that the adult will come to pick them up and care for them.

I chose to adopt my child after four years of fostering him. I had no idea what to expect when it came to the long-term damage he had experienced, which manifested itself physically, mentally, emotionally, and spiritually. I have had to reexamine each of my previously held beliefs: religious, spiritual, and even metaphysical ones. Music is one of the only things that has offered consistent reprieve and healing for both of us.

Parents often undergo a change in their own spiritual beliefs (as opposed to religious beliefs). Children who have experienced trauma in their lives may explore several established religious structures or attend one church. But often their inner spiritual search calls for more than a societal religious structure and more of an internal philosophy and personal source of faith, hope, and strength. When the birth parents have not provided their children with safety or basic needs, a patriarchal or matriarchal religious figure does not automatically comfort the child. Our search for meaning and significance in life changes, and our approach to relationships changes when we have to support and work with the abusers who harmed these children. Our perspective on why bad and good things happen can change when the abusers have more legal rights as birth parents than the children have as victims. My spiritual beliefs evolved by travelling this path and by having this experience. All that matters is that my child finds a source of faith and comfort, and finds a way to believe in something greater than us. It no longer matters if he goes to church each week. It matters that he has the inner fortitude to visit with his birth parents (per court mandates) and handle PTSD and anxiety that such a visit triggers.

For many, religion is a source of comfort, including rituals, hymns and prayers. Religions around the world have long recognized that music relaxes and heals. From the mantras of monks to prayers sung in the Catholic Church, music is part of a sacred healing structure. For youth who are jaded, repetition and routine can be comforting, but spirituality may be more important than organized religion. I believe in organized religion, but my experience is that religion is based upon a community of people who share a similar moral code. To believe, one must have faith. These children are not quick to believe blindly or to seek comfort in benevolent authority figures or to respond to a heaven-hell dichotomy. Before these children of trauma can take comfort in religion, they need to develop the "internal feeling that there is something more ... Spirituality results when one's faith has been activated" (Popcak). In my own experience, first fostering faith is the most important, and fostering spirituality is an act of nurturing and mothering. Regardless of our own background or beliefs, giving children control over their bodies, minds and spirits is crucial.

I have found that as a mother, my job is to help my son explore faith, respect, and strength as concepts. But I also need to guide him in the discovery of finding peace—something he has no familiarity with—before he can learn to be peaceful. Meditation and music can be a spiritual bridge to both religion and healing. Music can enhance children's ability to meditate, attend classes, and explore quiet time. My children (fostered and adopted) and I have tried various meditation classes: some were guided (recorded or live), and some were informal. Like music, the meditation has to mirror the children's needs. We have experimented with styles, moods, music, and exercise. I have used gongs, drumming, rock and jazz, multicultural compilations and stories, depending on whether we needed to stimulate, calm, heal, or escape. Two things always happened: first, the children picked music based on the social, emotional, or trauma need that was triggered. If they were angry, they selected fast or hard rock music. If they were sad or nervous, they chose soft classical music. If fearful, they often picked music with lyrics that made them feel strong. Second, the children made these choices voluntarily. If they became upset or lost control, they could escape. They sought out the opportunity to decompress, to release negative emotions, and to seek healing. They transitioned from slamming doors to calmly turning on music. They gained self-control, self-awareness, and healing; they found comfort in music. I admit to bias: I had originally thought that all youth would accept meditative music as a soothing influence. I was wrong. It does not matter what kind of music the children used. Children left our home with the CD that was best for them. The music the children chose was as individualized and unique as the children themselves.

Mothers use music to foster social and emotional healing. However, it would be naïve to think that music and love are enough to heal children who have suffered trauma. And we must not equate healing with permanent change. In my experience, even without formal therapy, therapeutic mothering with music can effectively change children who experienced trauma. It does not matter what sound or music is used. In my own meditation studio, I have found that classical and meditative music can help improve test scores, improve memorization, synchronize brain hemispheres, improve clarity and critical thinking skills, and achieve deeper sleep. My students report decreased insomnia; increased focus and achievement in academics, work, and life; and fewer headaches. For exercise-based meditations, or physical or emotional release of negative emotions, fast, modern rock or alternative music can serve as a safe release.

My domestic partner, the children's foster father, and I were often asked by professionals in charge of foster children whether we had a magic wand. They placed the most severe cases in our home as a last chance, and we always seemed to get positive results. I used to think love would make the difference. Now I think it was the music that made a difference, along with many other supports, of course. But the influence of music on the physical, mental and emotional changes in these children cannot be ignored. Neurological research demonstrates that music has positive effects on both the body and brain. It can positively affect mood disorders (Raglio et al.) and produce direct biological changes, such as reducing heart rate, blood pressure, and cortisol levels (Friedman). In the PBS documentary *The Healing Power of Music*, Spencer Michels reports on the power and versatility of music therapy in medical settings: "when former U.S. Rep. Gabrielle Giffords returned to Washington for [a] State of the Union address ... she had made a dramatic recovery after being shot in the head. Her family credits music therapy for helping to get her voice back." Although much more research on the neurological effects of music therapy is needed, what is known is that listening to music activates multiple regions in the brain. Scientists say the brain responds to music by creating new pathways around damaged areas. Michels notes the following: "music is now being used to help patients with a wide variety of illnesses [and] ...a growing number of studies do suggest music can aid healing in various ways. One recent scientific paper out of Harvard showed music therapy helped stroke patients regain speech ... other studies found music may improve heart and respiratory rates and blood pressure, as well as anxiety and pain." Music may also have a positive healing effect on a wide variety of illnesses, including epilepsy, multiple sclerosis, and Parkinson's disease (Raglio et al.).

Music can even help youth with ADHD. According to Tali Shenfield, "In 1985, half a million children were diagnosed with ADHD. Today, that [number] has increased to between five and seven million." Schools in particular are quick to label any child learning difficulties as having ADHD. Regardless of diagnosis and the symptoms, music appears to be a solution:

> When music is played, it produces a ... neuro-feedback loop ... Playing a musical instrument requires three motor control functions: Sequencing, Spatial organization ... and Timing. Music can spark the synapses, increasing the brain's dopamine levels. It is this ... that is responsible for motivation, working memory and attention regulation. ADHD brains have low levels of dopamine. However, listening to music increases dopamine levels, and can help ... patients to better function. (Shenfield)

Music therapy was developed by psychologists at the University of Michigan in the mid-1940s "to treat war veterans suffering from psychological issues such as PTSD" (Shenfield). It also works when applied to ADHD because children thrive on structure and routine: "Music has structure, and ADHD minds need ... structure to go through the daily activities of life. Music gives them ... organization to help them strategize, forestall and respond to the things around them" (Shenfield). According to music therapists, certain tones, rhythms, and vibrations can help treat medical and behavioural problems: "Brigham Young researchers found that when ... kids with ADHD listened to three 40-minute recordings of classical music a week, their brain waves moved to higher levels that allowed them to focus more ... 70 percent continued to show improvement six months later" (Cordes).

Rhythmic music can help children without ADHD to settle down, as rhythm is perceived differently by the brain, making children pay attention when things are said in a musical way (Cordes). It is now widely recognized that music impacts brain development, and its effects are being explored as a possible treatment for traumatic brain injury. Music can also activate the attention network on both sides of the brain, which can help overcome attention problems (Thaut and McIntosh). Music influences mood, reduces impulsiveness and restlessness, and alleviates anxiety and stress (Shenfield). All of these are traits of children who suffer from ADHD or PTSD.

Some experts in the field are questioning whether music also heals emotional suffering. According to Dr. Mike Friedman, the evidence suggests it does:

> *Research says yes. We now know through controlled treatment outcome studies that listening to and playing music is a potent treatment for mental health issues. Research demonstrates that adding music therapy to treatment improves symptoms and social functioning (and) demonstrated efficacy as an independent treatment for reducing depression, anxiety and chronic pain.*

Friedman's findings prove true in my own experience. My adopted son has overcome a tremendous amount of neglect and trauma, but his trauma responses are still triggered by different stressors. His stress level determines which music he chooses to play. He is now ten years old, but even as young as age five, his choices ranged between Steven Tyler's screams to soft meditation music sung in Hindi. The more stressed he is, the quieter the music he chooses. The happier he is, the more he leans toward rock music that he will sing.

Researchers are helping us discover the social and emotional power of music. It impacts us in ways that other sounds do not, and "using MRI technology, they're discovering why music can inspire such strong feelings and bind us tightly to other people." "Music affects deep emotional centers in the brain," says Valorie Salimpoor, a neuroscientist at McGill University (qtd. in Suttie). "Basically, when people listen to music with a familiar beat, they anticipate emotional peaks and enjoy it more" (Suttie). In many cases, teaching these children of trauma to anticipate emotional peaks is a key part of teaching them to control those same emotions. According to Salimpoor, "The dopamine release comes from having their predictions confirmed; this combination of anticipation and intense emotional release" may explain why people love music, yet have different tastes (qtd. in Suttie).

Ed Large, a music psychologist at University of Connecticut, agrees that music releases powerful emotions. According to Jill Suttie, Large looks at how variations in dynamics—slowing or speeding up rhythm, or softer and louder sounds—resonate in the brain and affect emotional response. Large argues that musical rhythms directly affect brain rhythms, and brain rhythms are responsible for how you feel. That is why when people gather and hear the same music, it is a shared emotional experience. Your brain literally synchronizes with the music. Perhaps that is why we were able to help our children slow down their emotional reactions.

Rhythm and those dynamics were a key part of mothering "Daniel" with music. He was a brain-injured teenager diagnosed with obsessive-compulsive disorder (OCD) and ADHD. Although his home was stable, his single mom needed a break. When he was placed in weekend respite care, he became angry and volatile, and he had allegedly harmed others. He could not watch television for more than three minutes without pacing in circles. He had emotions, hormones, and pent-up energy in body and mind. He had frantic bursts of speed, so I began with rhythm. We kept a steady pace while walking, hiking, and geocaching, and we listened to music in order to set that pace. I always gave him something to do with hands and feet simultaneously. We had one rule: keep a steady pace. No lagging behind or running ahead. He was responsible for walking the dog and throwing balls. Since I had a younger child in the house, it was necessary to impose a naptime, so Daniel lay on his bed, listening to music while tossing a ball to the beat, which slowed him down and gave him an activity that was a repetitive break from pacing. He began opting for quiet time outside of naptime. I focused on turning things that made him different into strengths as we sought rhythm-based activities. I taught him golf, which requires a steady rhythm. He struggled until I taught him to sing a version of Johann Strauss's "Blue Danube Waltz" while swinging. He found that the rhythm of his swing, timed to that tune, was not too fast or slow. He made the golf team, played in tournaments, and gained peer acceptance.

So, although mothers know music can be a positive influence for children, foster mothers and other caregivers know it can be an educational, psychological, and healing tool for children recovering from trauma. Whereas science has begun to verify music's healing effect, mothers have already been using it to foster social and emotional healing. As Michael Thaut and Gerald McIntosh suggest, "Scientists need ... to pay more attention to research that will benefit children, and to focus on disorders in which neurologic music therapy lacks rigorous study so far" (Thaut and McIntosh). Scientists, it seems, need to listen to their mothers.

WORKS CITED

Baker, Mitzi. "Music Moves Brain to Pay Attention: Stanford Study Finds." *Stanford Medicine News Center*, 1 Aug. 2007 med.stanford.edu/news/all-news/2007/07/music-moves-brain-to-pay-attention-stanford-study-finds.html. Accessed 21 Nov. 2017.

Boykin, Anne, and Savina Schoenhofer. *Nursing as Caring: A Model for Transforming Practice*. Jones and Bartlett Publishers, 2001.

Cordes, Helen. "Music Therapy: The Health Benefits of Music: Fascinating Findings on How Classic Music Can Help Kids with ADHD and Colicky Babies." *Parenting*, 2013, www.parenting.com/article/healing-tunes-the-health-benefits-of-music. Accessed 21 Nov. 2017.

Cook, Janet D. "The Therapeutic Use of Music: A Literature Review." *Nursing Forum*, vol. 20, no. 3, 1981, pp. 252–66.

Dorado, Joyce, and Vicki Zakrzewski. "How to Help a Traumatized Child in the Classroom." *Greater Good Magazine*, 23 Oct. 2013, greatergood.berkeley.edu/article/item/the_silent_epidemic_in_our_classrooms. Accessed 21 Nov. 2017.

Friedman, Michael. "Does Music Have Healing Powers?" *Psychology Today*, 4 Feb. 2014, www.psychologytoday.com/blog/brick-brick/201402/does-music-have-healing-powers. Accessed 21 Nov. 2017.

Janis, Byron. "A Healing Art." *The Wall Street Journal*, 7 May

2014, www.wsj.com/articles/a-healing-art-1399495645. Accessed 21 Nov. 2017.

The Healing Power of Music. Narrated by Spencer Michels, *PBS News Hour*, 27 Feb. 2012, www.pbs.org/newshour/show/the-healing-power-of-music. Accessed 21 Nov. 2017.

Popcak, Gregory. "Faith, Spirituality, Belief, Religion ... What's the Difference?" *Patheos*, 5 May 2014, www.patheos.com/blogs/faithonthecouch/2014/05/faith-spirituality-belief-religion-whats-the-difference/. Accessed 21 Nov. 2017.

Rose, Martha Joy. "*The Journal of Mother Studies*": A Peer Reviewed, International, Interdisciplinary, Open-Access, Digital Humanities Hybrid Project. MA Thesis, CUNY, 2015.

Raglio, Attardo, et al. "Effects of Music and Music Therapy on Mood in Neurological Patients." *World J. Psychiatry*, vol. 22, no. 1, 2015, pp. 68-78.

Ruddick, Sara. *Maternal Thinking: Toward a Politics of Peace.* Beacon Press, 1989.

Sacks, Oliver W. *Musicophilia: Tales of Music and the Brain.* Knopf. 2007.

Shenfield, Tali. "Healing Power of Music for ADHD Children." *KidsGoals*, 2 Apr. 2013, kidsgoals.com/adhd-in-children/healing-power-of-music-for-adhd-children/. Accessed 21 Nov. 2017.

Skwarecki, Beth. "Babies Learn to Recognize Words in the Womb." *Science Magazine*, 26 Aug. 2013, www.sciencemag.org/news/2013/08/babies-learn-recognize-words-womb. Accessed 21 Nov. 2017.

Suttie, Jill. "Why We Love Music." *Greater Good Magazine*, 12 Jan. 2015, greatergood.berkeley.edu/article/item/why_we_love_music. Accessed 21 Nov. 2017.

Thaut, Michael, and Gerald McIntosh. "How Music Helps to Heal the Injured Brain." *The Dana Foundation*, 24 Mar. 2010, dana.org/Cerebrum/2010/How_Music_Helps_to_Heal_the_Injured_Brain__Therapeutic_Use_Crescendos_Thanks_to_Advances_in_Brain_Science/. Accessed 21 Nov. 2017.

Villalpando, Nicole. "Program Connects Foster Kids to Music, Life Lessons." *Statesman* 14 Sept. 2012, www.statesman.com/lifestyles/parenting/program-connects-foster-kids-music-life-lessons/eFyZHjU5Y6Gc3zvozGsRiJ/. Accessed 21 Nov. 2017.

6.
Singing into Motherhood

The Power of Singing During Pregnancy, Birth and Postpartum

AMANDA MEHL WEST

This chapter presents the idea of singing as a powerful tool to ease a woman's transition into motherhood. In pregnancy, the birthing process, and the postpartum period, the act of singing can bring physical calm, connection, and empowerment to both mother and baby. Additionally, it can build trust and understanding between individuals (the mother and her baby, or partner, or birth assistant) or within a community (a mother's family, birth team, circle of friends, spiritual community, etc.). The transition into motherhood can be physically, mentally, and emotionally challenging. Music counteracts these difficulties and acts as a pathway for liberation and healing by connecting mind, body, and spirit, by releasing endorphins, by focusing thoughts, and by forging deeper emotional and spiritual connections. As scientific research demonstrates the physical, psychological, and emotional benefits of singing, there is a growing field of birth professionals and women consciously using song to facilitate the transformation into motherhood. This chapter surveys current worldwide work in the field, including that of music therapists, midwives, doulas, and educators. Additionally, the chapter offers examples of stories in which the act of singing successfully supported women in their pregnancy, birth, and/or postpartum experience. It is hoped that increased awareness of the benefits of such singing will lead to its practice becoming readily accepted, supported, and simply commonplace.

For four years now, I have been co-leading prenatal singing circles, under the name of Womb Song, in Santa Cruz, California. In these community circles, women meet regularly and practice simple

90

meditation and breathing techniques, then learn simple songs and lullabies from around the world in a call and response format. I am a musician by profession, and my co-leader, Megan Jacobsmeyer, and I are both trained doulas as well as mothers. During our time leading these Womb Song circles, we have witnessed firsthand again and again the power of music to inspire, uplift, connect, ground, and empower the women who employ their use. We had done some Internet browsing on prenatal singing, and knew we were not alone in this work, but I wanted to take the next step and formalize the information now offered here. I have been inspired and amazed but not surprised by what I have found, for it is clear that this form of medicine (for that is what it becomes) should be offered in every woman's journey into motherhood.

THE MAGIC OF SINGING TOGETHER

A National Public Radio story from July 2013 presents the findings of musicologist Bjorn Vickhoff, who, along with his team from Sahlgrenska Academy in Sweden, measured and charted the changes in choir members' heartbeats as they sang. The researchers were surprised at just how quickly the singers' heartbeats united as the tempo and phrasing of the music guided them into a shared rhythm. The synchronizing of these heart beats is one of the core elements in the power of shared music. Rituals around the world involve singing or chanting together— consider most church services or something as simple as singing "Happy Birthday." Singing together allows participants to experience a momentary sense of unity. Researchers have recently discovered that the "fetal heart rate ... changes with the physiological and psychological state of the mother" (Ivanov et al. 13641). So as a singing mother comes into that experience of calm and connection with a greater whole, so too does her baby.

ORIGINS

Although song has been used throughout human history, the origins of modern day prenatal singing can be traced to France in the 1960s and to a French classical singer and vocal instructor named Marie-Louise Aucher. Aucher developed an approach to singing she called "Psychophonie" and began to notice positive benefits in her pregnant students, which extended into birth and the postpartum (Potel, "Psychophonie in English"). According to Potel, Aucher connected with a young Michael Odent in 1976, the now famous French physician, author of fifteen books and leader in the field of obstetrics. Odent invited Aucher into the maternity unit of the French hospital where he was working at the time, and so began the first modern-day weekly prenatal singing workshops. Odent believed that women give birth more easily in the company of people with whom they feel comfortable (Kitzinger 184); he had the idea to include not only the pregnant women and their partners but also the nurses and midwives at the hospital (Dawid). That same year a midwife trained by Aucher created a prenatal singing group at another maternity hospital, Les Lilas near Paris, and these groups continue today (Potel, "Psychophonie in English").

Marie-Laure Potel, who also studied the Psychophonie method with Aucher and has worked musically with pregnant women for over twenty years, has written a book entirely devoted to the subject of prenatal singing titled *Le Chant Prenatal*, currently only available in French. Many prenatal singing groups continue in France today and are gaining popularity in the rest of Europe and around the world. A simple Internet search will uncover singing circles happening in Canada, Scotland, Australia, China, England, and across the United States (Plourde; Waldman; "Womb Song U.S.").

The Internet offers an easy way for ideas to spread globally. Many of the online writings about music, pregnancy, and childbirth have appeared within the last five years, and many of these cite a single video for their inspiration: a woman named Temple Cundall calmly singing with guitar and vocal harmony accompaniment by her husband, just before the homebirth of their ten-pound son. This video, uploaded to YouTube in December 2007 and viewed over two and half million times was obviously influential for many of its viewers. In the last twenty years, with the advancement of technology and the ability to study fetal development and brain function, a vast amount of scientific research has been confirming what humans have instinctively known for thousands of years: music is a powerful medicine, and singing offers its most highly potent form. With the support of scientific research, more Western professionals are incorporating song into their work with prenatal, birthing, and postpartum women, as singing begins to play a more evidence-based and socially embraced role in pregnancy, birth, and new motherhood.

PREGNANCY

Learning to sing lullabies in pregnancy benefited women in terms of relaxation, in feeling closer to their infants, in connecting with other pregnant women and in providing an additional tool for communication in the early newborn period. Some women described profound feelings of love and connection with the unborn infant while singing the lullabies ... it appears to be an enjoyable exercise for pregnant women and to have an effect on reducing maternal stress and encouraging infant attachment. (Carolan et al.)

These were the key findings from The Limerick Lullaby Project, which studied the effect of singing on prenatal stress. Participants in the Limerick study learned three lullabies through four group sessions with musicians. Qualitative in-depth interviews were conducted approximately three months later to capture the women's experiences. Rosario Montemurro tells a similar story in relation to a group of pregnant women in the village of Vilamarxant, Spain. The pregnant women and mothers of newborn infants discovered "a cascade of psychological benefits [for the mothers] ... After their babies were born, the mothers who had sung to their unborn infants found themselves more proficient at calming their newborns." As both of these studies demonstrate, prenatal singing can have a profound effect on women in numerous ways including the following: helping a mother tune into her body, encouraging and supporting mother-infant bonding, creating and offering a mental and emotional refuge, and reducing postpartum stress.

Prenatal singing provides a chance for a mother to learn how to breathe in rhythm and to consciously relax her muscles. Singing is done through a slow release of air, which automatically relaxes the body. Singing in tune and with ease also requires a relaxed jaw and throat (Bruser 68, 133). Many birth workers have made note of the correlation between the jaw and mouth, and the perineum (Fletcher; Gaskin; Skoko). Ina May Gaskin, one of the most revered and well-known midwives in the United States, approaches birth through something she calls "sphincter law"—an understanding she and her team have developed through three decades of experiences with over two thousand births at The Farm Midwifery Center in Tennessee. In her book *Ina May's Guide to Childbirth*, she writes the following:

> I noticed a strong connection between the sphincters of the mouth/throat and those of the cervix and yoni. A relaxed mouth means a more elastic cervix. Women whose mouths and throats are open and relaxed during labour and birth rarely need stitches after childbirth.... Most women can figure out how to relax their jaw more easily than their bottom.... Singing will maximize the ability of the body's sphincters to open. (178)

Another benefit of prenatal singing is that it strengthens communication channels between mother and baby, which nourishes and supports infant-mother bonding. Hearing is one of the first senses that the fetus develops, and it occurs between sixteen and twenty weeks in utero. French physician Alfred Tomatis extensively studied the ear, nose, and throat through his work with many singers. He was instrumental in developing the field of Audio-Psycho-Phonology which explores the inter-dependencies between the ear, voice formation, body and mind. One of Tomatis's fundamental ideas was that "the fetal ear responds to sound and uses the energy it receives ... to shape the developing nervous system and brain" (qtd. in Prada ix). He was fascinated by the experience of listening and the profound implications it has upon fetal development and mother-infant bonding. Tomatis writes, "the vocal nourishment that the mother provides to her child is just as important to the child's development as her milk" (*The Conscious Ear* 132).

Sheila Kitzinger notes in *The Complete Book of Pregnancy and Childbirth* that the "spectrograph of a baby's first cry can be matched with that of its mother's speech.... The baby has been listening to its mother's voice and has learned her speech characteristics" (79). Obstetrician-gynecologist Shawn Tassone notes several other studies that also draw this conclusion:

There is a silent conversation born from the physical fusion between you and your baby during pregnancy—an unspoken communication that deepens as you journey together toward birth.... Visualize the umbilical cord as a telephone wire that connects two receivers ... communication goes both ways, and encompasses physical, emotional, and spiritual connection ... transmitted through emotion-borne hormones [that] can also physically alter the state of your baby within the womb, after birth, and beyond.

These ideas suggest that the mother's voice is extremely important in fetal development. When a mother sings, her voice is amplified for her child in the womb and resonates through the mother's bones and the amniotic fluid, offering an even more powerful aural and vocal connection with the fetus than the spoken voice alone.

Today in the Western world, it is commonly understood that a healthy diet is important for a healthy pregnancy. Historically, other cultures have included a concept of healthy surroundings: what a woman sees, hears, feels, and thinks during pregnancy contributes to, or subtracts from, nourishment for a growing fetus. Giselle E. Whitwell—a board-certified music therapist, trained childbirth educator, certified birth doula through DONA (Doulas of North America), and prenatal parenting instructor with a career spanning over twenty-five years—offers further details. As the website for her organization, The Center for Prenatal and Perinatal Music, explains:

The Chinese had their Tranquility Centers, where mothers were encouraged to walk by the banks of the rivers to maintain their peace and serenity. The Hindus believed that mothers should be taught to transfer their thoughts to the fetus. Specially trained teachers shared this philosophy and gave mothers the necessary techniques in locations called Thought Rooms. Likewise, in Japan ... it was believed that the voices of the parents and extended family, their thoughts and feelings had an influence on the fetus; all disharmonious sounds were avoided.

Considering this, Whitwell writes that "Music, because of its nature and qualities, is most suitable for the task of nurturing the physical, emotional, mental and spiritual development of the unborn baby."
   Beyond the physical experience of singing, lyrics and melodies of a song can offer benefits for mental and emotional refuge. The 2014 documentary *Alive Inside*, exploring the profound effects of music on patients with Alzheimer's and dementia, demonstrates the power of music to connect us to other times and places, even other parts of ourselves. When singing is consciously and intentionally practised during pregnancy in a relaxing and supportive environment, the space and the presence it creates can be returned to during birth and postpartum through song. It is as if the songs become a wormhole in time. As one Womb Song participant later commented about her birth: "One moment in particular I was feeling that I couldn't take anymore and my whole body seemed to be coming apart...as I listened to the "Hollow Bamboo" song and went back to the circle of women in my mind, I found my place of strength again and was able to make it through."
   The benefits of prenatal singing extend not only into birthing but also into the postpartum period. Candice Sirak has discovered that singing prenatally affects the mothers' perceptions of infant temperament: infants who were sung to during pregnancy were perceived to be calmer overall than infants who were not sung to. Whether this was because the infants were in fact calmer or because the mothers were calmer and thus more available to attend to the needs of their infants, the results are the same: prenatal singing reduced postpartum stress levels for both mothers and children.

BIRTH

Things were not progressing so my Doula put on the Grease soundtrack. The entire room was singing and I felt it really helped put me at ease and back on course. (qts. In Lifeplustwins)

The benefits of singing during birth all contribute in one way or another toward increasing a labouring woman's comfort and reducing her experience of pain. Easing pain during birth makes for a more relaxed body, which makes for an easier labour, which makes for less pain, and the positive cycle continues (Simpkin, "The Birth Partner" 121). Music therapist and founder of Sound-Birthing prenatal program, Mary DiCamillo, explains that during birth music can "cue rhythmic breathing, assist the mothers in relaxation, prompt positive associations, and help focus attention on the music as a diversion from pain and hospital sounds."

Singing during labour eases pain by regulating breathing, relaxing the body, and helping open the cervix, which gives the mind a place of focus and connects the birthing mother with her birth team and/or with another place of strength and power. Sophie Fletcher, clinical hypnotherapist, doula, and author of *Mindful Hypnobirthing*, echoes Ina May's idea that vocalizing can help open the cervix. She has seen this practice work in her own experiences as a doula and has also heard similar stories from other midwives. Fletcher explains how singing different notes will activate different places along the spine, which, in turn, stimulates different parts of the nervous system, with those nerves branching off to one or more internal organs. Thus, certain notes that activate certain points along the spine can stimulate the cervical area. This may sound foreign to a Western understanding of the body, but it is fully accepted in other traditions. For example, traditional Chinese medicine advocates vocal toning to stimulate and tone bodily organs (Nakkach and Carpenter 15).

Elisa Benassi, a midwife and music therapist in Italy, inspired by Aucher's work, is developing singing as a method of pain relief during labour. Her explanation is that the vibrations from singing reduce muscle tension, which also reduces pain signals to the brain (Kurilko; Ridolfi). One of the most important tasks for a woman during her labour is to simply relax and allow her body to open to her baby. Writer, lecturer, and social anthropologist Sheila Kitzinger writes in *The Complete Book of Pregnancy and Childbirth* that "relaxation is vital for labor" (189). In a very physical way, the act of singing can assist with this work as the jaw and throat relax, and the notes resonate throughout.

Elena Skoko, a contributing author to this collection, lives nomadically between Croatia, Italy, and Bali, offering her *Singing Birth* workshops, which teach women the power of song in birthing and in their own lives. Skoko writes that a "woman's body is a complex yet poetical system that is able to respond to analogies, metaphors, symbols and gestures as well as to rational and mechanical stimulation." Music offers all of these forms of both physical and mental stimulation. Song lyrics give a worried mind something to focus on. In the Womb Song circles I lead, many of the songs we use are about surrender, trust, and opening, with lyrics like "I am feeling very open, like a flower in the morn, let my petals open, let my child be born," or "I am opening up in sweet surrender to the luminous love light of my babe."

The power of music links to memory, emotion, and experience, and can offer a portal into another time and place, helping connect a mother to a sense of calm and support if she is not feeling that in her birthing experience. As Molly, a Womb Song participant said:

> *Song really helped during my emergency C-section. I had brought many physical tools with me to help me deal with the birth; photos of nature, a cuddly blanket, etc. But they took all of these things away from me as they prepped me for surgery. They took away feeling in 80% of my body. They took away my knowledge, my power, and even my ability to see what was happening. But they couldn't take away song. As I desperately prayed my son would be safe, I sang a simple song: "Simply Trust. Don't the leaves flutter down just like that?" It got me through a scary time, and everything was fine in the end.*

I had a powerful experience with another one of our Womb Song moms who had been attending circles regularly. During her home birth, she texted to see if I might come and sing some songs with her and her partner. She had already been in early labour since the previous day and her contractions had stalled to almost nothing. She and her partner were sitting in despair on the couch when I came in with my guitar. I immediately got them standing and moving as we begin to sing the songs together she had become so familiar with during her pregnancy. Her spirit lightened and she smiled for the first time since I arrived. After another ten minutes, she felt a strong contraction. A few songs later, she felt another, and then another. Later that night, her baby was born in a beautiful home water birth and without forethought she greeted her baby with a song we sing in our Womb Song circles: "May the longtime sun shine upon you, all love surround you, and the pure, pure light within you, guide your way home."

Midwife Robin Lim has written of her observations of the universal instinct to bring song into birth. Lim is one of eleven midwives at Bumi Sehat, the famous birth center in Bali where six to seven hundred babies are born each year. She reflects on how the spiritual connections offered by song also help remind us of the sacred nature of birth.

POSTPARTUM

Still, I kept singing.... I was singing for her and for me without distinguishing the two ... that is the ultimate coping strategy. Every moment I was humming along, letting the music and words tumble out was a moment I wasn't thinking dreary thoughts. I wasn't thinking anything at all.... Singing also activates another overlooked coping strategy: breathing. Singing is breathing and breathing is life. (Miller 34)

Singing invariably continues its physical and mental benefits in the postpartum period, benefits that are magnified if singing has also been done prenatally. The early postpartum period can be one of the most emotionally powerful and overwhelming times in a woman's life. Singing the same songs she has been singing prenatally can keep her connected to a calm joyful space.

Studies have been done demonstrating the effects of songs sung to babies while they were in the womb and the calming effects they can have post birth (Partanen; Simkin, *Parents Singing*; Sirak).

Benefits are for both mother and baby, for as a mother calms, her baby can too, and vice versa. Penny Simkin, birth educator and doula based out of Seattle, has written extensively on the power of singing to children while in utero and the incredible benefits this can offer after a child is born (Simkin, *Parents Singing*; *The Birth Partner* 24). She recalls that her interest in prenatal singing began in the 1980s with inspiration from French pioneering physician and obstetrician, Michel Odent, and his book *Birth Reborn*. Odent's weekly prenatal singing circles inspired Simkin to begin her own. At that time, research on the capabilities of newborn babies—to recognize and have preferences toward familiar voices and sound— was just beginning to be published. She began suggesting to all of the students in her childbirth classes that they sing to their baby or play their favourite recorded music, with the thought that the baby will remember it and be soothed by it after birth.

One of Simkin's couples brought this to another level and chose one song that would become their son's song. They sang it frequently during pregnancy and when the birthing time came, they ended up needing a C-section. She writes the following:

> As the cesarean was underway, and the baby boy, crying lustily, was raised for the parents to see, the father began belting out the baby's song. Though the mother didn't have a strong voice under the circumstances, she also sang. The baby turned his head, turned his face right toward his father and calmed down while his father sang. Time stopped. As I looked around the operating room, I saw tears appear on the surgical masks. It's a moment I'll never forget, and it was that event that taught me the value, not only of singing prenatally, but also, singing the same song every day. (Simkin, *Parents Singing*)

Another doula attending our Womb Song circles in California recalled an almost identical experience she shared with a client. The couple had chosen a song they loved and sang it religiously to their baby each day she was in utero. In the end, this mother too had a C-section and as soon as the baby was out, both mother and father began singing the song to her. "Everyone in the room, the doctors, nurses and myself all started to cry," the doula recalls, "and the baby, she instantly stopped crying. It was so beautiful!"

A study from the University of Helsinki in Finland demonstrated this ability of babies' to recognize music they heard in utero for up to four months after their birth (Hoffmann). Twenty-four Finnish women played a particular melody to their babies in utero five days a week for the final trimester of their pregnancies. After the babies were born, their brains showed more reaction to the familiar melody both immediately and four months after birth than the control group. Contributing neuroscientist Eino Partanen, suggests "The mother's voice has more resonance than any other voice in the womb, and this may make it more likely that the baby will remember the melody... This can be quite useful when the baby needs to be comforted after it is born." (qtd. in Hoffmann).

Lullabies are a universal form of song passed down through generations of parents to their young. In this way, song offers another portal through time, connecting generations and offering a sense that one is not alone in the sometimes very lonely task of infant care. As Molly, a mother from our Womb Song circles shared:

> When I was a child, my mother rarely sang because she had been told she couldn't carry a tune in a bucket. However, she did sing me a special lullaby when I felt scared. Sadly, she passed away before my son was born. I miss her terribly and I search for small ways to connect my son to her. I find great comfort in singing the same lullaby every night to my son because it connects the generations. It reminds me how safe and loved she made me feel.

CONCLUSION

In closing this chapter, the following is clear: "One can never sing too much. It is one of the most complete modes of expression, involving mind, body and emotions." (Tomatis, *The Ear and The Voice* 26). The research and anecdotes offered here are by no means comprehensive, and it is my hope that this subject will continue to be explored in breadth and depth. But in the stories uncovered here, and from the years I have spent working with women as they move through pregnancy, birth, and into motherhood one thing is clear: song and singing offer a medicine that connects mind, body, and spirit, helping ease the often painful, always incredible, transition into motherhood. And news of this ancient medicine is spreading.

WORKS CITED

Bruser, Madeline. *The Art of Practicing: A Guide to Making Music from the Heart*. Three Rivers, 1997.

Carolan, M., et al. "The Limerick Lullaby Project: An Intervention to Relieve Prenatal Stress." *Midwifery*, vol. 28, no. 2, Apr. 2012, pp. 173-90.

Cundall, Temple "Woman Sings While In Labor." *YouTube,* uploaded by templetunes75, 24 Dec, 2007, www.youtube.com/watch?v=z3WA9iHz5ww . Accessed 21 Nov. 2017.

Dawid, Julie. "Why Sing?" *The Singing Midwife: Musical Pregnancy, Babies, Birth and Midwifery Musings*, thesingingmidwifedotnet.wordpress.com/sing-with-me/. Accessed 19 Nov. 2017.

DiCamillo, Mary. "Music Therapy Assisted Childbirth Helps Moms (and Coaches) Through Labor." *Personal Stories*. Musictherapy. org/about/personal_stories. Accessed 19 Nov. 2017.

Fletcher, Sophie. "Why Singing Will Help Kimberley Walsh Birth Her Baby." *Mindful Mamma UK*, 12 Jun. 2014, www.mindful-mamma.co.uk/why-singing-will-help-kimberley-walsh-brith-her-baby. Accessed 19 Nov. 2017.

Frandes, Ioana "From Conception to Birth 2 - Sensory Stimulation." *Prenatal Bliss*, 6 Nov. 2014, prenatalbliss.wordpress. com/2014/11/06/from-conception-to-birth-2-sensory-stimulation. Accessed 19 Nov. 2017.

Gaskin, Ina May. *Ina May's Guide to Childbirth*. Bantam, 2003.

"Health Shots." *National Public Radio*. 10 Jul. 2013, www.npr. org/sections/health-shots/. Accessed 14 Nov. 2017.

Hoffmann, Thomas. "Babies Learn Lullabies in Mother's Womb." *ScienceNordic*. 3 Nov, 2013. sciencenordic.com/babies-learn-lullabies-mother's-womb. Accessed 19 Nov. 2017.

Ivanov, Plamen Ch., et al. "Maternal-Fetal Heartbeat Phase Synchronization" *Proceedings of the National Academy of Sciences of the United States of America*, vol.106, no. 33, Aug. 2009, pp. 13641-2. http://www.pnas.org/content/106/33/13641.full

Kitzinger, Sheila. *The Complete Book of Pregnancy and Childbirth.* Alfred A. Knopf, 2008.

Lifeplustwins. "Singing in Labor." *Stand and Deliver: Reflections on Pregnancy, Birth and Mothering.* 14 Jan. 2008, rixarixa.blog-spot.com/2008/01/singing-in-labor.html. Accessed 19 Nov. 2017.

Lim, Ibu Robin. "Sing the Babies Earthside." *Pathways,* 2011, pathwaystofamilywellness.org/Pregnancy-Birth/sing-the-babies-earthside.html. Accessed 14 Nov. 2017.

Miller, Karen Maezen. *Momma Zen: Walking the Crooked Path of Motherhood.* Trumpeter, 2007.

Minson, R. "A Sonic Birth." *Music and Miracles,* edited by D. Campbell, Quest Books, 1992, pp. 89-97.

Montemurro, Rosario N. Rozada. "Singing Lullabies to Unborn Children: Experiences in Village Vilamarxant, Spain." *Birth Psychology Journal,* Fall 1996, birthpsychology.com/journals/volume-11-issue-1/singing-lullabies-unborn-children-experiences-village-vilamarxant-spain. Accessed 14 Nov. 2017.

Kurilko, Daria. "Sing to Reduce Labor Pain." *Genius Pregnancy.* 29 Dec. 2010. Web. 16 Jan. 2016.

Nakkach, Silvia, and Valerie Carpenter. *Free your Voice; Awake to Life through Singing.* Boulder: Sounds True, 2012. Print.

Odent, Michel. *Birth Reborn.* Souvenir, 1994.

Partanen, Eino et al. "Prenatal Music Exposure Induces Long-Term Neural Effects." *Plos One Journal,* vol. 30 Oct. 2013, doi: https://doi.org/10.1371/journal.pone.0078946

Plourde, Rhonda. "South Coast Singing Circle Classes to Begin." *South Coast Today,* 3 Sept. 2008, www.southcoasttoday.com/article/20080903/PUB02/. Accessed 14 Nov. 2017.

Potel, Marie-Laure. *Le Chant Prenetal.* Paris: Editions DesIris, 2012. Print.

Potel, Marie-Laure "Psychophonie in English." *Envie de Chanter.* 2008-2016. Web. 15 Jan. 2016.

Prada, Roberta. "To the Reader." *The Ear and the Voice.* By Alfred A. Tomatis. Scarecrow, 2005, pp. ix–xi.

Ridolfi, Elisa, "Universi Sonori—La Psicofonia e I benefice del canto prenatale." *Fanoperbambini.* 15 Apr. 2015, www.faboperbam-bini.it/web/universi-sonori-la-psicofonia-e-i-benefici-del-canto-prenatale. Accessed 19 Nov. 2017.

Rossato-Bennett, Michael, director. *Alive Inside: A Story of Music and Memory*. BOND/360, 2014.

Simkin, Penny. "Parents' Singing to Fetus and Newborn Enhances Their Well-Being, Parent-Infant Attachment, & Soothability: Part One." *Science & Sensibility,* 19 Feb. 2013, www.scienceandsensibility.org/blog/parents-singing-to-fetus-and-newborn-enhances-their-well-being,-parent-infant-attachment,-&-soothability-part-one. Accessed 14 Nov. 2017.

Simkin, Penny. *The Birth Partner; A Complete Guide to Childbirth for Dads, Doulas, and All Other Labor Companions*. Harvard Common Press, 2008.

Sirak, Candice. "Mothers' Singing to Fetuses: The Effect of Music Education." Dissertation, Florida State University, 2012.

Skoko, Elena. "Free Your Mouth and Your Os Will Follow" *Singing Birth Workshop PDF*, www.singingbirth.com/workshop. Accessed 19 Nov. 2017.

Tassone, Shawn A. "The Two-Way Umbilical Cord: Bonding with Your Baby Before Birth." *The Llewellyn Journal*, www.llewellyn.com/journal/article/2421. Accessed 19 Nov. 2017.

Tomatis, Alfred A. *The Conscious Ear: My Life of Transformation Through Listening*. Barrytown, Station Hill, 1991.

Tomatis, Alfred A. *The Ear and the Voice*. Scarecrow, 2005.

Vickhoff, B., et al. "Music Structure Determines Heart Rate Variability of Singers." *Frontiers in Psychology*. 9 Jul. 2013, frontiersin.org/articles/10.3389/fpsyg.2013.00334/full. Accessed 19 Nov. 2017.

Waldman, Maya. "Womb Song," singingforeveryone.co.uk/groupsandchoirs/wombsong.php. Accessed 19 Nov. 2017.

Whitwell, Giselle E. "Prelude." *Center for Prenatal and Perinatal Music*, 2007-2016, www.prenatalmusic.com/pages/prelude.php. Accessed 19 Nov. 2017.

"Womb Song U.S." www.wombsong.com. Accessed 19 Nov. 2017.

7.
Singing Birth

From Your Voice to Your *Yoni*

ELENA SKOKO

> Restoring the right to storytelling to the voices that have
> been denied, in order to interrupt their void and silence,
> their absence from the stage of the time, rebuilding the
> memory so that every single voice can speak by itself and
> for itself, and while doing so, express its own being.
> —Michela Zucca, anthropologist
> (Translated by the author)

Childbirth is part of women's lives, and it is one of the most
transforming experiences for women. It happens through the
same canal where women experience sexual pleasure, a place
of wonders called "*yoni*" in Hindu culture, and it is indeed a
continuation of women's sexual life in its full orgasmic potential.
Today, science proves the importance of modulated voice for the
wellbeing of women, children, men, couples, communities, and
the human species in general. The melodious maternal voice has
a special effect on humans; it is in the roots of our linguistic and
social behaviour. Yet singing during childbirth still needs to be
understood properly as a beneficial and powerful practice used
by women and by traditionally and medically trained midwives
and obstetrician-gynocologists who provide maternity assistance.
Until recently, women used to sing and dance during important
moments of their social and individual lives, including childbirth.
One does not have to be a professional singer to sing while having
a baby. Spontaneous singing is part of our human nature and
culture. Making peace with our own ancestors is the first step to

setting our voices free in order to regain our dignity as childbearing women and mothers.

FINDING MY VOICE

I had mixed feelings toward Slavic Istrian (Croatian) folk songs and dances. I loved them, but I also felt ashamed to perform them. My grandfather would ask me to sing with him "our way" (*po našu*), and we would perform typical nasal chirping duets in front of other family members. He would cry afterward while my mother and her sisters would hide their tears, and my cousins would chuckle. I felt my voice was powerful in that it could induce deep emotional states in others, but I also felt there was no space for it to be expressed freely for me in urban setting. I stopped singing.

I started singing again at the university in Bologna (Italy), where I formed a psycho-noise-punk'n'roll band called CUT together with my colleagues at the Faculty of Languages. I resonated with the international bands of the riot grrrl movement—L7, Babes in Toyland, Sleater Kinney, Bikini Kill, Pussy Riot—as well as with "angry women" (Juno), including Nina Hagen, Diamanda Galás, Lydia Lunch, and Exene Cervenka. I loved to perform my anger, and I would paint my face, crotch, and legs in blood red when I performed. When I graduated, I had to choose between my two passions: research or singing. Since both were unprofitable, and each would guarantee an income that would mean mere subsistence, I chose the band and went underground. After six years, three albums, and a period of female power exploration through performance and embodiment that included onstage group rituals, rock'n'roll, fashion, and multimedia, my bandmates felt overwhelmed. Meanwhile, I ended up one month in a hospital, back in my hometown in Croatia, with an inflammation in my right ovary. The doctor threatened a partial oophorectomy if I did not rest. I was twenty-seven years old at the time. I stopped singing again.

I used to nurture my ears with Billie Holiday, Ella Fitzgerald, Anita O'Day, Peggy Lee, Esther Williams, Big Mama Thornton, and other ladies singing the blues. It felt so right to my soul. The blues was a foreign kind of music to me, as was the English language, but it felt so close. There was something special in the old school blues that rang my bell. As Naomi Wolf puts it:

> Ragtime, and then jazz and blues, also introduced a new frankness about discussing the vagina, and female sexuality in general. Blues lyrics in particular were filled with African American slang for "vagina" ... These slang terms were usually encoded in metaphors: the clitoris was a bell that needed a ring; the vagina was a hot frying pan, or a butter churn that needed to be beaten, or a hot dog bun in need of a hot dog.... Rather, the metaphors that both male and female blues singers used about the vagina consistently cast female desire as strong, steady, positive, sometimes funny—just as male sexual desire is often portrayed as very funny—and obviously in need of gratification, as well as deserving satisfaction. (222-23)

In 2007, I moved to Bali (Indonesia), where I met a man in a local restaurant. He asked me what I was doing. I said, "I want to sing the blues." He paused and said, "I am a bluesman." Junior Wells gave Bluebird this nickname when he was playing harp in his band in Chicago. After some time, we formed the band Bluebird & Skoko, and recorded an album. Our "Trust Your Mojo, Sista" is an ode to love, passion, and sexual mystique. We would sing, play, create, make love, and howl to the moon all night long with stray dogs gathering under our gates and wailing with us. Then we made a baby. Our daughter Koko was born in 2009 in Bali. I described our story in my book *Memoirs of a Singing Birth*. She came out as she came in—while I was singing in ecstasy.

BIRTHING WITH SONG

When I got pregnant, I laughed in joy and delight. It was the craziest thing I had done in my life. When I realized I was doing a crazy thing that I did not know anything about, I started searching for help. My mother gave birth in a hospital. The little she described was not encouraging. My grandmother gave birth four times at home, with the help of her mother and her husband holding her from the back on their wedding bed. This birthing scene created an icon in my head that I cherished during pregnancy and birth. My great-grandmother was a village community healer, but she could not lend me a hand from the heavenly meadows. (She would call it "*livada*," a big field where ancestors' souls gathered.) I did not want to give up my freedom while giving birth. I found a midwife who nourished me with love during pregnancy and assisted with the birth of my baby using kind words and songs. She encouraged me to be and to act as a lioness—and to sing. She would not tell me what to do, but she would be a mirror where I could see myself as a capable and competent woman who was transforming herself into a mother.

MOTHERING WITH SONG

I sang my baby to Earth, and I continue singing to her whenever she feels distressed. We sing together when we are happy, as we make up our own music and lyrics. During the first years with Koko, I discovered that some frequencies and rhythms could calm her down. It is the "mother's voice" that all mothers discover, as it is so beneficial and immediately soothing to babies and children. Fathers know this as well, and they can tell amazing stories while inducing sleep. Researchers have addressed this phenomenon and have recognized the mother's role in shaping the linguistic and socioemotional functioning of children to form the life-long patterns of human socialization (Dissanayake). As Sandra Trehub explains,

> Mothers sing regularly to infants, doing so in a distinctive manner marked by high pitch, slow tempo, and emotional expressiveness. The pitch and tempo of mothers' songs are unusually stable over extended periods. Infant listeners prefer the maternal singing style to the usual style of singing, and they are more attentive to maternal singing than to maternal speech. Maternal singing also has a moderating effect on infant arousal.

Since the 1970s, research has explored the mother-baby auditory link before birth, focusing on the hearing capacity of the fetus in the womb. The mother's voice is reported to be the most intense acoustic signal measured in the amniotic environment influencing the wellbeing of the fetus, the development of the brain and auditory system, and the social and emotional development of the child (Fifer and Moon).

This phenomenon is well known today, and prenatal educators motivate future parents to speak and sing to the baby in the belly in order to create the foundation for a familiar acoustic environment for the baby's birth and early infancy (Simkin). The prenatal market has embraced this idea, and now a plethora of soundscapes for the bellies is available, resulting in mothers wrapping themselves in sound equipment hoping to increase their offspring's IQ. However, it is not the music itself, least of all music transmitted through pregnancy belts, that makes babies happier or more intelligent: it is *their own mother's voice* (Jahn et al.).

As humans, we are perfectly equipped to make music based solely on the features of our body; the instruments can be considered as accessories. Our innate ability to sing and dance, and to use these capabilities to engage intimately and socially, is part of our human nature. The infant's brain does not distinguish between music and language; actually, it treats language as a special case of music (Koelsch et al.). It appears that if mothers want their children to improve their communicative and intellectual skills, they should start singing as soon as possible.

VOICE AS INSTRUMENT

Since the origins of our species, the voice has played a crucial role in human musical activity. The human physical constitution (mainly the orofacial musculature, laryngeal anatomy, along with the neurological control over pitch, intensity, contour and duration of sounds produced by it), which enables us to produce vocal modulated sounds, represents a consistent heritage dating back to at least one million years ago. According to the Oxford paleoanthropologist Iain Morley,

> In contrast to the prevailing trend in Western music of
> the last few hundred years, instruments (anthropogenic

sound-producers) are not fundamental to musical production; the human body has the potential to constitute
an excellent instrument in its own right, both melodic
and percussive. Instruments constitute an accessory to
these existing human capacities; the origins of musical
behaviour would not have relied upon the invention of
instruments. (152)

Babies usually like a simple repertoire connected to prenatal and
natal memories, but I remember Koko did not choose her birth
song as her favourite one, although I sang the same song all the
way through labour and birth. Instead, I would make up monot-
onous, repetitive, wordless lullabies that had an instant effect.
Meaningless onomatopoeic expressions worked magic both in
cheerful play as well as in emergencies. Scholars Stephen Malloch and Colwyn Trevarthen have named this mother-baby vocal
interaction as "communicative musicality." They also emphasize
that the role of this primal musical communication taking place
in infancy creates patterns for affective relations and a sense of
community belonging well into adulthood. Genevieve Vaughan, a
feminist theoretician of the gift economy, considers mother-infant
bonding and interactions as the foundation of future linguistic and
social patterns; she also advances the possibility of this primal
relationship being the essence of social bonding, one which relies
on mutual gifting rather than monetary exchange.
    Some spiritual communities, such as the Orthodox Jewish
Lubavitchers, have specifically coded singing in their religious
and social practices. Ethnomusicologist Ellen Koskoff gives some
examples of their "*nigunim*" (singular "*nigun*"), vocally modulated melodies that are the very expression of the worshipers' faith
and spirituality. The songs can have a happy atmosphere, or they
can express yearning; many are performed using "vocables," or
syllables without referents in spoken language. Koskoff chooses
examples that include repetitive lyrics such as "yam ya di di di yam
bam ya di di di yam bam bam bam" for the happy melody, and
"yi ya ma ma ya ma ma ma ma ma ya ma ma" for the melancholic
melody in one of the most favourite yearning "nigun" (Koskoff
110-11). However, the women's voice ("*kol isha*" in Hebrew) in

this community is prohibited on those occasions where men are present, since it is perceived as sexually promiscuous (*"ervah"*) (Koskoff 95).

SCIENCE BEHIND THE VOICE

It is not the content or the grammar of the vocal expression that matters in emotional bonding and stress reduction; it is the familiar—and especially maternal—comforting and rhythmical voice that makes our oxytocin rise. I turn to neuroscience in an effort to give back some authority to women's and maternal singing:

> Since each vertebrate clade contains famously vocal members, language in the sense of human's unique ability to use recursive grammar may be unlikely to stand alone in its ability to release OT [oxytocin]. It is at least as likely that prosodic cues are responsible for the observed similarities in OT release between touch and human speech, and that non-linguistic social vocalizations facilitate attachment via the release of OT or related peptides in many other species. Nonetheless, two grammatically identical instances of human language differ in meaning depending on tonality, who is speaking, who is listening and the nuances of the relationship between them. (Seltzer et al. 4)

The use of modulated voice, similar to the touch, has a direct effect on the neurohormone oxytocin. Known also as the "hormone of love," oxytocin plays a crucial role in childbirth and breastfeeding, but it also it affects our innermost humanity, our physical and socioemotional functioning and wellbeing, as individuals, couples, families, communities, and as a species. The research on the therapeutic properties of singing on mother-infant bonding as well as in other social and pathological situations has been explored and documented in Kay Norton's book *Singing and Wellbeing: Ancient Wisdom, Modern Proof.* Norton points out how, therapeutically, the singing repertoire that works best varies according to the cultural background of each individual. The beneficial properties of singing, and especially community singing, are one of the emerging fields

111

of research in the UK, where scholars at the University of Oxford are producing scientific evidence on the topic (Pearce and Launay).

The exchange of oxytocin between the mother (and father) and the child passes through their voices, and it is mutually responsive. When the mother is out of reach, her voice is soothing for her child, like the embrace of her cuddling arms. When the mother is overwhelmed and exhausted, the cooing and wooing of her baby's smiling face works as an immediate lift, and raises her levels of oxytocin. I remember that my baby's crying voice was also able to induce a stressful reaction in myself, as was the effect of my angry voice on her. She would look at me in awe and suspension until my voice would become cheerful and my face positively expressive again. I would, of course, feel guilty. During pregnancy, both mother and baby produce oxytocin that passes through the placental barrier in a two-way communication. Once they become two separated bodies, their amorous bonding continues through their vocal exchange as well as through skin-to-skin contact, "but a strikingly similar hormonal profile emerge[s] in children comforted solely by their mother's voice" (Seltzer et al.). Vocalizations, then, may be as important as touch to the neuroendocrine regulation of social bonding in our species.

My voice was transformed during childbirth and motherhood; it became somehow lower and warmer. In the expulsive phase of labour, weird sounds were coming out from my throat; they were very deep, as if coming from the underworld. These sounds could be contrasted with high-pitched sounds, resembling a teakettle, I had made a few hours previously when my midwife delicately remarked how much "energy" I had and advised me to bring it downward. I explored a plethora of sounds during labour, and many came unexpectedly. I remember using my voice expressively and quite creatively during my daughter's conception, and these rehearsals came in handy when she was ready to reveal herself through the very same passage of my body. I was uninhibited when I was giving birth; my voice went where I had never been. I could physically experience and acoustically express the connection with other mammal "mommas." I would sound like a lioness, a tigress, a hog, a momma bear, a queen cat, a bitch, a bird, and a whale. I had a feeling that I could pick up frequencies from the world of the ancestors: I had a circle of grandmothers and great-grandmothers all the way back to the first birthing hominids humming in my ears.

I distinctively remember the moment I embraced the sensuality of my situation. I started moaning and groaning as if I were making love. The more I felt sensual the closer I was to opening up. I felt my entire childbearing body was responding to my voice; it was both physical and spiritual.

I could not have gone on with my vocal voyage if I did not have a supportive environment. I wished I had been brave enough to do it all by myself, possibly in an ancient cave that was used to serve this purpose, but I was not. Although in the Slavic tradition (in some rural and isolated places well into 1960s) women were giving birth alone (Vondraček-Mesar), convinced that their baby could give birth to itself (Gasperini), a few branches broke from the tree that had connected me to my ancestral mothers' experiences. I tried at least to find a matching soul that would like singing and music while being an expert in gentle birth assistance. I found it in Ibu Robin Lim, a poetess midwife. If the birth centre Bumi Sehat that she founded in Bali was not an ancient cave, it was the place where women gave birth freely and where midwives were singing and were supportive to vocal childbearing expressions. I kept in touch with Ibu Robin, and I occasionally witnessed births at Bumi Sehat. What I was able to notice, apart from reassuring faces and overall stable poses of both younger as well as senior midwives—even in critical situations—was their changing voice. When they had an everyday conversation they had a normal voice, but as they entered a room where a woman was giving birth, their voices would become sweet as mead, caressing as a feather, and very melodious. It was not an infant-directed speech; they would not infantilize a woman in any way. They would use a mother tongue, a mother voice, a mother pitch. Not the "motherese" in the sense of expressive exaggeration: no, it was a kind but firm vocal support, such as a mother would use who is encouraging her child to take her first steps, feed herself, go beyond her boundaries, and become independent.

Scholars may continue to treat these skills as "unconscious," both in mothers as well as in midwives, but they are highly effective and experiential; they belong to deeply rooted human patterns of interaction. I have met other senior singing midwives—Canadian Betty-Anne Daviss and American Carol Gautschi—and I field recorded their favourite birth songs during a coffee break at a conference (available on my website, www.singingbirth.com). Betty-Anne told me about her experience with Indigenous midwives in Guatemala who regularly sang special songs both to mothers and newborns. Carol had a repertoire in which spiritual songs went along with her own birth-themed songwriting production. There are also singing obstetrician-gynecologists, such as Dr. Carey Andrew-Jaja, who continued the singing tradition passed on by his senior mentor, not because it was evidence based but because they both liked it, and their patients seemed to enjoy it (Mosbergen). In a hospital in France in the 1970s, a then-young obstetrician-gynecologist, Michel Odent, and a French singer, Marie-Louise Aucher, founder of the "psychophonic" method, started a choir as part of an unstructured prenatal education program (Cardinale and Durieux). Their intuition, to include group singing as part of maternity assistance, was much appreciated both by pregnant women and by midwives (Odent).

If singing can be part of a humanized maternity assistance, why not encourage parturient women to indulge in this beneficial expression of their childbearing and motherly skills? As Morley explains, "Musical experience can gain much of its value from a sense of a profoundly personal response coupled with the sense of shared experience; meanwhile, when practised alone, it can act as a surrogate for interaction and shared experience."

Women often spontaneously start singing, as well as vocalizing, humming, and moaning melodiously while in labour. As a singer and advocate for human rights in childbirth, I happen to hear stories of women being silenced and ridiculed when singing in labour and childbirth, especially in medical settings. These anecdotes leave me deeply saddened, and I intend to do more research on the subject. Attitudes reflecting aversive reactions against woman's singing voice in labour have to do, in all its complexity, with historically determined gender interrelations as well as with power and pleasure issues. It is a women's secret, brought to light in recent times, that birth can not only be sensual but orgasmic (Davis and

Pascali-Bonaro). Some healthcare providers do not understand or cannot come to terms with this notion.

The voice is a powerful tool during childbirth, but it is also very personal. I have met a singer who was afraid to use her voice so as not to harm her child, as she felt her voice was too powerful. There are many singers' anecdotes that tell about their voice changing during pregnancy and childbirth—some experiencing long lasting transformation and some coming back to normal quickly. When you are a professional singer and your performance is tied to standards you are supposed to deliver, standards based on nonpregnant conditions, then some anxiety may occur when addressing pregnancy, childbirth, and motherhood that involve physical changes of the singer. But there is no other way than arrange for a birth setting so that little or no interference takes place. Harsh, disrespectful, or harmful assistance during delivery may produce damage to the abdominal and genital areas, influencing the ability to use the voice or perform, as in the case of an opera singer affected by chronic flatulence after childbirth (Hooton). Abuse and disrespect during childbirth in hospital facilities are widespread, and can happen both in low-income as well as in high-income countries (WHO). It is not the birth itself that is harmful to the vocal ability, but the poor quality and the inappropriateness of the maternity assistance. If a Caesarean birth happens to a singer, she can face some extra challenges (Pitman Will).

YOUR *YONI*; YOUR VOICE

Few people know that our yoni is directly connected to our voice. I prefer to use the term "yoni" instead of "vagina" because it is more precise and inclusive. When I was giving birth, afraid of my vagina exploding, Ibu Robin invited me to touch my Yoni (she "pronounced" it with the capital letter). This term previously felt so "new age" that it would never come from my mouth without intellectual embarrassment. But when I touched my ... *Yoni*, I felt a pride—unrelated to the vagina word. There was nothing compared to the feeling of glorious wonder, the sense of amazement with my own body, and the euphoria in the moment I realized another living being was coming out from *Her*!

Yoni is a Sanskrit term for the fascinating area between female legs up inside the lower abdomen. It stands for the vulva (external genitals including labia majora, labia minora, urethra, and the complete clitoral body; the "vagina" (internal muscular and tubular tract and the female prostate); and the inside reproductive organs (cervix, uterus, ovaries, Fallopian tubes). In all its anatomical, poetical, spiritual, philosophical, and practical aspects, *yoni* is the female principle itself. On the other side there is *"lingam,"* the male principle. Their mutual interaction produces the love of the Universe. I borrow from another culture as I do not know any other term in the five languages I speak that expresses the same complexity, beauty, and respect for human genitals as those of *yoni* and *lingam*.

During my pregnancy, I discovered the mouth-vagina connection for the first time in books of Ina May Gaskin, the mother of spiritual midwifery. I was fascinated. Based on her experiences with birthing women, Gaskin acknowledges that women who were able to widely open their mouth, loosen their jaws, and protrude their tongues had a more rapid cervical dilatation than those who could not. If a woman was "smooching" with her partner during labour, she had a better chance for making it quicker and, eventually, painless than a woman who was not. When a couple, while in early labour, made love, the outcomes were far more promising than for couples who had not made love. Even self-stimulation of the vulval area and/or of the nipples has positive effects on women's labour (Komisaruk et al., "Women's Clitoris").

Undoubtedly, there is much oxytocin involved, as well as dopamine and endorphins. The anticipation of pleasure and orgasm boosts woman's euphoric and blissful states moved by the levels of dopamine and opioids/endorphin release (Wolf). This sparkling cocktail of hormones enhances the feeling of security and intimacy promoting showers of oxytocin that regulates all the birthing and postpartum activities. If a "sexually assertive, self-aware woman is much more focused, motivated, energised and biologically empowered" (Wolf 77), this condition might indeed affect her ability to successfully and pleasurably give birth—from cosmic orgasm to orgasmic birth.

But there is more about female biology that we have to acknowledge. Science has finally, without lessening bias, addressed the female body in its own peculiarity. We know now that the female genital system is an intricate multidirectional neural freeway for pleasurable sensations interconnected between the head and our entire orgasmic body (Komisaruk et al., *The Science of Orgasm*). Three sets of nerves run along the spine and directly connect our brain with our genital area. These include the pelvic nerves that convey sensations to the brain from perigenital skin (the area of our pubic hair), perineal skin (the area from the vaginal opening to the anus, often damaged when episiotomies are administered), vagina and cervix; the pudendal nerves that reach the clitoris (the densest nerve supply in the body) and perigenital skin; and the hypogastric nerves that zoom in from the stomach to the cervix and the uterus. And then there is a bonus—the nervus vagus, which connects our auditory apparatus (ears), the pharynx (from the back of the nasal cavity deep inside the throat), and the larynx (the "voice box") down to the cervix and the uterus. This connection creates a freeway from your voice to the *yoni*. The nervus vagus remains active even in case of spine damage, and conveys pleasure and orgasm from the genitals (or even the skin of the shoulder) to the brain and vice versa, since it runs independently from the spine.

The vagus nerve is the key to scientifically understanding the "singing birth." Not only is our mouth connected to our vagina, but our voice is essential to our experience of pleasure and of childbirth; it has a direct intimate influence both on ourselves and on others, including our children and men. It is now scientifically confirmed what women and men always knew: singing is empowering and highly sensual and has benefits for general health, sexuality, conception, and birth. Our mouth gets sensual by performing modulating melodies, and our *yoni* opens up by hearing love songs. Rural folks all over the word performed spicy duets during the day so to "light the fire up" in the night, mutually gifting each other with all degrees of pleasure. This is a potential reason why, in modern times, the "crooners" such as Frank Sinatra and Elvis Presley, had a strong, even physical, impact on women (for the benefit of the music industry). Our sexual organs, in unison with our six senses, are even able to choose the right mate for procreation, as described in detail by Catherine Blackledge's in her book *The Story of V.* But today the knowledge of singing as an intrinsic part of our childbearing capacities has been neglected, facing stigma when spontaneously performed.

It appears that our uterus and cervix respond to our mouth and ears. The childbearing woman has all her senses enticed: she remembers everything people around her said and the tones they used during birth. As we know, babies hear as well. When the woman expresses herself vocally in those moments, she is hearing herself and interpreting her own voice: is it reassuring and pleasant, or is it frightening and an expression of pain? This multifaceted information might have a direct influence on the outcomes of her birth.

When women in childbirth are treated in respectful, competent and loving way, the motherly, vocally modulated, voice may contribute to creating conditions for them to give birth on their own terms, allowing their children to experience love and freedom from the very start.

WORKS CITED

Blackledge, Catherine. *The Story of V: A Natural History of Female Sexuality*. Rutgers University, 2003.

Cardinale, Marie-Jo, and Annie Durieux. *Bien dans ma voix, bien dans ma vie*. Le Courrier du Livre, 2004.

Davis, Elizabeth, and Debra Pascali-Bonaro. *Orgasmic Birth: Your Guide to a Safe, Satisfying, and Pleasurable Birth Experience*. Rodale, 2010.

Dissanayake, Ellen. *Homo Aestheticus: Where Art Comes From and Why*. Reprint edition. University of Washington, 1995.

Fifer, William P., and Christine M. Moon. "The Role of Mother's Voice in the Organization of Brain Function in the Newborn." *Acta Paediatrica (Oslo, Norway: 1992). Supplement* 397, 1994, pp. 86-93.

Gaskin, Ina May. *Ina May's Guide to Childbirth*. Bantam, 2003.

Gasparini, Evel. *Il matriarcato slavo. Antropologia culturale dei protoslavi*. Firenze University Press, 2010.

Hooton, Christopher. "Opera Singer out of Work after Surgery Left Her Unable to Sing Due to Chronic Flatulence." *The Independent*, 23 Jan. 2014, www.independent.co.uk/news/weird-news/

opera-singer-out-of-work-after-surgery-left-her-unable-to-sing-without-farting-9080793.html. Accessed 15 Nov. 2017.

Jahn, Michael, et al. "Music Devices for the Fetus? An Evaluation of Pregnancy Music Belts." *Journal of Perinatal Medicine*, August 1, 2015, pp. 639-773, *PubMed*, https://doi.org/10.1515/jpm-2015-0074.

Juno, Andrea. *Angry Women*. Juno, 1999.

Koelsch, S., et al. "Children Processing Music: Electric Brain Responses Reveal Musical Competence and Gender Differences." *Journal of Cognitive Neuroscience*, vol. 15, 2003, pp. 683-93.

Komisaruk, B.R., et al. "Women's Clitoris, Vagina, and Cervix Mapped on the Sensory Cortex: fMRI Evidence." *The Journal of Sexual Medicine*, vol. 8, no. 10, 2011, pp. 2822-830.

Komisaruk, B.R., et al. *The Science of Orgasm*. Johns Hopkins University, 2008.

Koskoff, Ellen. *A Feminist Ethnomusicology: Writings on Music and Gender*. University of Illinois Press, 2014.

Malloch, Stephen, and Colwyn Trevarthen. *Communicative Musicality: Exploring the Basis of Human Companionship*. Oxford University Press, 2009.

Morley, Iain. "A Multi-Disciplinary Approach to the Origins of Music: Perspectives from Anthropology, Archaeology, Cognition and Behaviour." *Journal of Anthropological Sciences*, vol. 92, 2014, pp. 147-77.

Mosbergen, Dominique. "This 'Singing Doctor' Has Sung to Every Newborn He's Delivered." *The Huffington Post*, 14 July 2014, www.huffingtonpost.ca/entry/singing-doctor-carey-andrew-jaja_n_5585562. Accessed 15 Nov. 2017.

Norton, Kay. *Singing and Wellbeing: Ancient Wisdom, Modern Proof*. Routledge, 2016.

Odent, Michel. "The Evolution of Obstetrics at Pithiviers." *Birth*, vol. 8, no. 1, 1981, pp. 7–15.

Pearce, Eiluned, and Jacques Launay. "Choir Singing Improves Health, Happiness – and Is the Perfect Icebreaker." *The Conversation*. 28 Oct. 2015, theconversation.com/choir-singing-improves-health-happiness-and-is-the-perfect-icebreaker-47619. Accessed 15 Nov. 2017.

Pitman Will, Andrea. *Pregnancy and Postpartum: A Guide for*

Singers. Arizona State University, 2013.

Seltzer, Leslie J., et al. "Social Vocalizations Can Release Oxytocin in Humans." Proc Biol Sci, vol. 277, no. 1694, 2015, pp. 2661-2666.

Simkin, Penny. "Beautiful Music: The Benefits of Singing to Your Baby, Before and After Birth | Pregnancy & Birth." *Pathways to Family Wellness Magazine*, 2013, pathwaystofamilywellness.org/Pregnancy-Birth/beautiful-music-the-benefits-of-singing-to-your-baby-before-and-after-birth.html. Accessed 15 Nov. 2017.

Skoko, Elena. *Memoirs of a Singing Birth*. Self Published, *lulu.com*, 2011.

Trehub, Sandra E. "Musical Predispositions in Infancy." *Annals of the New York Academy of Sciences*, vol. 930, 2001, pp. 1-16.

Vaughan, Genevieve. *The Gift in the Heart of Language*. Mimesis International, 2015.

Vondraček-Mesar, Jagoda. "Rađanje bez ičije pomoći u nekim južnoslavenskim krajevima." *Etnološka tribina*, vol. 23, no. 16, 1993, pp. 173-82.

Wolf, Naomi. *Vagina: A New Biography*. Virago, 2012.

World Health Organization. "Prevention and Elimination of Disrespect and Abuse during Childbirth." *WHO*, 2014, www.who.int/reproductivehealth/topics/maternal_perinatal/statement-childbirth/en/. Accessed 15 Nov. 2017.

8.
Land of My Mothers?

Clara Novello Davies as "Mam"[1] and Musician

RACHELLE LOUISE BARLOW

The wind held up above his head the sound of the choir from the Chapel for me to hear, and gave it back, but in those few notes I heard the rich, male voice of the Valley, golden, brave, and clean, with heart, and with loftiness of spirit, and I knew that their voice was my voice, for I was part of them as they were part of me, and the Valley was part of us and we were part of the Valley, not one more than the other, never one without the other. Of me was the Valley and the Valley was of me, and every blade of grass, and every stone, and every leaf of every tree, and every knob of coal or drop of water, or stick or branch or flower or grain of pollen, or living creature, or dust in ground, all were of me as my blood, my bones, or the notions from my mind. (Llewellyn 231)

Although women in Welsh history have received increasing attention in recent decades, the participation of women in music remains underexplored. Choral singing, in particular, has occupied a central position in Wales since the mid-nineteenth century when coal mining resulted in both rapid industrialization and population expansion in South Wales. Here, choral singing provided a unique framework for cementing social relations and galvanizing community spirit. However, Welsh choirs have since become stereotyped. Today, choral singing is often equated with a singular image of nationhood, one that is indelibly linked to a working-class conception of male identity; even the national anthem boldly states that Wales is the "land of my fathers." By contrast, this chapter interrogates this paternalistic view by examining how Clara Novello Davies (1861-1943) promoted female singing to national and international audiences. Despite establishing the Royal Welsh Ladies' Choir—a pioneering female choir with a bourgeois membership—in 1883, Clara's longstanding musical career is often overshadowed by that of her son, composer Ivor Novello (1893-1951). In terms of success, her choir won chief prizes at both the Chicago World's Fair (1893) and the Paris Exhibition (1900), yet her personal legacy has since been forgotten. Drawing upon her autobiography, among other sources, I examine how Clara negotiated the dual role of being a "mam" and a musician. Moreover, Clara contested a number of contemporary ideologies regarding domestic responsibility and social visibility. Invoking a historical ethnomusicological perspective, I show how Wales was also the "land of my mothers."

LAND OF MY FATHERS

The quotation that opens this chapter was reproduced from a novel by Richard Llewellyn (1906-1983) titled *How Green Was My Valley*, a narrative that depicts the life of a family, the Morgans, living in a coal mining community in a Welsh valley. Though written in 1939, the story is a nostalgic reflection upon an earlier period in South Wales, when the narrator, Huw Morgan, was a young boy. Recalling the struggles placed on family life, Huw traces the transformation from the utopian vision of a pastoral green valley to one that is blackened by the reality of an expanding coal mining industry. Although music is not the main focus of the narrative, Llewellyn shows how the struggle of industrial life is punctuated with moments of music making that promote communal accord and a unified identity. In particular, it is choral singing that is noted especially as a focus not only for social recreation but also, as the quotation above indicates, as a marker of national identification.

What is particularly interesting in this novel is the ambiguity surrounding location as it relates to music and society in South Wales. This ambiguity is illustrated in Llewellyn's failure to name his valley—showing how a familiar place serves to represent a cultural identity that is homogenous and typical of any Welsh valley during the late Victorian era. The immediate popularity following the book's publication within Wales indicated that this identity was familiar, and it was, therefore, accepted as a true reflection of life in the South Wales valleys. In 1941, this notion of an industrial Welsh identity was promoted to a much wider international audience when John Ford, an established American film director, adapted the novel for the screen for Twentieth Century Fox. Featuring a star cast that included Maureen O'Hara, Walter Pidgeon, and Roddy McDowall, the film was awarded five Oscars (including one for Outstanding Motion Picture) in 1942.

Such success in the international arena raised awareness of Wales, its people, and its economic output with new audiences. That being said, John Ford's adaptation promoted a singular, gendered representation of choral singing in Wales. From the outset, a connection is established between music and life in the valleys, since the opening credits are accompanied by a rendition of "*Rhyfelgyrch Gwŷr Harlech*" ("The March of the Men of Harlech"). Less than five minutes into the two-hour-long film, the viewer is introduced to the musical element of Welsh industrial life: coal-blackened miners stand in line to collect their wages before walking humbly from the site of the mines to row upon row of houses, where the woman of the household (the "mam") is waiting to amass the family budget before helping her husband and sons to wash away the residue of a hard day's toil. Importantly, the representation of this sequence in film is complemented by music that is essential, not ancillary, to the narrative. As such, the music is created by—and for—the men themselves. From the moment they leave the mines to the moment they cross the threshold, they sing together in harmony.

Here, John Ford's decision to include the sound of male voices singing "Men of Harlech" at the opening of the film is significant for a number of reasons. First, it calls upon a sense of national identity that was created in an earlier period of Welsh history. The connection to an historical narrative is crucial; although the song represents the tale of a fifteenth-century battle for the throne between the Lancastrians and the Yorkists at Harlech Castle (situated in North Wales), its adoption throughout the nineteenth century as an anthem not only for the proclamation of a national identity but also for communal singing serves to highlight how the song

was adapted to suit the changing demographics of an industrialized Wales. That is, it serves as what Philip Bohlman would call
an "unofficial national anthem" (111).[2] The second reason that
"Men of Harlech" is noteworthy in terms of both Ford's vision
and Llewellyn's narrative is linked to gender. By using male-only
versions of songs, the film projects a singular vision of music and
working-class masculinity to both national and international
audiences, and, simultaneously, cements the patriarchal image
of Wales as the "land of my fathers."[3] It is worth noting that the
book (without the aid of audiovisual technologies) also associates
men with choral singing.

It may be questioned how relevant a 1939 book and a 1941 film
are to the concept of national identity in contemporary Wales. In
the late twentieth century and to some extent in the twenty-first
century, the participation of women in Welsh choral singing has
often been significantly marginalized or, in some instances, completely absent from accounts concerning the musical practice in
Wales. According to *The Welsh Academy Encyclopaedia of Wales*,
published in 2008, "the male choir is regarded as a characteristically
Welsh institution. It found congenial soil in the country's populous
mining valleys, metallurgical centres and quarrying districts ...
[and] fulfilled similar roles to football teams in providing a focus
for local identity and opportunities for disciplined collective expression" (Davies et al. 532). Although it cannot be denied that the
practice of choral singing in Wales developed along gendered lines
from a unified approach first performed in mid-nineteenth-century
chapel choirs, sources, such as the one mentioned above, fail to
acknowledge the development of female choirs alongside their male
counterparts, which perpetuates the notion that choral singing in
Wales has historically been linked only to men.

By contrast, this chapter seeks to uncover Wales as the "land of
my mothers." Interrogating the paternalistic perspective often called
upon to represent Wales, I examine how Clara Novello Davies
promoted female singing to national and international audiences
with her Royal Welsh Ladies' Choir. Despite leading this pioneering female choir between the early 1880s and late 1930s, Clara's
longstanding musical career is often overshadowed by that of her
son, composer Ivor Novello. Having built a reputation throughout

his lifetime as a successful playwright, actor, and composer, Novello's legacy continues to be remembered in the present day with the prestigious Ivor Novello Awards. Since 1955, the Ivors have been presented annually by the British Academy of Songwriters, Composers, and Authors (BASCA) in association with PRS for Music to recognize excellence in British and Irish songwriting and composing. The musical legacy of Ivor Novello's mother, however, has been largely forgotten. Drawing upon her autobiography, and other sources, I examine the successes of Clara's female choir by focusing upon two case studies—the Chicago World's Fair (1893) and the Paris Exhibition (1900)—in order to show how she negotiated the dual role of being a "mam" and a musician.

CLARA'S NOVELLO IDEA

Clara Novello Davies was born in Canton, Cardiff, to Jacob Davies and his wife Margaret (née Evans). Like many families living in South Wales during the nineteenth century, the upbringing of Clara's parents was influenced by the two main facets of Welsh life: religion and mining. The family had strong religious connections, since Clara's maternal great-grandfather, the Reverend William Evans of Tonyrefail (1795-1891), was known for his unique style of pulpit recitative, while his son, also called William Evans, was a leading deacon at a Calvinistic Methodist chapel. Although religion functioned here as a form of employment, as well as faith for both, the latter William gained wealth through farming land at Parc-Coed-Machen in St Fagans, near Cardiff. Here, the involvement in religious leadership coupled with the involvement in profitable agricultural work ensured that William's family occupied an elevated social position in the local community.

Margaret's social status was to be altered, however, when she married Jacob Davies. The pair first met in chapel when Jacob was a seventeen-year-old miner, an occupation that was considered by Margaret's parents to be inadequate to support their daughter. Despite attempts to separate the couple, Margaret's marriage to "a young fool of a miner who [could not] even buy her bread let alone butter" (Novello Davies 9) prompted her father to disown her. Such outward signals concerning the division of social class between the couple did little to dissuade them, particularly Margaret, who used her background by educating Jacob, principally a Welsh speaker, in the use of the English language. Moreover, she turned the house into a quasi-private school in order to increase the family income, and secured employment with better wages for her husband.

However, one area in which Jacob did not require assistance was music. From a young age, he could be heard singing in chapel, and he began to conduct the village choir at the tender age of twelve. Enthusiasm for music was demonstrated also by the couple's daughter, Clara. Jacob and Clara often spent weekends together at the local Salem Chapel, located in Canton, where both musical and religious interests were fostered. Jacob played a leading role in the chapel, as both a precentor and a leader of the Band of Hope singing sessions.[4] Clara's own musical abilities developed significantly as she became recognized officially as the chapel's harmonium player, playing all services from the age of ten. She became conversant with the activities of the chapel choir, since the harmonium was situated in the gallery with singers on both sides. Singing was a particular passion for both father and daughter. Jacob was interested in the positive effects of singing and following the visit of an American evangelist named R. T. Booth, he set up the Cardiff Blue Ribbon Choir in 1880 for the cause of temperance.[5] Once again, Clara's musical skills were nurtured as she became the official accompanist for the choir's performances at national *eisteddfodau*[6] and at choral competitions held at the Crystal Palace in London.

Following her 1883 marriage to David Davies, a solicitor's clerk who sang in the Cardiff Blue Ribbon Choir, Clara fulfilled the role of a housewife; she notes in her autobiography that her retirement from public engagements in order to do so was presumed (Novello Davies 56). This was not an uncommon expectation for married Victorian women, particularly those who belonged to the middle class. In 1854, a lengthy narrative poem by Coventry Patmore (1823-1896) was published in London. Titled "The Angel in the House," the poem depicts the vision of an ideal woman. As a wife and mother, she obeys and adores her husband, promotes his wellbeing while simultaneously allowing her own life to be filled by the responsibilities of motherhood, social engagements, religion, and domestic management. This idea of a fixed domestic ideology was well established by the late Victorian era with a proliferation of household help manuals and etiquette guides published to teach women how to behave in social situations. In this matter, involvement in musical practices was somewhat problematic, since music performances in general did not reflect the domestic ideology presented to women; pursuing a career as a professional or semi-professional musician was particularly difficult for "middle- and upper-class women who were firmly discouraged from any kind of public exposure or career" (Fuller 315). Despite the fixed nature of contemporary ideologies regarding domestic responsibility and social visibility, Clara was not an "angel in the house."

Mimicking the precedent set by her mother, Clara canvassed to secure a better job for her husband David, since his salary was insufficient to support the newly married couple. More importantly, she furthered her musical interests and created an income by teaching private vocal lessons. In the same year, Clara established the Welsh Ladies' Choir, as it was first known, with encouragement from her father. Less than a year into her marriage, following the death of both her mother and her first child Myfanwy Margaret, who lived only for a few weeks, Clara was introduced to the art of choral conducting by Jacob. She recalls that "perfection in singing had always been [her] father's aim," and concepts of the qualities that signalled worthy performances came from hearing a variety of visiting "world-famous singer[s]" (Novello Davies 58). According to Clara, "father was never too poor to afford front seats for us both at every concert" (58). Although it was possible to hear both male and female solo artists on the stage in the late nineteenth century, the idea of seeing and hearing an all-female choir was seemingly innovative. She explains in her autobiography:

One day he was looking over some part songs which the publishers had sent for his approval, and calling me over to him he said: "Look here, Clara. These glees are for female voices only!" His tone of surprise was not to be wondered at—in those days when men monopolised most of the good things in life. "Did you ever hear of such a thing?" he continued.... I went over the parts and was enchanted as father. "Why don't you get your pupils together and form a ladies' choir", he went on. "But who ever heard of a woman conductor?" I asked incredulously. But the idea had a great thrill for me, and I decided to try. Thank God for father who always had vision and was keen on innovations, whose sole thought about women was not the one prevalent in those days – that they should be tied to the home—but was only too pleased to have me follow along his own lines of endeavour. (Novello Davies 59)

The notion of creating a female choir at this time must not be undervalued. Wales was a patriarchal society in which male musical practices, particularly in terms of choral music, were the privileged and expected form. Such an initiative also belonged to a greater consciousness regarding respectability in the nineteenth century when the idea of women on stage provoked mixed responses. Therefore, the formation of a female-only choir led by a female conductor can be viewed as a conscious subversion of such patriarchal values. The members of the newly formed Cardiff-based choir—comprised of approximately seventy women—were drawn largely from Clara's private pupils. The advantage of using her pupils in this manner meant that consistency in terms of tone, pronunciation, and breath control was achieved with ease, since each singer had received identical training. Significantly, each singer belonged to an elevated social class. In other words, the financial burden of musical tuition was exclusive in two ways: excluding those classes who were unable to pay and marking music as a social distinction for those classes who were. For women in the late Victorian era, voice lessons were socially desirable yet financially burdensome. This reflects a marked contrast from the aforementioned stereotype concerning working-class male voice choirs in Wales.

WOMEN OF HARLECH

The formation of Clara's Welsh Ladies' Choir was significant in the development of Welsh choral music, especially in relation to the achievements of the choir in the international arena with its performances at the World's Fair held in Chicago in 1893 and the Paris Exhibition of 1900. International exhibitions have attracted scholarly attention because, as Burton Benedict notes, they allowed nations "to project an image of unity for their own people and to present to the world at large" (5). Further, international exhibitions provided a framework in which the power relationship between the colonized and the colonizers could be displayed. In terms of music, non-Western sounds of the exoticized Other were favoured by visitors and audiences. In this context, the inclusion of Welsh music at such exhibitions was unusual. Moreover, it is surprising that the Welsh chose choral music, which could have been interpreted as essentially colonial music being used to characterize their national identity. However, originating in the nonconformist colonization of the industrialized valleys, the Welsh choir represented a unique combination of religious difference and social solidarity at a critical moment during the Industrial Revolution.

In Chicago, the World's Fair commemorated the four-hundredth anniversary of the "discovery" of America by Columbus in 1492. Chicago was an important centre for Celtic migration; Irish immigrants in particular played a significant role in the city's political and musical realm.[7] Welsh communities were well established in North America at the time of the exposition, as the relevant census reported 267,160 individuals with Welsh ancestry resident in the states by 1900. As a tribute to this immigrant community, the World's Fair featured an *eisteddfod* that was co-ordinated by the National Cymmrodorion Society. The word "*cymmrodorion*" is formed from "*cyn-frodorion*," meaning "earliest natives." Consisting of a four-day program (5-8 September), the initiative was designed to promote Welsh culture at an international level. The secretary of the society, William ap Madoc, was a key figure in its successful realization. To encourage interest, ap Madoc circulated ten thousand pamphlets (both in Welsh and English) throughout Wales. He asked the following: "Will the Welsh people neglect this grandest and most exceptional opportunity of exhibiting THEIR literary and musical characteristics? 'THEY WILL NOT!' is the united voice of the Cymry of America and their descendants, and we pray that the same will be the voice of GWALIA" (*World's Columbian Exposition* 7).

Despite the circulation of the open invitation, Clara recalled receiving a personal invite for her choir to participate. Although the obvious benefits of being involved included promotion for the Welsh Ladies' Choir as well as for Welsh choirs in general, the financial burden of travel and accommodation was unsurprisingly great. For Clara, the decision to compete required careful consideration for another reason: she had recently given birth to a son, David Ivor Davies ("Ivor Novello," born 15 January 1893). With the support of her father and her husband in terms of childcare for young Ivor, Clara agreed to participate and began to raise sponsorship for the venture. In this matter, the princely sum of 500 pounds was offered by Lascalles Carr, editor of the local newspaper *Western Mail*, whereas the remainder was achieved through fundraising concerts arranged by the choir.

Like all *eisteddfodau*, the Chicago Eisteddfod required all entrants for the choral competitions to learn a number of test pieces. In this case, the test pieces were "The Spanish Gipsy Girl" (arranged by Walter Damrosch) and "The Lord is my Shepherd" (arranged by Franz Schubert). According to Clara, the former piece is "one of the most difficult things ever written for ladies' voices ... [as] it calls for quick dramatic attack and technique of every description ... the voices blend in perfect simulation of the tambourine's prolonged shaking" (Novello Davies 91). Despite many of the choristers suffering with seasickness on the journey from Southampton to New York, Clara attempted to continue rehearsals aboard the ship in order to ensure her choir was ready to face its competitors. For the female choral competition, there were two other entries: The Cecilians, from Wilkes-Barre, and The Scranton Ladies. Both Wilkes-Barre and Scranton are known as settlements for Welsh immigrants.

Greeted with a standing ovation, Clara's choir was the last of the three women's choirs to compete. Believing that the previous ensemble—The Cecilians—had delivered a "perfect" rendition of its test pieces, Clara was doubtful about her own choir's performance. To her surprise, however, John Thomas, harpist to Queen Victoria, announced on behalf of the adjudicators that the Welsh

Ladies' Choir had won the Ladies' Choral Prize of 300 dollars.[8] Amid the stateside celebrations of cheering, hats being thrown into the air, and invitations for the choir to perform across America, details regarding the choir's success was communicated back to Wales via telegrams sent to Lascalles Carr. In the afterglow of the competition, Clara and her choir embarked upon an unplanned tour to Kansas City, Buffalo, and Niagara Falls, which, though important for the promotion of the choir, kept Clara away from her parenting responsibilities.

Although it might seem logical for musical ensembles to gain recognition in the international field following national success, the opposite was true for Clara's Welsh Ladies' Choir. Even though the choir was known in Cardiff prior to the Chicago Eisteddfod, recognition in the broader national context was lacking. This was remedied in 1894 when Clara received an invitation to perform before Queen Victoria at her residence in Osborne House on the Isle of Wight on 8 February 1894. This was an important engagement for the female choir; no other Welsh choir had been honoured in this way. In the following year, the Treorchy Male Choir—a choir made up largely of miners and colliers—performed for the Queen on 29 November, whereas the Rhondda Glee Society (winner of the male choral competition in Chicago) was invited to sing on 23 February 1898. Thus, it was a bourgeois female choir that was first to be recognized with a royal title; from the time of their command performance, Clara's choir became the Royal Welsh Ladies' Choir.

Whereas the Chicago Eisteddfod allowed Welsh-Americans to assert their right to promote a native identity on one side of the Atlantic, the Paris Exhibition of 1900 offered a different opportunity for musical exhibition on the other. Comparable to the Chicago World's Fair, the Paris Exhibition was an international fair that took place between 15 April and 12 November. Although Clara notes in her autobiography that choirs in Wales were invited to participate in the Exhibition (139), contemporary accounts in the media suggest a more complicated reality. On 13 May 1900, Laurent de Rille, head of the Music Commission for the Exhibition, sent a letter to Paul Barbier, a professor of French at Cardiff University, inquiring whether or not it would be possible to include Welsh choirs at the

Exhibition. The suggestion was taken seriously, and a conference was organized accordingly, to which representatives of a number of Welsh choirs were invited. The conference committee concluded that it would be "desirable" to be represented at the Paris Exhibition, and it suggested in particular that an international contest should be organized following the precedent set at the Chicago Eisteddfod. It is clear that the relationship between competitive spirit and communal singing in Wales was an important factor to consider when representing musical practice outside of Wales. That being said, the organizing committee did not follow the suggestion of arranging a contest. Instead, the Welsh singers—the Royal Welsh Ladies' Choir and two Welsh male choirs (namely the Rhondda Glee Society and the Barry District Glee Society)—were afforded the opportunity to present a concert at the Trocadéro Hall in Paris.

Social class is pertinent here. The distinction between the social backgrounds of the choristers from France and those from Wales was observed by Clara: "The French male choristers struck me as being of the bourgeoisie, and very different from our sturdy Welshmen, many of whom were miners" (Novello Davies 140). Of course, Clara's own bourgeois female choir was also very different from the Welsh male choirs. In terms of the relationship between choral performance and national identity, the Paris Exhibition allowed the Welsh choirs to promote a different sense of nationhood; the choirs were able to select their own songs free from the restriction of competitive regulations. Without the need for test pieces, the repertoire performed by the Royal Welsh Ladies' Choir was more closely linked with a sense of native identity; it contained several songs in the Welsh language, including the following Welsh folksongs arranged for the choir by David Emlyn Evans (1843-1913): "*Y Deryn Pur*" ("The Gentle Dove"), "*Llwyn Onn*" ("Ash Grove"), and "*Clychau Aberdyfi*" ("The Bells of Aberdovey"). Interestingly, the choir performed a joint item with the male choirs: "The March of the Men of Harlech." As I discussed earlier, the piece is especially associated with a Welsh construction of masculinity. The involvement of the female choir in this performance underscores the ways in which women were actively involved in a stereotypical representation of male identity in Wales for an international audience.

LAND OF MY MOTHERS?

Having received recognition in the form of awards and congratulations in both Chicago and Paris, Clara and her choir had acquired a reputation as a leading female ensemble on the international stage.[9] Despite holding a musical career for over six decades, the personal legacy of Clara Novello Davies and her pioneering choir has been largely forgotten from narrative records in Wales. In some ways, this lacuna is related to the general representation (or lack thereof) of women in the musical history of Wales. On the other hand, however, the legacy of her son, Ivor Novello, has maintained a place in the cultural memory of the people of Wales.

To conclude, I would like to draw attention to a contemporary event held in Cardiff Bay on 3 December 2014. Authored by a Cardiff-based writer, Arnold Evans, *Novello & Son* depicts Clara's life, focusing particularly on her musical achievements and her (sometimes strained) relationship with Ivor. Although the factual framework of this musical revue is taken largely firsthand from Clara's autobiography, Evans admits that his depiction of her life may not have been entirely accepted by Clara herself. He says: "I don't know if *Novello & Son* is a true portrait of Clara. What I do know is that she would insist that it wasn't. She'd hate some of the words I've put in her mouth, cringe at the moments when she lets her guard down. And, of course, she'd be outraged by the bits I've made up." The construction of myth alongside the representation of reality is notably clear. Moreover, he uses his brief program note to draw the audience's attention to Clara's social standing and her position as a woman. Evans explains that the revue is a tribute not only to the life of Clara but also to "those of her generation who never allowed such minor obstacles as class distinction, sex discrimination or the occasional world war to stand in their way."

Taking place in the Western Studio, a small theatre situated within the iconic Wales Millennium Centre, the single performance of the revue in this venue was well attended, especially by those belonging to the older generations.[10] What is most interesting in the context of this chapter is the representation of Clara and the reception of the event portrayed in the press. In particular, it

133

is the relationship between a female and a male, Clara and Ivor (played by Rosamund Shelley and Christopher Littlewood, respectively), that is especially noteworthy. Although the title of the tribute—*Novello & Son*—suggests that Novello, the role assumed here by Clara, occupies the superior position in this partnership, the hierarchical relationship is reversed in reality. In a review published by *Wales Online*, the show is framed immediately in terms of Ivor's fame rather than solely on Clara's success (Smith). For example, the title reads "Ivor Novello's Mother Is Brilliantly Captured in Stage Show" and the by-line refers to the "Cardiff Entertainer's Famous Mum" (Smith). Although the adjectives "brilliant" and "famous" indicate a sense of approval from the article's author Mike Smith, he later says that "Rosamund Shelley is superb as the driven, talented, egocentric, bitchy, at times pompous and, ultimately, out of her depth product of a Welsh Methodist family." Considering the lack of negative press regarding Clara and her choir throughout her lifetime, it must be questioned how much truth there is in this depiction exposed to audiences in the twenty-first century. A negative portrayal is framed in terms of a positive reception.

The show's repertoire is also of interest. Arnold Evans has chosen for Clara (played by Shelley) to sing only songs composed by Ivor, despite the fact that Clara herself composed a number of songs and her choir sang a diverse repertoire of songs in English and in Welsh. However, Evans' choice provided a particularly poignant moment when Shelley began conducting the audience as if they were the long-established members of the ladies' choir, and accepting the role assigned to them, members of the audience sang aloud. The choice of song—Ivor Novello's wartime classic, "Keep the Home Fires Burning"—is significant: at an event signalled to remember the lifetime successes of Clara Novello Davies, it is her son's song that is audible. In this manner, Ivor, rather than Clara, is heard sonically, a symbolic gesture, since it confirms also that the legacy of Ivor is remembered and a living memory of his music is alive at this time. Despite the advances of Clara Novello Davies and her Royal Welsh Ladies' Choir in the realm of Welsh music, once again, the women of Harlech are marginalized in order to perpetuate the myth of Wales only as the "land of my fathers."

ENDNOTES

[1]"Mam" is the Welsh word for mother.

[2]According to Bohlman, "unofficial national anthems serve all the functions of a national anthem, but they do not have the top-down sanction to represent the nation beyond its borders" (111).

[3]The opening lines of the official Welsh national anthem read "*Mae hen wlad fy nhadau yn annwyl i mi. Gwlad beirdd a chantorion, enwogion o fri.*" The English translation reads as follows: "The old land of my fathers is dear to me. Land of poets and singers, and people of stature."

[4]Following the religious reforms of the nineteenth century, the issue of temperance became pertinent when the temperance movement was initiated in England and Wales. Although the focus for social reformers was placed at first upon individuals, strategies aimed at social groups soon emerged. This was linked especially to social class; reformers, who were predominantly middle class, believed that the behaviour of the working classes needed to be addressed (especially in relation to temperance) in order to stabilize society as a whole. In this matter, the Band of Hope played a crucial role. Though associated with the temperance movement, Band of Hope leaders did not focus solely upon the issue of alcohol consumption. Instead, they "aimed to inculcate a new cultural identity in their young members, to facilitate the absorption of the upwardly mobile working-class families into respectable society" (Shiman 49).

[5]The Blue Ribbon Movement was initiated by Francis Murphy in the United States during the 1870s, and was part of the greater Gospel Temperance Movement and general focus on temperance in the late nineteenth century. As this may suggest, the movement was associated with abstinence from alcohol, and those who joined the movement wore a blue ribbon on their lapel as a public marker of this decision. The movement initially took the form of meetings held in public halls, where "rousing speeches," "personal testimonies," and "collective song[s]" were presented. Richard T. Booth, who was himself a reformed drinker, imported the movement to Britain in the 1880s. He launched a Blue Ribbon campaign, which lasted for five years because of its widespread appeal at this time. See "Blue Ribbon Movement" (Blocker et al. 107-09).

[6]An *eisteddfod* (pl. *eisteddfodau*) is a Welsh competitive festival of music and poetry.

[7]Between 1903 and 1922, Captain Francis O'Neill (1848-1936), an Irish-born policeman, published a significant number of Irish traditional folk melodies that were collected from the Irish diaspora in Chicago. His main collection *The Dance Music of Ireland: 1001 Gems* (1907) remains both highly regarded and well used by Irish traditional musicians.

[8]The other music adjudicators were Ben Davies (1858-1953, a Welsh tenor); William Tomlins (conductor of Chicago's Apollo Music Club from 1875 to 1898); D.J.J. Mason (director of the Wilkes-Barre Oratorio Society); William Courtney (a British-born tenor living in New York); John Gower (also British-born, a cathedral organist living in Denver, Colorado); and Mary Davies (1855-1930, a Welsh soprano who was well-known in the fashionable London music scene).

[9]In Paris, the Royal Welsh Ladies' Choir was awarded the Grand Prix for its efforts and Clara was presented with a gold wreath of laurel leaves by Camille Saint-Saëns (1835-1921). The laurel leaves were donated to St. Fagans National Museum of History by Ivor Novello in 1943. Clara also received a Sèvres bowl (worth 80 pounds) from the French Government (*Western Mail*, 24 July 1900). Moreover, her skills as a conductor made an impact in Paris. As it was reported in *The Musical Times*, a "lady conductor was doubtless something of a novelty to the French folk" (1 September 1900). Louis-Albert Bourgault-Ducoudray (1840-1910), the president of the Paris Conservatoire, was one such person who was impressed by Clara. He reportedly commented "she possesse[d] the exquisite delicacy of feminine sentiment, and the energy indispensible for forcing her will on a large number. I have never heard such efforts of choral interpretation ... as those that she obtains" (Novello Davies 142). Accordingly, Clara was offered a position to teach at the Conservatoire, but she declined.

[10]The location of the venue in Cardiff Bay is significant, since a statue of Ivor Novello was erected there in 2009. Created by Peter Nicholas (1934-2015), the 7 foot bronze sculpture features Ivor seated and looking over his shoulder towards the Wales Millennium Centre. The statue cost 80,000 pounds to build, an amount

that was raised through an official charity named the Ivor Novello Statue Fund. An equivalent statue memorializing Clara Novello Davies does not exist.

WORKS CITED

Benedict, Burton. "International Exhibitions and National Identity." *Anthropology Today*, vol. 7, no. 3, 1991, pp. 5-9

Blocker, Jack S., David M. Fahey and Ian R. Tyrrell. *Alcohol and Temperance in Modern History: An International Encyclopaedia.* Vol. 1, ABC-CLIO, 2003.

Bohlman, Philip V. *Focus: Music, Nationalism, and the Making of the New Europe.* 2nd ed., Routledge, 2011.

Davies, John, et al., editors. *The Welsh Academy Encyclopaedia of Wales.* University of Wales Press, 2008.

Fuller, Sophie. "'The Finest Voice of the Century': Clara Butt and Other Concert-Hall and Drawing-Room Singers of Fin-de-siècle Britain." *The Arts of the Prima Donna in the Long Nineteenth Century*, edited by Rachel Cowgill and Hilary Poriss, Oxford University Press, 2012, pp. 308-27.

Llewellyn, Richard. *How Green Was My Valley,* [1939], Simon and Schuster, 2009.

Novello Davies, Clara. *The Life I Have Loved.* William Heinemann, 1940.

Shiman, Lilian Lewis. "The Band of Hope Movement: Respectable Recreation for Working-Class Children." *Victorian Studies*, vol. 17, no. 1, 1973, pp. 49-74.

Smith, Mike. "Ivor Novello's Mother Is Brilliantly Captured in Stage Show." *Wales Online.* 4 Dec. 2014, www.walesonline. co.uk/whats-on/arts-culture-news/ivor-novellos-mother-brilliant-ly-captured-8225265. Accessed 15 Nov. 2017.

The World's Columbian Exposition International Eisteddvod, Chicago, 1893: Cais a gwahoddiad cenedlathol ac eisteddfodol/ A National and Eisteddvodic Call and Invitation. Chicago: Rand McNally, 1891.

9.

Que Vivan Las Mamas

Las Cafeteras, Zapatista Activism, and New Expressions of Chicana Motherhood

DAVID EICHERT

What does it mean to be a mother along the border between Mexico and the United States? Mexican and Mexican American mothers have long found themselves politically and socially marginalized by their societies because they fall outside of established power dynamics. This systematic disenfranchisement is nothing new: during colonization, for example, the Spanish imposed the strict *castas* system, which ranked people in the Spanish colonies by race and "purity of blood," thus disenfranchising Indigenous and mixed blood (*mestizo*) mothers. Patriarchal norms reinforce a system of uncompromising gender roles that continue to define the role of a mother as very limited and powerless. Violence and poverty, endemic to many communities in Northern Mexico, disproportionately impact mothers while racist politicians in the United States often blame immigrant mothers from Mexico for many of their country's political ills. Moreover, Mexican American mothers continue to face legal and societal barriers in the United States, regardless of citizenship or education levels.

In response to these systemic challenges, the Chicana feminist movement (as well as the larger Chicano Movement) has fought since the 1960s against harmful cultural forces in an effort to improve the lives of Mexicans on both sides of the border. Musicians in particular have played an important role in the creation of a Chicano and Chicana (often simplified to Chican@) identity. They have combined traditional Mexican instruments and styles with modern musical genres to address a wide range of social, political, and economic problems faced by the Mexican community (Alvarez and Widener 227). Although this Chican@ tradition of creating songs about social issues is not new, a recent group from East Los Angeles called *Las Cafeteras* brings a fresh and unexplored perspective to the issues faced by many Mexicans and Mexican Americans. In particular, many of the band's songs explore the challenges faced by Mexican mothers on both sides of the border by asserting a strong transnational solidarity against the forces that marginalize these women.

This chapter examines the music of Las Cafeteras and its messages about transborder Chicana motherhood. Furthermore, special attention will be given to how the band challenges existing power dynamics of gender-based violence and economic limitations and how they envision through music an ideal world that recognizes the political potency of the Chicana mother.

BACKGROUND

The musicians of Las Cafeteras started making music in 2005. The various members of the group, which now features two women and four men, first met while taking music classes at the Eastside Cafe in El Sereno (the easternmost neighbourhood of Los Angeles). The group decided to write music promoting an idealized sense of community inspired by Chican@ activism, and eventually released its first album, *It's Time*, in 2012 (Gutierrez). The group's name comes from the Eastside Cafe, but it is feminized to show the band's commitment to making music about gender equality (Phillips; Romero).

Las Cafeteras's choice to use traditional Mexican musical styles to convey a political message is nothing new. Chican@ musicians have been writing music about social causes for decades, both for use in public demonstrations and as part of a community discussion on identity and politics. Many groups fuse traditional Latin musical styles with a variety of modern genres, such as rock, R&B, hip-hop, punk, or jazz, and the names of many of these groups reflect themes of resistance, Indigenous identity, and self-determination, which are so important to the Chican@ Movement (e.g. Rage Against the Machine, Quetzal, Ozomatli, Delinquent Habits, Funky Aztecs, The Filthy Immigrants, etc.) (Loza, "Assimilation" 147).

The music of Las Cafeteras is heavily influenced by the *son jarocho*, a regional musical style from Veracruz, and it is particularly important for Chican@ music and identity. During the second half of the twentieth century, the *son jarocho* experienced a resurgence in popularity in Mexico and quickly crossed the border into California, where early Mexican American musicians such as Los Lobos and Ritchie Valens adopted the style. Las Cafeteras relies heavily on the *son jarocho* to convey their political messages; they employ traditional instruments like the *jarana*, a small guitar, and the *tarima*, a wooden box with sound holes upon which musicians dance, to create percussion (*zapateado*). Other instruments include the *quijada*, a dried jawbone of a donkey or horse, and the *marímbula*, a plucked key box bass (Viesca 725-26).

The *son jarocho* was created during the era of colonization. It combined the various musical influences in Veracruz, such as music from the Spanish, the Indigenous populations of southeastern Mexico, and Africans taken to the New World. The first documentation of *son jarocho* as a distinct musical form occurred in 1776, when it was banned by the Spanish Inquisition during a period of strict Catholicism for allegedly being blasphemous and immoral. Later, following the Mexican War of Independence in the early 1800s, *son jarocho* was an important part of the creation of a Mexican identity that was neither wholly Spanish nor Indigenous, especially among the country's *mestizo* population. This history is particularly important for Chican@ musicians like Las Cafeteras, who see the *son jarocho* as a kind of resistance music that survived and flourished despite colonial cultural oppression (Loza, "From Veracruz").

By taking *son jarocho* music styles and using them to express solidarity with mothers on both sides of the border, Las Cafeteras pays homage to a centuries-old struggle against exclusion and disenfranchisement. Furthermore, Las Cafeteras's use of the *son jarocho* connects the music to a larger Chican@ activist tradition that peacefully challenges oppressive power dynamics while supporting mothers and other marginalized groups. Specifically, in many of the songs the musicians of Las Cafeteras decry the violence and economic disadvantages faced by many mothers along the border, and simultaneously praise and emphasize the idealized potential of mothers to act as political agents in their communities.

MOTHERS AND VIOLENCE

A consistent theme in the music of Las Cafeteras is the violence and discrimination faced by mothers on both sides of the border. This violence—resulting from gang activity, harsh legal barriers, or other forms of discrimination—is a particularly vile part of the systemic limitations restricting Chicana mothers. However, by telling the stories of mothers affected by violence, Las Cafeteras seeks to bring attention to the plight of these women and to create a tool that will inspire individuals to rally for political change.

For example, in the song "*Mujer Soy*," Las Cafeteras target one of the worst problems facing mothers in Mexico: the pandemic of femicide occurring in the northern *maquiladora* towns on the U.S.-Mexico border. For the musicians, this phenomenon, caused by the intersection of poverty, globalization, and patriarchy, is one example of the forces disenfranchising and harming mothers.

Since the early 1990s, hundreds of women and mothers have been brutally murdered in Ciudad Juárez—a major manufacturing centre south of El Paso, Texas, and the second-largest metropolitan area on the U.S.-Mexico border. These murders are often shrouded in mystery, and investigations can be stalled for months until body parts are found floating down the river or in mass graves (Cave). Often the mothers and family members of murdered women are unable to properly grieve because of government restrictions on access to the bodies. One mother even recounted that government authorities barred her from visiting a morgue, and produced conflicting accounts about how many murdered girls were held inside (Cave).

There are many causes of this violence, including drug-related gang violence and jealousy from romantic partners and other men. One study found that a third of studied bodies had been sexually assaulted (Cave). These problems are not specific to Ciudad Juárez either: on average, six women are murdered every day in Mexico, with relatively high impunity for the criminals. For instance, only 24 percent of all femicides in 2012 and 2013 were investigated by police; only 1.6 percent of the crimes resulted in sentencing. Furthermore, femicide is simply the most extreme form of violence against women in Mexican society, where over 60 percent of women have been abused and where more than a third of women have been victimized by male partners (Matloff).

Las Cafeteras addresses these issues in "*Mujer Soy*" by using the femicide epidemic as a symbol of the Mexican woman's larger fight against oppression. The song opens with a timid and plaintive *son jarocho* instrumental introduction, followed by powerful language evoking the many challenges faced by Mexican women in Ciudad Juarez:

> *Las niñas, las niñas y las mujeres,*
> *sólo pedimos justicia.*
> *Nos dejan, nos dejan con los quehaceres*
> *y un golpe de caricia.*
> *Caminar, caminar es peligroso*
> *en los desiertos de Juárez.*
> *El Gobierno es poderoso*
> *mientras mueren las mujeres*

> Girls, girls and women,
> we only ask for justice.
> They leave us, they leave us to our chores
> and hit us with a caress.
> Walking, walking is dangerous
> in the deserts of Juárez.
> The Government is powerful,
> whereas women die.

Las Cafeteras continues, incriminating the *maquiladora* system and declaring the following:

> *Yo no vengo a disculparme: mujer soy y lo seré. Sólo vengo*
> *a declararle que quieta nunca estaré.*

> *En la casa, la calle, el desierto,*
> *hay maquiladora.*

En la casa y en la calle, el desierto,
hay maquiladora.

I didn't come here to say I'm sorry: I'm a woman and I'll always be. I just came to tell you I'll never stay still.

At home, in the street, in the desert,
there are maquiladoras.
At home, in the street, in the desert,
there are maquiladoras.

The *maquiladora* system is often blamed for creating the conditions that have allowed the femicide epidemic to become so widespread. Following the signing of the North American Free Trade Agreement (NAFTA) in 1994, the number of *maquiladoras* (factories) along the U.S.-Mexico border increased dramatically to meet the sudden demand from American corporations. As workers (mostly female, and often young mothers with children) from poverty-stricken areas of Mexico migrated to these border towns in search of work, massive metropolitan areas arose with little public transportation, not enough electricity, and poorly-lit dirt roads. This combination of inadequate infrastructure and hundreds of female migrant workers walking home from work late at night increased the risk for greater violence against women (Pantaleo 350). Moreover, the *maquiladora* system has been widely criticized by activists for having created a "consume and dispose" cycle of young female workers who work until they lose their utility and are then replaced by fresh hands (Fragoso 163).

From the perspective of Las Cafeteras, the violence in Ciudad Juárez is endemic of a larger systemic problem that reduces the bodies of mothers to objects that can be violated and discarded without punishment. Las Cafeteras also points to the Mexican government, which allowed for the expansion of the *maquiladora* system and which has failed to stem the murders of mothers and daughters in Ciudad Juárez and throughout Mexico.

In response, Las Cafeteras offers words of support. Instead of reducing them to a valueless body, the mothers of "*Mujer Soy*" are given a voice and a purpose:

Cada paso, cada paso que camino
Me lleva a la libertad.
Llegaré a mi destino,
Donde en paz podré estar.
Vivo lucha, vivo lucha mujerista,
Mi existir tiene razón.
Sobrevivo en la conquista,
Tengo grand fuerza y pasión.

Mujer soy y lo seré.

Every step, every step
Takes me towards freedom.
I'll reach my goal eventually,
Where in peace I'll be.
I live, I live a pro-woman fight,
My existence has meaning.
I survive in conquest,
I have great strength and passion.

I'm a woman and I'll always be.

Las Cafeteras also addresses other forms of violence in its music. For example, in addition to the very real threat of sexual assault and murder faced by mothers in Northern Mexico, there are also legal barriers that create dangerous conditions for mothers who choose to immigrate to the United States. Since 1994, when the United States government enacted harsher measures to enforce border security, migrant deaths as a result of exposure have dramatically increased. In order to avoid border fences and evade border security, migrants are obliged to travel longer distances over more dangerous terrain, which requires the need for more water and food. This is especially trying for mothers with children or menstruating women, and female migrants are 2.7 times more likely to die of exposure than men (O'Leary 112-17).

Las Cafeteras addresses these risks in the plaintive song "*Ya Me Voy,*" which recreates the desperate and perilous journey experienced by many Mexican immigrants to the United States. The song opens with a quiet and pained female voice, as the migrants, driven by economic desperation and violence, choose to cross over into the United States:

Ya me voy sin dinero
Ya me voy, yo no quiero
Pero ya me voy

I am going without money
I am going, I do not want to
But I am going

In addition to telling the story of marginalized individuals (Mexican migrants to the United States), Las Cafeteras also draws attention to the various forms of sexual violence threatening migrant mothers, including rape and sex-work-related exploitation, via a mournful dialogue between a mother and her child:

Ya me voy, yo no quiero
Sin dinero, por mi sueño
Ya me voy (ya me voy)
En la tarde ya me voy (ya me voy)
Por la luna ya me voy (ya me voy)
Tengo frío pero voy
ya me voy

No te vayas no te vayas
No te vayas mi madre
No te vayas (no te vayas)
Con la cara maquillada (no te vayas)
Con la boca muy rosada (no te vayas)
Con tu negra minifalda
Ma no te vayas ma
No te vayas

I am going, I do not want to
Without money, for my dream
I am going (I am going)

145

In the afternoon I am going (I am going)
By the moon I am going (I am going)
I am cold but I am going
I am going

Do not go do not go
Do not go my mother
Do not go (do not go)
With made-up face (do not go)
The very pink mouth (do not go)
With your black miniskirt
Do not go mama
Do not go

In addition to the various weather-related risks experienced by all migrants crossing to the United States by foot, Mexican mothers also take the risk of sexual assault while crossing the border. Too often, border crossing guides (also called *coyotes*) will threaten to abandon female migrants in the desert if they do not exchange sex for continued help. This treatment is not limited to adult women either; some migrant mothers tell stories of being coerced to surrender their teenage daughters to *coyotes* in exchange for continued direction. To make matters worse, these migrant mothers often cannot report their rapes or the rapes of their daughters to authorities in the United States for fear of deportation, which allows these kinds of crimes to continue unpunished (Joffe-Block).

Furthermore, cross-border trafficking is a perverse forms of gender-based violence that harms Mexican mothers. The American market for Mexican sex workers is nothing new. During Prohibition in the United States, northern Mexico became the place for American men to find amusement in the numerous bars, clubs, and brothels that sprung up to meet demand (Lacey). As a result of immigration policies in the twentieth century which excluded women, many single mothers and abandoned women unable to find other forms of work were obliged to turn to sex work in order to support their families (Rosas). This trend has continued to this day: for example, a recent study of Mexican sex work found that the overwhelming majority of women were single mothers, many coming from poverty-stricken areas of Mexico in search of a better life. The desperation of many of these women puts them at greater risk for exploitation and trafficking into the United States (Bender).

By choosing to emphasize the stories of marginalized Mexican mothers, Las Cafeteras is magnifying the voices of disenfranchised women whose experiences are often ignored or co-opted by oppressive cultural and political forces. Because the violence faced by these mothers has many causes (legal barriers, patriarchal influences, neoliberal economic policies such as NAFTA), Las Cafeteras seeks to highlight their challenges and inspire solutions.

ECONOMIC CHALLENGES

In addition to describing the violence faced by mothers along the border, Las Cafeteras also recognizes the economic challenges and barriers that colour the experiences of many Chicana women. This includes both the day-to-day struggles of a mother to provide for her family as well as the larger systematic disenfranchisement that creates unique challenges for Mexican mothers.

Las Cafeteras, continuing to bring attention to the stories of people on the margins of society, devotes several songs to the daily struggles and victories of working mothers. For example, in their song "*Cafe Con Pan*," Las Cafeteras connects a seemingly inconsequential, maternal activity (the preparation of coffee and bread for a morning meal) to ideas of strength and supreme communal importance (including one line that declares that mothers who prepare breakfast are *fuertes luchadoras* [strong fighters] for the community, a term usually associated with professional wrestling). Similarly, the band dedicates their song "*Trabajador Trabajadora*" to "mothers, who sacrifice to make ends meet" as well as to a long list of different daily workers (farmworkers, teachers, students, activists, spiritual leaders, etc.). Furthermore, the song points out that it is mothers (and, as also noted in the song, single mothers) who fill many of these roles and form an essential part of the economy and society.

The message of gratitude and appreciation for working mothers in "*Trabajador Trabajadora*" counters a larger, negative perception of Chicana mothers in American media, which often stereotypes

Mexican mothers as foreign or parasitical, which includes, for example, the recent "anchor baby" debate during the 2016 U.S. Presidential campaign or the racist laws in states along the border (Barro; Bermúdez et al.). Latina mothers also face unique societal challenges in the United States, such as earning 56 cents for every dollar earned by a white man in the United States, which results in thousands of dollars in lost income every year (O'Brien). America's system of mass incarceration, which imprisons one in every eighty-eight Latino men, also hurts Mexican mothers, who are obliged to provide for families and households without the financial and day-to-day support of husbands or male family members (Schlossberg). The overtly positive and grateful message of *"Trabajador Trabajadora"* instead envisions a world where mothers are appreciated and valued for the work they do, both in the community and for their families.

Las Cafeteras also critiques macrolevel economic forces that disenfranchise the Chicana mother (such as NAFTA, as previously mentioned). For example, in *"Ya Me Voy,"* Las Cafeteras recreates the pains faced by impoverished Mexican women left behind by migrant husbands and sons. In a hypothetical conversation, a husband announces that he is compelled to migrate north out of economic need:

Ya me voy, yo no quiero, sin dinero
tengo miedo pero voy
Para el norte ya me voy
Por el jale ya me voy (ya me voy)
No se a donde pero voy
Ya me voy

I am going, I do not want to, without money
I'm afraid but I am going
To the north I am going
By the pull I am going (I am going)
But I don't know where I am going
I am going

In response, his wife pleads for him not to leave her:

No te vayas mi querido
Con cariño te suplico
No te vayas (no te vayas)
A morir en las montañas (no te vayas)
El desierto no perdona (no te vayas)
Y tampoco Arizona (no te vayas)
No te vayas

Do not go my dear
With fondness I beg you
Do not go (do not go)
To die in the mountains (do not go)
The desert does not forgive (do not go)
Nor Arizona (do not go)
Do not go

This conversation represents decades of similar discussions that have happened between husbands and wives, or sons and mothers, in Northern Mexico, and demonstrates in some small way the economic necessity that has separated thousands of families.

Economic migration between Mexico and the United States is nothing new: during the first half of the twentieth century, it was mostly Mexican men who crossed the border to work seasonal jobs in the United States, leaving behind wives and children for months at a time. This arrangement was formalized with the Bracero Program in 1942, which brought in hundreds of thousands of men to work the fields and factories during World War II. Although women and mothers were forbidden from working in the United States, they were an essential part of the Bracero Program, since they were tasked with staying home and caring for dependent children and elderly members of the family, thus enabling their husbands to work. The work was dangerous—both for the men who crossed the border and for the mothers left behind in Mexico, who suddenly lacked social and financial stability. In some cases, men chose to abandon their families and establish new families in the United States, thus stranding Mexican mothers on the other side of the border in a "married-but-single" limbo without remittances or knowledge of her husband's whereabouts. In all cases, there were no resources dedicated to helping these mothers care for their children or household, which put untold psychological and financial pressures on these women (Rosas).

In many ways, economic disenfranchisement goes hand-in-hand with the violence faced by mothers on both sides of the border. Because Chicana mothers are often viewed as expendable—by gang members, government leaders, *maquiladora* managers, *coyotes*, etc.—their lives and their stories are not valued, and they find themselves on the margins of society. In response, Las Cafeteras uses music to directly address these systemic problems.

MOTHERS AS POLITICAL AGENTS

Finally, the music of Las Cafeteras is connected to a strong underlying message of solidarity among mothers on both sides of the border. This idea of unity, a consistent theme of the Chicana feminist movement, is central to the work of Las Cafeteras as the band seeks to reimagine the Chicana mother as a political agent. Instead of being acted upon by colonial powers and patriarchal oppression, the Chicana mother is portrayed as a powerful and potent force for good in her community and the world at large.

For example, the band rewrote the words to the traditional *son jarocho* folk song "*La Bamba*" to focus on revolutionary Chicana values. This feel-good anthem, dubbed "*La Bamba Rebelde*," decries racial profiling and discrimination while declaring:

Que vivan las mujeres de East L.A.
Porque bailan La Bamba, que bailan la bamba...
Como las Zapatistas, como los Zapatistas
Yo lucharé, yo lucharé, yo vencere

Long live the women of East L.A.
So they can dance La Bamba...
Like the Zapatistas, like the Zapatistas
I will fight, I will fight, I will overcome

The choice to use "*La Bamba*" as a platform for their activist declaration is an obvious one, since the song is arguably the most well-known *son jarocho* song in the United States thanks to Ritchie Valens's popular 1958 adaptation. By remixing "*La Bamba*," Las Cafeteras joins a long tradition of musicians on both sides of the border who have used the music to express their heritage and Mexican ancestry. The reference to the Zapatistas, as well as the overarching themes of the song that closely mirror radical Zapatista ideology, connect the struggle of the Chicana woman in the United States to the counter-globalization and pro-equality battles that are so important to the Chican@ movement.

Other than traditional musical styles such as the *son jarocho*, perhaps the most important influence on Chican@ activist music is the ideology of the Zapatistas. In 1994 the Zapatista Army of National Liberation (*Ejército Zapatista de Liberación Nacional* or EZLN) declared war against the Mexican state. Based mostly in Chiapas, the southernmost state of Mexico, the group consists of thousands of Indigenous men and women who espouse a libertarian socialist ideology based on radial participatory democracy that opposes economic globalization and marginalization by Western and postcolonial powers. The Zapatista war with Mexico has been largely defensive, and true to their creed of nonviolence, many of their military actions have been largely symbolic. For example, in 2000, the Zapatista Air Force "bombed" a federal military encampment with thousands of paper airplanes (Meyer and Ndura-Ouédraogo 12).

The Zapatistas are also radically dedicated to gender equality in all aspects of the movement. This was clearly outlined by Zapatista leader Subcomandante Marcos in one of his earliest communiqués, when he wrote about "the double subjugation of women" who were marginalized because of their gender in a community already marginalized by the North American Free Trade Agreement (NAFTA) and the federal Mexican state (Govea 66). Gender equality was also outlined explicitly from the beginning of the rebellion, when the Zapatistas announced the women's revolutionary law alongside its other foundational revolutionary laws. This law outlines the rights of women to fair pay, decisions about childbirth and marriage, political involvement, healthcare, and education, and even though many Indigenous women are unaware of the specific protections that the law affords them, its mere existence has become a symbol of fair lives for women (Castillo; Speed et al. 3-4).

The Zapatista women's movement draws on Western feminist ideologies while preserving and reclaiming Indigenous traditions that were lost with the imposition of European culture (Hymn 2). This hybrid form of Indigenous feminism, with an emphasis on creating a movement for everyone by everyone through communalism and consensus, has proved instrumental for many Chican@ activists and musicians, such as Las Cafeteras, who have used Zapatismo as a framework for their own activism (Govea 66; Marquez 79).

The Zapatista uprising was an important paradigm shift for the Chican@ movement in the United States, since "no longer was the movement looking to an indigenous past for its inspirations. It was now a group of living, indigenous peoples from southern México who were challenging the dominant power relations in the new, neoliberal world order" (Marquez 79). It is only logical, therefore, that Las Cafeteras heavily employs Zapatista ideology in its messages about mothers as political agents.

Perhaps the most explicit example of Zapatista influence in the music of Las Cafeteras can be seen in the music video for the "beautiful dope remix" of *Mujer Soy*, released in 2015 and remixed by local Los Angeles DJ Yukicito. The music video for the song, which was meant to "reclaim the dance floor with empowering dance music" (Iseli), follows a day in the life of a Chicana single mother and community activist from East Los Angeles named Maryann Aguirre. One important message of the music video is the multiplicity of roles played by the Chicana single mother. Aguirre must be and is an excellent mother, employee, leader, and community member from the moment she wakes up to the moment she falls asleep. The influence of Zapatista and Chicana ideology on the video is obvious, as can be seen in the posters announcing, "*Sin las mujeres no hay revolución*" (Without the women there is no revolution) and "*Mi existencia es mi resistancia*" (My existence is my resistance). The message is clear: Mexican mothers like Aguirre are strong, multidimensional, and not invisible as they resist borders and categories that would otherwise ignore them. Even though forces from society and the government have historically restricted the political efficacy of Mexican mothers, they are capable political agents whose voices deserve to be heard.

Furthermore, the choice to remix *"Mujer Soy"* is highly symbolic. The remixed song and music video demonstrate solidarity with the women of Mexico and create a unified transborder voice in support of motherhood and women. The remix also suggests a continuation of the Mexican mother's struggle—even though a physical border has been crossed, there still is work to be done. Finally, the choice to feature Aguirre is deliberate and follows in the grand tradition of using media to portray the lives of subjects who would normally be ignored by the dominant culture. "Imagine," the video concludes, "a world where we saw every womyn's story, vision, strength, passion, dignity, labour, courage, resiliency, leadership, freedom, [and] power. What would the world look like?"

In conclusion, Las Cafeteras uses its music to actively oppose dominant societal and political forces that oppress and marginalize Mexican and Mexican American women. There are many layers of resistance in the music—such as the choice to employ and remix the cross-cultural musical style of *son jarocho*, the decision to feature microlevel stories of mothers as a way to critique large transnational inequalities, or the frequent references to Zapatista promother political ideology. By telling the stories of violence and struggle and empowerment that are so common to the experience of Mexican mothers, Las Cafeteras seeks to praise and honour the sacrifices made by mothers on both sides of the border.

WORKS CITED

Alvarez, Luis, and Daniel Widener. "Brown-Eyed Soul: Popular Music and Cultural Politics in Los Angeles." *The Struggle in Black and Brown: African American and Mexican American Relations During the Civil Rights Era*, edited by Brian D Behnken, University of Nebraska, 2012, pp. 211-36.

Barro, Josh. "Just What Do You Mean by 'Anchor Baby'?" *The New York Times*, 28 Aug. 2015, www.nytimes.com/2015/08/30/upshot/just-what-do-you-mean-by-anchor-baby.html. Accessed 15 Nov. 2017.

Bender, Steven. *Run for the Border: Vice and Virtue in U.S.-Mexico Border Crossings*. New York University, 2012.

Bermúdez, J. Maria, et al. "Mejor Sola Que Mal Acompañada: Strengths and Challenges of Mexican-Origin Mothers Parenting Alone." *Journal of Divorce & Remarriage*, vol. 52, no. 8, 2011, pp. 622-41.

Cave, Damien. "Wave of Violence Swallows More Women in Juárez." *The New York Times*. 23 June. 2012, www.nytimes.com/2012/06/24/world/americas/wave-of-violence-swallows-more-women-in-juarez-mexico.html. Accessed 15 Nov. 2017.

Castillo, R. Aída Hernández. "Zapatismo and the Emergence of Indigenous Feminism." *NACLA Report on the Americas*, vol. 35, no. 6, 2002, pp. 39-58.

Fragoso, Julia Monárrez. "Serial Sexual Femicide in Ciudad Juárez, 1993–2001." *Aztlan*, vol. 2, 2003, pp. 153-78.

Govea, Melissa N. "Zapatismo and Community-Based Social Change: Toward a Feminist Global Praxis?" *Cultural Politics and Resistance in the 21st Century: Community-Based Social Movements and Global Change in the Americas*, edited by Kara Z. Dellacioppa and Clare Weber, Palgrave Macmillan, 2012, pp. 61-78.

Gutierrez, Juan. "Best L.A. Musicians by Genre." *L.A. Weekly*. 3 Oct. 2013, www.laweekly.com/music/best-la-musicians-by-genre-4167163. Accessed 15 Nov. 2017.

Hymn, Soneile. "Indigenous Feminism in Southern Mexico." *The International Journal of Illich Studies*, vol. 2, no. 1, 2010, pp. 21-34.

Iseli, Julie. "Identity, Love, Culture, and Las Cafeteras." *Gypset Magazine*, 1 Apr. 2015, http://gypsetmagazine.com/identity-love-culture-and-las-cafeteras/. Accessed 15 Nov. 2017.

Joffe-Block, Jude. "Women Crossing the U.S. Border Face Sexual Assault with Little Protection." *PBS Newshour*, 31 Mar. 2014, www.pbs.org/newshour/nation/facing-risk-rape-migrant-women-prepare-birth-control. Accessed 15 Nov. 2017.

Lacey, Marc. "The Mexican Border's Lost World." *The New York Times*. 31 July 2010, www.nytimes.com/2010/08/01/weekinreview/01lacey.html. Accessed 15 Nov. 2017.

Loza, Steven. "Assimilation, Reclamation, and Rejection of the Nation-State by Chicano Musicians." *Postnational Musical Identities: Cultural Production, Distribution, and Consumption in a*

Globalized Scenario, edited by Ignacio Corona and Alejandro L. Madrid, Lexington Books, 2008, pp. 137-50.

Loza, Steven. "From Veracruz to Los Angeles: The Reinterpretation of the 'Son Jarocho.'" *Latin American Music Review*, vol. 13, no. 2, 1992, pp. 179-94.

Marquez, Oscar. "La Otra Educación: Hip-Hop, Zapatismo, and Popular Education." *Cultural Politics and Resistance in the 21st Century: Community-Based Social Movements and Global Change in the Americas*, edited by Kara Z. Dellacioppa and Clare Weber, Palgrave Macmillan, 2012, pp. 79-98.

Matloff, Judith. "Six Women Murdered Each Day as Femicide in Mexico Nears a Pandemic." *Al-Jazeera.* 4 Jan. 2015, america.aljazeera.com/multimedia/2015/1/mexico-s-pandemicfemicides.html. Accessed 15 Nov. 2017.

Meyer, Matt, and Elavie Ndura-Ouédraogo. "Love-Force and Total Revolution: Twenty-First Century Challenges to Global Nonviolence." *Exploring the Power of Nonviolence: Peace, Politics, and Practice*, edited by Randall Amster and Elavie Ndura-Ouédraogo, Syracuse University, 2013, pp. 1-15.

O'Brien, Sara Ashley. "78 Cents on the Dollar: The Facts about the Gender Wage Gap." *CNN.* 14 Apr. 2015. Web. 28 Dec. 2015.

O'Leary, Anna Ochoa. "Close Encounters of the Deadly Kind: Gender, Migration, and Border (In)security." *Migration Letters*, vol. 5, no. 2, 2008, pp. 111-21.

Pantaleo, Katherine. "Gendered Violence: An Analysis of the Maquiladora Murders." *International Criminal Justice Review*, vol. 20, no. 4, 2010, pp. 349-65.

Phillips, Erica E. "Las Cafeteras on the Strict Rules of Son Jarocho Music." *L.A. Weekly.* 30 Dec. 2011, www.laweekly.com/music/las-cafeteras-on-the-strict-rules-of-son-jarocho-music-2402575. Accessed 15 Nov. 2017.

Romero, José. "Las Cafeteras Presentan su Primer Álbum con Son Jarocho." *La Opinión.* 3 Nov. 2012, laopinion.com/2012/11/03/las-cafeteras-presentan-su-primer-album-con-son-jarocho/. Accessed 15 Nov. 2017.

Rosas, Ana Elizabeth. "Breaking the Silence: Mexican Children and Women's Confrontation of Bracero Family Separation, 1942-64." *Gender & History*, vol. 23, no. 2, 201, pp. 382-400.

Schlossberg, Tatiana. "New York City Bar Association Urges Reduction of Mass Incarceration in Report." *The New York Times*, 28 Sept. 2015, www.nytimes.com/2015/09/29/nyregion/new-york-city-bar-association-urges-reduction-of-mass-incarceration-in-report.html. Accessed 15 Nov. 2017.

Speed, Shannon, et al. *Dissident Women: Gender and Cultural Politics in Chiapas.* University of Texas, 2006.

10.
Parenting Outside the Mainstream

Indie Rocker Moms

JACKIE WEISSMAN

The stereotypical image of the sex- and drug-fuelled rock star is the diametric opposite of the stereotypical image of motherhood. Yet woman rockers have always found ways to support themselves, their children, and their creativity. Oftentimes, this is accomplished by finding supportive family models outside the mainstream. Sometimes, this approach is kept secret. At other times, it is thrust forward as an act of rock 'n' roll rebellion. This chapter explores the issues indie musicians encounter, and draws primarily on research and experiences I captured during the making of my recent documentary film, *Rock N Roll Mamas*. Over seven years, the film examines the lives of Kristin Hersh from the bands Throwing Muses and 50FOOTWAVE (and a solo performer), who homeschooled four children while living on a tour bus; Zia McCabe from The Dandy Warhols, who relied on her husband, the band guitar's technician and merchandise seller, for childcare; and up-and-coming hip hop MC, Ms. Su'ad, a single mom who depended on family and other single mothers with mixed success. The chapter also includes insights from prominent rock critics and authors, such as Evelyn McDonald and Ann Powers, who provide valuable research regarding rock musician mothers throughout history.

Although rooted in the story of rock 'n' roll moms, this chapter challenges the more universal notion that there is an ideal mothering or parenting style, and highlights the worldwide struggle of women who try to balance their passion for their children and their art.

JACKIE WEISSMAN

PUBLIC MOTHER'S STORIES:
WHY I MADE *ROCK N ROLL MAMAS*

Throughout history, women's stories, especially those of mothers, have been kept hidden, outside of the public eye. Society has a vision of the perfect mother as both doting and selfless, or as a corporate multitasker who does it all. There are few public visions of a creative mother. What are these women's lives like?

In an effort to explore this mystery and to better understand how to balance my own creative inner needs with the needs of my toddler, I started making a documentary film called *Rock N Roll Mamas* in 2003. I did this because I had a difficult time finding mothers' stories and locating role models whom I could emulate as a creative person and parent. As a result, I went on a seven-year journey making the film, which took me to many places and introduced me to many musician mothers. Ultimately, I was lucky enough to follow three rock mamas off and on through brief periods in their lives: Ms. Su'ad, Kristin Hersh, and Zia McCabe. Through the course of my filmmaking journey, I learned from all these women's stories.

I share these stories as a way to educate and empower creative mothers and validate their own choices as a parent and creative person, or simply as a person juggling career and creativity. Bringing mothers' stories out into the light gives them power. As Adrienne Rich has profoundly stated, "only the willingness to share private and sometimes painful experience can enable women to create a collective description of the world which will truly be ours" (3).

MS. SU'AD

I begin with Ms. Su'ad, the first subject in the film, whom I followed the longest. I met Ms. Su'ad at a small local performance in Portland, Oregon, at benefit for a political cause, where she was a completely engaged and energized performer. In the audience, there was a little boy dancing. He certainly piqued my curiosity, as I do not see many young children at shows dancing alone. Then Su'ad called him up on stage to dance with her; this boy was her son, Moses. They danced together to her strident, lyrical rhymes;

What I am is,
the fearfulness of symmetry,
What I am is,
the fluidity of poetry,
What I am is,
the open book you cannot read,
What I am is,
me, me, me.
In this life I stand on my own two feet,
use the gifts God made me to hit the streets.
(Su'ad, "What I Am")

This incident was truly heartwarming—a rock 'n' roll tableau not seen often, an MC mother rocking out with her four-year-old son. It was a perfect dichotomy of the power and energy of hip hop mixed with the sweetness of maternity.

Ms. Su'ad is a dynamic, impressive performer and person. The name of her first EP was "The Urban Superwoman Is a Savage." She has bravado, to say the least. As a single, black mother in her early twenties, Su'ad seemed to have endless energy and passion. When I first started following her, Su'ad worked fulltime as a paralegal while Moses was in daycare, and then gigged and recorded on weekends while managing her music career at night. I mention Su'ad's race only because she comes out of a long history of strong, black women who are heads of their households. Although this does not give her—and the many others before and after her—wider social and political power, it does often imply leadership and responsibility within her (their) community (Rich xxvii). Led by her mother's example, Su'ad learned from a young age that she was capable of surviving and succeeding as a single mother with a burgeoning musical career and a day job.

Su'ad comes out of a strong tradition of single mother musicians in hip hop, and rhythm and blues. Ann Powers, NPR rock critic, music commentator, and a mother herself, discussed this aspect of rock n roll history in her interview for *Rock N Roll Mamas*:

I think historically in the beginning with R&B and early rock 'n' roll, the first few women who were successful often

had children, especially African American performers like
Ruth Brown or Aretha Franklin, who had a child when
she was a teenager. They oftentimes had children young,
and it wasn't really integrated into their performing lives.
It's more that the extended family would help and care
for these children.... But they weren't considered spent
once they had a child. That was just part of what women
did. At that time, that was the only option before the
pill. A lot of women had children young and then sort
of put them away or put them with their mom or their
sister and then went out and had their careers. (*Rock N
Roll Mamas*)

Su'ad and Moses seemed to move to a new place every time I
filmed them (about twice a year). During an early film shoot, Su'ad
was living with her backup singer, Adrienne, also a single mom
to a toddler. This arrangement seemed to work out well for both
Su'ad and Adrienne, as they shared childcare. Together, they could
book gigs and go over song arrangements during their time off.
They also helped each other with cooking and cleaning, essentially
acting as surrogate partners to each other during this time. Su'ad
said this about their living arrangement:

Yeah, it's great. I'm always like, "She's my wife." It works
out really good. The kids get along well and we help each
other out. And then we can talk about music and when
she's tired or burnt from the day, I can pick up a little bit of
the slack and hang out with the kids or whatever is needed.

Su'ad's experience is typical of an indie musician-parent trying
to make it. She worked all the time, whether working at her day
job, building her music career, or parenting. As a result, she was
exhausted and stressed: "I'm tired after work and I drive home
through traffic 'cause I work out in the suburbs. I drive home in
traffic or I take the bus and then pick [Moses] up, and I'm just tired
at night. Working eight hours a day, I want to have something to
give [Moses] at the end of the day but I'm just stressed and like
'Ahh.' But you just get tired and depressed."

Su'ad then decided to take a more part-time job so she could have more time with Moses and additional time to devote to music. She clearly loved spending time with her son, but she was also very driven to build her music career:

> I haven't been on email like I should; I haven't been on the message boards like I should for the last month. I have been hibernating with Moses, and I took time. I cut my work schedule, not forty hours a week, and I've just been in the house with him and writing and stuff.... I was burnt out from doing so many shows throughout the summer and the beginning of the fall that I was enjoying taking a break. Then one morning, I woke up and panicked; I was like, "Wait I'm falling off; I'm not out networking with people." Because that is how you keep your name in there, and you have to spend that time just on the Internet talking to friends. I know so many good MCs, and I know a lot of big names and it's like if I was just stepping it up more, I could be doing more, but I don't have the time. I have to do it slow.

At our next filming, Su'ad worked all day as a paralegal. She then took a half-hour bus ride home, picked up a bite for herself at a convenience store, and then picked up Moses from his babysitter. When she and Moses get back home, Su'ad prepared for a "big gig" opening for The Coup. Doing a lot of multitasking, Su'ad booked more gigs on the phone while getting dressed and playing with Moses (now four years old). She and Moses were living with Su'ad's mother now, who provided childcare in the evening when Su'ad has gigs. This situation worked well for her, but she was still juggling many things with her do-it-yourself ethic of making records, managing her own music career, and her all-encompassing day job.

Sometimes before a gig, Su'ad would rush over to the copy shop and make copies of inserts for CDs to sell after the show. She occasionally would miss sound checks because of this or because her car would not start or because she would be running late to get Moses to childcare. It can be a chaotic lifestyle.

As I filmed Su'ad, the chaos seemed to be taking its toll on her and her lifestyle. She stopped living with Adrienne, or her mother, and got her own apartment. I initially thought this seemed like a positive step, but the more I filmed Su'ad, the more I saw that she was less focused and more frenetic. I feared that this must be the reason her personal support was waning. The last time I saw Su'ad's apartment, it was filled with garbage bags full of music equipment and recording gear.

During my next shoot with Su'ad, she was getting ready for her first gig in a year. She no longer had a car and had to juggle getting rides with her mom, friends, or band mates. She had hired a new backup singer, a friend, to replace Adrienne. An older, eight-year-old Moses waited around in the apartment while Su'ad practised with her new DJ. Moses entertained himself by watching TV, playing basketball, and getting snacks.

At this point in time, Su'ad was not the confident superwoman I had been entranced by years earlier. She was jittery and fluttering all around her apartment. She went from spending time with Moses, getting him snacks and looking over his job chart, to wrangling cable and then practising song after song with her new DJ. Her computer was having problems, so she called her building super-intendent, who often gave her computer assistance. She chatted with him while he troubleshot; she asked to use his phone as her phone had been shut off. She was doing this gig so she could pay her phone bill this month.

She needed a phone so she could try to find a ride to her gig and someone to watch Moses. After multiple phone calls to Moses's dad, her mother, and others, Su'ad eventually got a ride with her mother to meet and drop off Moses with his dad at her gig. She had missed sound check, so mingled a bit in the greenroom while listening to the other performers on her bill.

When it came time for Su'ad's performance, she went on but was clearly a bit more flustered than she had been at past performances. Working with all new people and the brief rehearsals had taken a toll on Su'ad's confidence as well as on her performance. There were some problems with the microphone and some mistakes in the songs, which Su'ad covered up expertly. Her momentum picked up a couple of songs into the set, and she eventually won the crowd over by doing call and response while dancing.

When Su'ad finished her performance, she ran to the restroom and stayed there, even when finding out that a reporter, who had been clearly intrigued by her performance, wanted to interview her. It seemed as if Su'ad was upset and exhausted and that she wanted to sequester herself. I could not figure out why, and was confused and worried.

After this performance, Su'ad and Moses moved to Seattle, and I did not see them for about a year. Su'ad had music connections there and a high-powered corporate job. She was excited to try living in a larger city in order to make more money and get a bigger jump start to her music career. I was happy for Su'ad and hopeful that she could make it work there.

About two years later, I heard that Su'ad was back in town, and I interviewed her. She told me that living in Seattle was extremely challenging. Without her family and friends as a support network, Su'ad felt very alone and struggled with Moses, and became depressed. She ultimately decided to move back home:

> I was working at a really high profile business with a job that was ... [high pressure]. They hired me to streamline their whole process, and I was really unhappy. It was different for Moses, being away from his dad. It was a new kind of struggle for me because I'm okay with struggle. I like to struggle when it's something that I'm striving for, that I believe in, and the thought of it makes me excited, but obtaining that sort of position didn't make me happy.

Back in her home city, Su'ad continued to struggle with depression. She did not have a job, and lived in hotels. Moses began living more and more with his father.

I saw Su'ad again about a year after that. She had recently graduated from a rehab program for drug dependency, and was upbeat and confident. Su'ad had not performed since before her rehab stint but was doing a lot of writing she was proud of and had been published in a *Writers in the Schools* anthology. Moses lived fulltime with his father, and Su'ad saw him a lot during the week and on the weekends. Su'ad was working fulltime as a customer service agent at a tech company. Su'ad's work and music careers were on the upswing until her support system started collapsing, and then crumbled upon her move to a bigger city. This ultimately led to Su'ad's depression and her drug dependency in Seattle.

For any type of parent who is establishing a music career or for any type of creative endeavour, having a stalwart support system, family, paid help, or a spouse is of the utmost importance. Without these helpers, having time to create and the ability to earn money—and then parent—is almost impossible. According to some scholars, it is fairly common for young, black, single mothers like Su'ad to struggle with depression (Atkins).

My film's other two subjects, Kristin Hersh of Throwing Muses and Zia McCabe of The Dandy Warhols, exemplify the importance of having a strong support network in the life of a working musician. To be clear, these women also have the advantage of being white and in long-term relationships, both of which contribute to their ability to make a fulltime living from their music.

KRISTIN HERSH

Kristin Hersh started her band, Throwing Muses with her half-sister, Tanya Donnelly; they began in 1985 while Kristin was still in high school. Kristin was the singer, songwriter, and guitarist for the band. After becoming extremely popular in Boston and Newport, Rhode Island (where Kristin and the band are from), the band became the first American band to sign to the English label 4AD. They were later contracted by Warner Brothers in the United States (McDonnell).

Kristin grew up in a commune. After receiving a head injury during a bicycle accident, she began to "channel songs":

> When I was fourteen, I started hearing songs and it wasn't good. It was unsettling. I had always wanted to be a scientist. In fact, I had started college early, and I was a biology major. I was trying to ignore the songs as hard as I could ... I've come to grips with the fact that songs just play. They just write themselves and they don't shut up if I don't somehow make of record them.

At the age of eighteen, Kristin had her first child, Dylan. She ended up losing custody of him after a long, difficult legal battle. During this time, Kristin was diagnosed with bipolar disorder, which she has been treating with various different remedies, including medication and acupuncture (McDonnell).

I met Kristin in 2006 when she was on tour with 50FOOTWAVE. She invited me onto her tour bus and introduced me to her three-year-old son, Bodhi, whom she was lovingly cuddling. Then, this soft-spoken and gentle woman apologized. A couple of hours before I met her, Kristin had pulled out her own tooth with a pair of pliers, and apparently was still recovering. I was immediately spellbound; this woman is hardcore, I thought. The juxtaposition of this offstage and onstage Kristin, channeling her loud, fierce songs, was intriguing. In fact, Kristin created 50FOOTWAVE after Throwing Muses stopped recording because of lack of funds. She performed solo but found that she was "channeling" much more aggressive songs that would not work with her solo acoustic music:

> But there were still songs that were more aggressive, that were harder. And kind of me wearing my influences on my sleeve. It sounded like the songs that I was listening to as a teenager. And it happened that the Muses bass player, Bernie, was getting antsy at the same time, so we moved to LA and shacked up with the drummer, Rob Allers. What they brought to these songs was not just a reflection of these songs' intrinsic sound; it was something more than that. Which was kind of what I was looking for, so now I'm kind of following 50 Foot Wave to see what it does next.

Kristin is the mother of four boys: Dylan (eighteen), Ryder (thirteen), Wyatt (eight), and Bodhi (three). The last three are with her husband and manager, Billy O'Connell. Billy drives the tour bus and arranges Kristin's touring and recording schedule, whereas Kristin plays, records, and writes music, all while homeschooling her three boys. Kristin has always toured pregnant and folds mothering into her musical career:

> I didn't think it was anyone's business particularly because

I've always toured pregnant and I do whatever I have to do … But you know I do videos pregnant, and I'm on the road up until my eighth month usually. The babies go out on tour when they are three or four months old. They're quite portable at that age, and I have my doubts as to how healthy it is for any of us but they have their family around I think more than most kids do and that's healthy. (qtd. in McDonnell)

Kristin, Billy, and their boys live a primarily nomadic lifestyle:

We're never anywhere for very long … I would tour forever if I could. I mean it's hard. To live for that two hours of music is romantic and it drives you. It's hard for me to sit still as a person and touring has exacerbated that part of my personality. Touring is an extreme example of restlessness, and it feeds itself. You get used to seeing a new world every day. And sometimes I bring my family and sometimes I don't, but either way, it's fast and it's music and I like that. (qtd. in McDonnell)

Kristin and Billy have been through a lot on the road over the years. They have struggled with lack of money as the music business changes from selling albums through record stores to selling music digitally directly to customers:

We had left LA looking for America. We found it just outside Cleveland. It was amazing. The people were brilliant. We just wanted to raise our kids there and escape. It didn't work out that way. We lost our house in a flood. We were wiped out in a day. All the money we'd saved from touring, all our retirement funds, all the kids' college funds were gone in one afternoon. We were deeply, deeply, deeply in debt. We went on tour for a year. We stayed homeless. It was sort of a perfect storm. It was just as the industry was beginning to fail. So the tour and record both lost money, so I was even deeper in debt. We had to live on credit cards to feed the kids. It was an interesting life lesson—not a practical lesson, because we already lived small—but a life lesson. Because poverty's a big monster. I was hungry. Pictures of me then, I looked old and brittle. (qtd. in McDonnell)

I caught up with Kristin and her family again in Portland, Oregon, where they settled for a year. Her sons Ryder (fifteen) and Wyatt (ten) were studying, while her youngest son, Bodhi (five), baked with Kristin. There was a fire in the fireplace, and the family's three dogs were milling about. It was a quiet, sweet, domestic scene.

Kristin had stopped curating the boys' homeschooling curricula, and she now let them decide on their own learning projects. Previously, she was getting school age curricula from the various states they lived in and was implementing it. After a while, she felt that it wasn't that relevant to her boys' lives, and now they could choose their own curricula to study. Ryder, Wyatt, and Bodhi, Kristin's boys were still living at home then, and were all very curious and studious, so it was no trouble for them to find subject matter that interested them.

During this visit, Ryder and Wyatt were writing a cookbook of their favourite recipes and dishes that they had on tour. Wyatt was keeping a garden and learning Icelandic while Bodhi was studying all types of fish and reptiles. The boys had travelled to every single state in America except Hawaii and Alaska, and had been to many countries overseas. Each boy was very bright and sensitive, articulate and thoughtful. Ryder, the eldest at home, took care of the other two boys when his parents were gone. He was an expert cook while Wyatt, the second oldest boy at home, loved planting and gardening. Bodhi, the youngest, described himself as "obsessed with fish."

Kristin's family is a self-contained family unit with no outside help. They take care of each other and get along well together. They have their own family jargon, as they are together so much:

They [the kids] just think that nobody will ever understand. They can be aloof and suspicious. But it's true their lives are very different from most of the kids they meet. They live on a tour bus. Even the other children of rock bands are usually of rich rock bands. Usually the only musicians that can afford to have kids are rock stars. It's very different. They have nannies. They have their own bus. They only tour a couple of months a year. Wyatt says we're just the gypsy people. I guess if it works for them, it works for me.

Ryder, Kristin's second oldest son, would often babysit for his younger brothers when his mother and father were at shows or recording. He had mixed feelings about the family's nomadic lifestyle:

I can pretty much adapt to being on tour. I can just adapt to most of what's going on, the stressful touring lifestyle. I know my way around so many places. I drive across the country. I know clubs in almost every state.... We never really stay in the same place. I never really get a chance to make friends or anything like that. I make friends all over the country and in other countries. I get to live a nice life. It's different from most people I know but still nice.... I really like that my family is so close. We always stay together wherever we go really. We just shuttle across in the tour bus or minivan or whatever. I don't really have much privacy. This is the first house [in Portland] where I've had my own room. I do a lot of reading, and escape into my own world. If I want privacy, I go the library or go out to get coffee. I feel like I have pretty cool parents. I'm pretty happy to be in this family even though some things aren't as good; the good outweighs the bad I think.

After the year in Portland, Kristin and her family returned to the road. I caught up with them one last time, about a year later. They were abandoning their roaming lifestyle and bought a new home in Rhode Island. I was with them the day they moved back to where Kristin grew up:

This is my new house in my old home. This is the island where I grew up. I haven't lived here in a long time. Here my kids get the nature that I grew up with. The ocean was a given to me. I had no idea it wasn't like that for everyone. It's the prairie, it's the woods. It's what you do and it's clean and healthy. It's balance and math and you learn to save the whales early. I want them to have that. I want them to have these gardens to grow their own vegetables. I want them to have grandparents. If it means that I have to work at 7-Eleven, it's a good reason to work at 7-Eleven.

A desire for their children to experience stability, however, appeared to be only part of the story behind this dramatic change. The music industry was changing, and Kristin's and Billy's ability to make it on the road was being tested. Right before they moved, Kristin's tour bus broke down, and they experienced another major financial crisis. They were rethinking how to make a living in the music industry. Billy spoke about the changes they were thinking of making:

I think the music business is at a crossroads. We've already been through the crossroads. We're further along, and now we have to make retroactive decisions, and we need to create stronger bonds with the fans. We need to make it about artists, songs, and fans.... The Internet has always been about cutting out the middle man. We've always tried to be available and accessible by the people who appreciate the music. Because it's not a star thing; it's not about being famous for us. It's just proselytizing for us; it's about the getting the music heard.... A lot of people say that music should be free, but that's ignoring a lot of realities. Artists need to feed themselves too. The art of recording is a talent. And there is money that we just have to say is necessary to feed the process, and it's not huge money. Nobody needs to make a fortune. We just want to live above the poverty line. One of the ideas we're talking about is having a monthly subscription service for fans. Kristin has about ten thousand people on her mailing list now that we can send messages to. We're seeking a very modest monthly subscription to Kristin, supporting her career. Having said that, Kristin needs to branch out and do other things too. She is writing one book, and she's written a children's book. She got other books to write and has a series of essays and monologues; she is starting to do a life performance.

About this, Kristin said the following:

> There are good people in the good music business and they are struggling. I see no reason to stop. I feel like they need me and I need them. If we can work, then we should. Sometimes it all falls apart. Particularly if you don't want to play the game and I really don't want to play the game. And I disappear myself, I know, but the music business is not music. It's the opposite of music ... Maybe if I took out the idea of a record label, and then I made the money from the CDs, and it didn't matter how few I sold, I could at least stay on the road, stay in the studio. It's a lot to ask to be a working musician. It's crazy; it should never have occurred to me in the first place. But music did occur to me, and there were always people behind the scenes ready to make it happen, and now I have to make it happen. It would be ideal if I could keep being a musician obviously. People have asked me to write books. The whole idea sounds offensive to me; writers should write books. Writers struggle the way musicians do. They shouldn't be coming to me and asking for me to write a book. But if it would pay for me to make a record, I would do anything.

Part of Kristin's and Billy's answer to the changing music industry was creating the subscription service CASH Music. With CASH Music in place, Kristin could tour and record without being on a label.

> When CASH started, it was not only to facilitate giving music away, like 50FOOTWAVE has always done. It was for other musicians to be offered a set of tools with which they can circumvent the recording industry and reach fans directly. It's a pretty simple idea. It's all based on that urge people have to keep the music going. It's not purely a giving

urge; it's this idea that they have an energy that could help turn the music that's in the ether into the music that's in their ears. It's completely reworked the way I function as a professional. Since the studio bills are paid by the audience, I have no one with an ear to the salability of the material. I can go to my lab and perform these experiments. And the outcome is only supposed to be truth, for lack of a better word. No one is interested in anything but that. And that's what I was essentially interested in all along. But even to play the game a little bit, you backpedal, you apologize; you alter your results until something palatable is the outcome. I should have never been interested in palatable; it doesn't come natural to me. (qtd. in McDonnell)

Although Kristin and Billy seemed to have found an answer to their concern about the music industry, Rhode Island did not stay home for long. About a year later, they moved to New Orleans, which proved to be a much better hub. Billy taught music management and marketing at Loyola University. Kristin loved the musical city with its history and characters (Duerden). And Bo, Kristin's youngest, was happy to have a permanent home:

Everything changed after Bo, my youngest, was born, she says of her six-year-old. It's like he said to me, "OK, I see what you've got going on, but things are going to change now I'm here." He asked me when we were going to stop going places. I told him that if we stopped going places, the adventures would end. But he just said, "Yes, Mom, when are the adventures going to end?" (qtd. in Duerden)

Ironically, a stable physical home has also come with a new and unexpected change. In 2013, Kristin and Billy split up after twenty-five years of marriage. Kristin now divides her time between New Orleans and her native Rhode Island. Understandably, this breakup has been very hard on her.

Kristin immersed herself in work; she completed and toured another album with the Throwing Muses, Purgatory/Paradise; and she recently completed another book about her friendship with Vic

Chestnut called *Don't Suck, Don't Die: Giving Up Vic Chestnut.* Because her sons are older now, touring is easier.

> The two older sons are grown and live on their own, whereas the two younger ones live in New Orleans. Kristin's career is thriving. Her emotional health is also more stable now as she successfully completed a posttraumatic stress therapy called EMDR (eye movement desensitization and reprocessing) which has alleviated her bipolar disorder. About this, she said wryly, "This is a relief. There is nothing wrong with me anymore, which is sort of a problem in itself." (qtd. in Duerden)

ZIA MCCABE

After watching the documentary *Dig!*, I noticed in the credits that Zia McCabe, the rowdy, effervescent, woman keyboardist in The Dandy Warhols, was pregnant. Zia (and the rest of the band) was known for performing naked and for being fond of partying. Eventually, I found out later, Zia was the band's party instigator, "Secret Agent McCabe." I wondered how and if Zia's life—and that of the band—would change after she had a baby. As such, I reached out to Zia, and explained how I would love to follow her through her first couple of years parenting on tour.

Zia is the only woman in The Dandy Warhols. At the time she had Matilda (Tildy), no other band member had children. Travis, Zia's husband, is also the guitar technician and merchandise seller for The Dandy Warhols, which means he is also deeply intertwined into band life. Zia has stated that she is "most open book person in the band": "Our fans have grown up with us. Now a lot of them have their own kids. We really let everyone be part of the family.... We had a contest to guess Matilda's weight when she was born and whoever was closest got an autographed baby t-shirt. I think it's fun to include our fans in our lives."

The band has acted as a surrogate family for Zia, Travis, and Matilda—a support system, as well as a built-in social life. Zia discussed the band's participation in her pregnancy and in Matilda's growing up:

Travis would go to the bar that everybody drinks at, and you know that book that tells you everything that happens while you are pregnant, and he would say, "today she got her teeth buds." Our lighting guy feeling her kick and maybe that's the only baby he'll ever feel kick. These are people that aren't planning on having families, and they get to have this family because of Matilda. They've brought it up on multiple occasions, and that's been great. The more people that can be part of Matilda's immediate family, the better.

Having as much support as possible is necessary during the hectic lifestyle that is a professional midlevel band. The band has provided this for Zia as best it can. Even with the band's assistance, Zia has had to juggle her pregnancy around the band's album and touring schedule, as there is no formal maternity leave for an indie band:

Basically we decided when Monkeyhouse was coming out [*Welcome to the Monkey House*] that we'll promote it for as long as it needs, and we'll get pregnant right as we finish promoting it. It worked out perfectly; we were lucky. We finished promoting Monkeyhouse in February, got pregnant, recorded *Odditorium*, and then toured that summer pregnant. We came home, finished the album one week before Matlida was born, and then I had six weeks maternity leave. After that I came in and did promo shots, shot a video, did a little bit of rehearsing, and then we did our first road trip show down the West Coast.

As an integral part of the band, Zia needed to discuss her pregnancy with the other members of the band and work it out.

I definitely didn't want to surprise anyone with being pregnant. Nobody knew this [the band] was going to last ten years. I'm married now. I'm going to have a baby. We're going to have to work this out. We were all just hoping by the time Tildy came we could afford two tour buses. Stuff would be a lot easier for us if the band was just one notch more successful. That didn't happen, but we did hit a spot where we feel like we have a consistent career and can count on this success for several years to come. The band was cool with this and me. They've all got serious relationships. They are totally not in a party mood.

Certainly having Matilda on tour shifted Zia's demeanour and that of the band as a whole. Before she had Matilda, Zia was known as Secret Agent McCabe and was all about getting the party started. Zia's bandmate, Brent DeBoer, said that after Matilda was born, "Secret Agent McCabe [didn't] come out much anymore."

Zia's role in the band has certainly changed but it has not gone away altogether:

> I've definitely proved otherwise that that's not how it used to be, but it's just not what I do as my fulltime lifestyle. It's definitely something that we worked out that one night per tour: Travis takes Matilda and I get to go and wake up with a horrific hangover ... When you are pregnant you think you are turning into an angel, and you're never going to party again and you're never going to stay up late and have a hangover because you are a perfect vessel for this child. And then you have the kid and you go, I do like hanging out with these friends, and I do like going out and getting rowdy. I am in a rock band, and this is what I am happy doing. I never expected to stop to become a mom. You just slowly realize that you have to pick and choose.

When I started filming Zia and her family, her daughter, Matilda was almost two. The Dandy Warhols were in their twelfth year together, and were touring Europe for the summer. Zia's husband also joined them on tour.

The band was doing a summer festival tour, which entailed flying into Paris and then taking a train to Normandy where they had an off day and then a festival date. The day after the festival date in Normandy, they all took a train back to Paris, where they had another festival to play. After that, they travelled to Amsterdam, where the band played a club. Clearly, it was a lot of travelling with a paucity of down time for that week. This gruelling schedule as an adult alone can be very tiring; with a two-year-old, it is especially challenging.

Zia and Travis took turns watching Matilda, with very little sleep for anyone. Typically, the family woke up late and then spent the day walking around or exploring their new location. Zia and Travis brought many special toys packed solely for tour, which Matilda had not seen before with which they would engage her. They clearly loved playing with her and being together as a family in the many new cities. Touring was a big adventure for them all. When that failed to keep Matilda occupied, they would get out the DVD player and play some movies.

Travis left for shows a couple of hours before Zia, so Zia would get ready while he was there or when Matilda napped. Then Zia would shuttle Matilda to shows in her car seat/stroller travel system. They would play and nap on the way to the show and then meet Travis at their trailer.

Having a partner who helps with childcare helps Zia smoothly manage her professional life. Although Zia can afford to be in the band fulltime with no day job, The Dandy Warhols is still a midlevel band, so spending money on a nanny for Matilda while on tour is out of reach. As Zia said, "If I didn't have Travis, I don't think I could do this. Without the money, you have to buy your support."

Ann Powers said this about indie rock parenting on tour:

> If you are a grassroots artist on the road, it's by hook or by crook. In that case what you really need is a supportive mate. If not a mate, a sister or someone who is willing to share so intensely and in fact be the dominant care giver at that time. And then you have to have a lot of faith that your choice is okay for your kid, I think. Because in that case your kid is going to have to be flexible and ride around in a van or an SUV or something that's not that comfortable. (qtd. in *Rock N Roll Mamas*)

At this time, in 2006, The Dandy Warhols toured for about two weeks at a time every summer and other times during the year.

Zia and Travis usually embarked on this tour without a nanny and took turns with the childcare. Occasionally, they would bring a nanny with them on tour, but usually, when they were both busy, they would ask a friend of the band or sometimes their tour manager to watch Matilda. Luckily, their summer tours were primarily festivals, in which the band's sets are shorter, so this type of patchwork childcare was fairly easy to find.

Their schedule varied when they were home, however. The band usually practised for about two hours a day and then did other things with their lives. Some of the band members were in other bands, whereas others wrote music or started business ventures.

Zia joined a playgroup with two other mothers she met in prenatal yoga. They would meet together and engage in such activities as finger painting or reading stories. Afterwards, they would all go out and have lunch together. These two moms were a big support system for Zia when Matilda was a toddler: "It's great to be going through this with two other moms that have kids that are two weeks away from Matilda's birthday. We went through prenatal yoga together. I've never had two girlfriends that were friends.... It's amazing the support."

Now that Matilda is a toddler and Zia and Travis have their rotating childcare schedule in place, they are vague about planning for future school options. They generally live in the moment, the present, because the future is unpredictable and difficult to plan for. Zia explained it in the following way:

> Courtney's [lead singer in The Dandy Warhols] great in history. Most of the history I know, I learned from Courtney. He's a good storyteller and has a fantastic memory for details. So I've always kind of pictured Courtney teaching her a lot of history lessons. Pete [guitar player in The Dandy Warhols] is someone who would stumble around in nature with her [Matilda]. All of them of course would teach her about art. She's immersed in music.... I really like the idea of her getting her education in part from these people. They're really a wealth of information. So we'll split; do some school, do some travel ... But you can't plan it. Who knows? I might be back going to school fulltime,

doing something else. You can't plan in a rock band that far ahead. You don't really get to plan a future other than trying to save as much money as possible.

As the years passed, the band continued to tour and record. They gained a large following in Europe as well as Latin America and Australia. Then, in 2007, Courtney, the lead singer of the band, got married, and in 2010, he had a baby, so recording slowed down while he was on paternity leave.

During this time, Zia recorded an album with her bandmate, Pete, and also started a side project, a country band called Brush Prairie, in which she was the lead singer. She was DJing quite a bit under the moniker DJ Rescue. Zia was excited about both opportunities. "I'm in a country band called Brush Prairie. I don't know what the earning potential is for this. I think it's just an opportunity to learn how to be in a band outside The Dandy Warhols."

Zia got started in The Dandy Warhols when she was nineteen and still in school; it was her first band. She knows how fortunate she has been:

> Okay, you had a band right before you turned nineteen, and you have not had a second job since about four years after that. Just getting that out of your life as a musician is way more than people that are way more qualified than me who have worked way harder than me have ever come close to. I want to consider myself lucky for just having that and I don't want to assume that that's just what life is like for a musician. I'm trying to be realistic as much as I'm trying to envision that as my reality.

When Matilda started preschool, Zia and Travis became free during the day. Travis started going to school full time in video production. Zia continued to practise with The Dandy Warhols and her new band, Brush Prairie. As the future of The Dandy Warhols is uncertain, Zia has started pursuing other jobs, including work in film production as a personal assistant and a second assistant director:

A midlevel band being together for ... years and to be making an income, a salary, is incredible but it's also, the stability, year by year, is less dependable. You can't count on it. We have no interest in stopping, but this is time we start putting out our Best Of [album]. I don't want to assume that now that Courtney has a kid, he wants to go back to that [writing music and touring]. I want to make sure the band is my priority, but I want to make sure we both have plenty to do outside of that.

The band is changing as well. All band members are married, and two other members have children. They decided to get off their major record label, Capitol, and to form their own label, Beat the World. About this Zia said the following:

Getting off the major label was a lot like moving out of your parents' house. You've got to keep track of the stuff yourself, and you start appreciating the stuff you took for granted before. And that's what we did as a band, and we're starting to mature in that respect and are really starting to make it run as a business. It's still unstable because it's music and it's art and making it stay as a business is unstable no matter how you look at it. And none of us have made enough to retire if another dime never came in. We're just making it happen as long as we can. None of us want it to ever, ever end.

The next time I saw Zia, she was performing at a birthday party for herself with Brush Prairie. She told me that she and Travis separated after twelve years of being together. I am completely shocked by this news, as their partnership was pivotal in making touring with a toddler a workable situation, and they seemed very happy together; they were an extremely compatible couple. However, Matilda was now in school full time, and they did not bring her on tour as much. About her separation, Zia said the following:

I felt like when I married Travis, he's a really good person, loyal and helpful and hardworking. I knew he'd make a great dad and a great partner for however long he was going to be a great partner for. But I also felt like, I want to fall in love again. I want lots of adventures in my life and we had a ton of adventures together. But I just felt like we got a point where we weren't improving, we weren't having more adventures. We were kind of starting to live our own lives a little bit. And I was just ready to move on and I didn't want to be married anymore.

After the separation, both Zia and Travis sorted out the custody situation for Matilda. The adjustment was challenging as Zia had been used to sharing childcare with Travis during the day. Zia's main challenge, she said, was loss of control of Matilda when she was in Travis's care:

The hardest part about all of that is giving up the control. Matilda now is with Travis half the time, with what food he buys, what television and movies he allows her to watch, when her bedtime is, how many baths etc. That was something I was very controlling of in particular, no additives, no hormones, no milk etc. Travis was going along with this when we were together, and it's probably slided now that we are apart, and that is something I just have to let go of.

Ultimately, Travis and Zia divorced amicably, and decided on equal custody every other week. Zia has let go and has moved on; she has dated other men while still having a good relationship with Travis. Matilda is happy; she has close relationships with both parents.

Zia and Matilda have a great time together. Zia has begun taking her on tour more now that she is older so they can experience travel together. Zia clearly loves being a mother but also loves being a gregarious musician, a sexy woman, and an outgoing person. Although Zia's personality has changed now that she is a parent, now that Matilda is older, she has integrated fun and change back into her life.

WHAT I LEARNED: PARENTING AND HAVING A CAREER ARE DIFFERENT FOR EACH INDIVIDUAL

I started this project to find role models that could teach me how to balance being a creative professional and a mother. Making music and parenting are both difficult pursuits. What these women's stories ultimately taught me, perhaps unsurprisingly, is that there is no one way or one magic answer. All of these women are driven to be the best they can be; they all are willing to do what they need to do in order to make that happen. Sometimes, this means that they, their relationships, and their professional lives suffer.

Despite their different styles, career paths, and economics, these women are all dedicated parents as well as musicians. They are each devoted to their children, and it showed. All of the children I followed were thriving, tremendously sweet, articulate, and bright; they were all well-adjusted. Even though their lifestyles seem unorthodox, these children get to spend a lot more time with their parents than do most children.

As I was preparing to finish the film, I thought these women's stories did contain a universal lesson: without a strong support network, parenting and engaging in a creative profession, such as, music is not possible. Kristin and Zia had support, and although they still faced challenges, they thrived. It was heartbreaking, in contrast, to watch Su'ad, who lost her support network and struggled through depression and addiction. But in the end, Su'ad persevered, and got her life back on track, though whether that life includes music is unclear. Meanwhile, both Kristin's and Zia's marriages broke up. What I see now is that being a musician and a parent is just like having any other type of career and being a parent. Things happen and change in life, and shifts occur. Marriages break up, children grow up, and careers are maintained, or they change. This is what life is. However, because a musician's lifestyle is inherently an unstable one—one with late nights, usually without a consistent paycheck, living from gig to gig—these changes in lifestyle can have tremendous implications. A simple change or challenge that a parent in a successful double income partnership has can ultimately wipe out a freelance musician parent. I am thankful that these women, however, are brave enough to embrace life in their own unique ways and share their stories. Knowing others are out there trying, sometimes struggling, sometimes succeeding, could inspire others to forge their own unique path.

WORKS CITED

Atkins, Rahshida. "Self-efficacy and the Promotion of Health for Depressed Single Mothers." *Mental Health in Family Medicine*, vol. 7, no. 3, 2010, pp. 155-68.

Dig! Directed by Ondi Timoner, Interloper, 2004.

Duerden, Nick. "How Throwing Muses, Kristin Hersh Found Her Own Muse of Peace."

The Independent, 19 Oct. 2013, www.independent.co.uk/arts-entertainment/music/features/how-throwing-muses-kristin-hersh-found-her-own-muse-of-peace-8889456.html. Accessed 16 Nov. 2017.

Hersh, Kristin. *Don't Suck, Don't Die: Giving Up Vic Chestnut.* University of Texas Press, 2015.

McDonnell, Evelyn. "Interview: Kristin Hersh Revisits the Early Days of Throwing Muses in her New Memoir, Rat Girl." *The Providence Phoenix*, 8 Sept. 2010, thephoenix.com/Boston/music/108160-interview-kristin-hersh-revisits-the-early-days-o/. Accessed 16 Nov. 2017.

Rich, Adrienne. *Of Woman Born: Motherhood as Experience and Institution.* Norton, 1986.

Rock N Roll Mamas. Directed by Jackie Weissman, Rock Mama Films, 2013.

Su'ad, Ms. "What I Am." *the urban superwoman is a savage*, Ms. Su'ad, 2004.

11.
Consciousness-Raising in "Anchorage"

Witnessing the Mother and Spinster in Conversation

LORI WALTERS-KRAMER

"Leroy got a better job so we moved
Kevin lost a tooth now he's started school
I got a brand new eight month old baby girl
I sound like a housewife
Hey Shell, I think I'm a housewife."
—Michelle Shocked (1988)

In *Rhetorics of Motherhood*, Lindal Buchanan contends that "discourses about mothers, mothering, motherhood permeate U.S. political culture" (xvii). She points to Margaret Sanger's birth control presentations, Diane Nash's civil rights discourses, and texts surrounding legislation of the Unborn Victims of Violence Act to illustrate the potentiality of these discourses within the public sphere. Other scholars of rhetoric have studied motherhood discourses in antiwar activism (Edwards and Brozana; Knudson), anti-slavery efforts (Harris), and the environmental movement (Peeples and DeLuca; Stearney); they have excavated an array of political, social, and cultural domains in which audience members' attitudes about the issue at hand may have been shaped to some extent by the rhetors' references to motherhood. The texts they examine are the typical texts of the rhetorical critic: speeches, books, newspaper articles. Yet the lyrics above, from Michelle Shocked's song "Anchorage," demonstrate that music can also be a vehicle for maternal discourses. Musicians, too, can turn to motherhood as a rhetorical tool to reach personal or political ends.

Michelle Shocked is not recognized as a musician who highlighted (or even paid attention to) motherhood. However, she peppered her albums with songs about maternal issues, such as abortion ("Prodigal Daughter"), stillbirth ("Stillborn"), and children ("A Child like Grace"). Motherhood was, in fact, a topic that she threaded throughout her albums, as were issues, such as homelessness, racism, and oppression. In the 1980s and 1990s, Shocked's music and her activism mirrored her commitment to social justice and shaped her image as an advocate for the marginalized. She stated that her recorded music—particularly the music broadcast on radio—was a mechanism to get fans to her performances where she could pontificate about political matters. In 1990, she claimed, "My agenda is to use the music to sell the agenda. I call that subversion" (Aiges L6). Much of her music is not overtly political. Rather, it is subtly political because of Shocked's reliance on metaphor and ambiguity (Walters-Kramer).[1]

"Anchorage," the song that helped her generate a large fan base in the late 1980s, is an example of activist rhetoric because, I argue, it functions to raise consciousness about the master narrative that expresses the proper unfolding of a female's life that persists within the constraints of a patriarchal context. Both the Mother and the Woman (specifically, the Spinster) are recognized in the song's narrative, which offers a wide and diverse audience potential moments for identification. Shocked employs a feminine rhetorical style in both sound and lyric while she juxtaposes motherhood and spinsterhood. In so doing, Shocked presents the audience with an opportunity to adopt a feminist sensibility.

MUSIC AS RHETORIC

As I have previously written and will summarize here, music has long been understood as rhetorical, though not always explicitly studied as such. Plato, Isocrates, and Cicero addressed the persuasive potential of sound and music (Katz 88; Winn 26), yet for thousands of years, scholars who invested in understanding and theorizing rhetoric focused on discursive texts because these texts were considered to be the most essential tools within the political sphere (Poulakos and Poulakos 33). There were exceptions to this norm, however. In the seventeenth and eighteenth centuries, scholars of music "typically discussed [music] in terms of affect and rhetoric" (McClary 20). In the twentieth century, philosophers such as Susan Langer (101) and Theodore Adorno noted their appreciation for music as rhetorical. Adorno, for example, acknowledged music's relationship to language: "music resembles language in the sense that it is a temporal sequence of articulated sounds which are more than just sounds. They say something, often something human. The better the music, the more forcefully they say it. The succession of sounds is like logic: it can be right or wrong" (1).

Music is a form of rhetoric imbued with meaning; it may be the vehicle for an argument, explicitly through lyric or more implicitly through sound or performance. It can be a resource employed or consumed daily that influences audiences in subtle yet compelling ways. Because the norms and values of a community can be and are expressed in music (Attali 5; Citron 3; Frith 135), it can perpetuate the status quo and the ideologies and practices that comprise a community. It is a resource that can be—and has been—used by people advocating or resisting change. By its very nature, music is always political and never innocent (McClary 25; Attali 5).

Because gender is a critical component of culture and because music can (re)produce culture—and according to Jacques Attali, even forecast the future (20)—the performance, content, and even business of music can be examined to excavate latent messages about gender and their potential influence on women's social and political positions. George Upton may have been the first to write extensively about women in music, as he focused on how women have influenced the music of composers such as Bach, Beethoven, Chopin, and others (33). Unlike Upton, Sophie Drinker, also one of the first to write on the topic, has focused on female musicians' acceptance into or refusal from secular and religious spaces over thousands of years. Unlike Upton, whose book's popularity is reflected in its multiple printings, Drinker's writing was considered subversive for unearthing the barriers female musicians have faced. Her writing survives today because her essays were passed among scholars in the early twentieth century (Wood vii).

In the late 1980s and 1990s, several books were published describing women's obstacles in the popular music industry (Bowers and Tick; Sara Cohen; O'Brien). Others scrutinized and theorized music from postmodern and/or feminist stances (Citron; McClary), and summarized the history of women in music (Neuls-Bates). Whereas scholars, such as those noted above, acknowledge the creation, performance, and business of music as gendered, Susan McClary's treatise on "feminine endings" illuminates the gendered nature of the sound of music. McClary points to the seventeenth century when "composers worked painstakingly to develop a musical semiotics of gender: a set of conventions for constructing 'masculinity' or 'femininity' in music" that has endured" (7).

RHETORICS OF MOTHERHOOD

A rhetoric of motherhood is at work when motherhood, mothers, or mothering are folded into a text by a rhetor, perhaps a rhetor who appreciates that in any given audience, multiple connotations of "mother" are at work. The meanings listeners assign to "mother" are guided by culturally embedded assumptions about—and expectations of—motherhood. In short, motherhood is more than a biological fact; it is also a symbolic construction. That is, motherhood is a product of symbolic systems in which understandings of motherhood have been negotiated and constructed. As a result, meanings of motherhood are historically contingent and are not universal or biologically bound. Meanings of motherhood can, and do, morph over time. In fact, current connotations of motherhood within the United States emerged between the seventeenth and nineteenth centuries when "maternal instinct, domesticity, sexual disinterest, empathy, morality, and self-sacrifice" were believed to be natural characteristics of females (Buchanan 15).

Buchanan adopts Roland Barthes's notion of "cultural code" to capture the power of Mother as a symbolic construct. As a cultural code, the code of Mother is always present, guiding daily practices. It is, to use another of Barthes's terms, an ideology and like any active ideology, the code of Mother may constrain action or thought. The enormous weight of this cultural code is recognized by Buchanan when she claims, "Mother is easy to invoke but difficult to resist" (7). That symbolic weight provides Mother with its persuasive power. The concept of motherhood has enough symbolic force that its use can generate a "visceral and emotional response" from the reader or listener (Harris 301).

Importantly, Mother is an ideology crafted within a patriarchal context and as a result, is laden with assumptions about gender. Adrienne Rich has acknowledged this aspect of Mother: "Motherhood is coded in ways that ... produce serious rhetorical consequences" (qtd. in Buchanan 21). Buchanan concurs with Rich: "Rhetorics of motherhood ... impede [women], always/ already positioning them within the gendered status quo" (5). The rhetorical consequences of the code of Mother vary. In fact, rhetorics of motherhood can also "benefit women, giving them authority and credibility" (Buchanan 5). This supports Wesley Buerkle's claim that maternal discourses that involve a "play between talk of women's liberation and obligation" can be promising or a liability (27). After studying several texts in which a rhetoric of motherhood was present, Buchanan concludes that "maternal rhetorics may be used to promote conservative, progressive, or feminist ends" (22). Hence, feminist and rhetorical scholars are motivated to examine the ways in which the code of Mother can empower and/or disempower women.

Motherhood is a code that any rhetor can employ. It is as available to mothers as it is to women who are not mothers; it is as available to men as it is women. For example, media outlets have relied on the cultural code of Mother to frame individuals as good or bad mothers (Hasian and Flores). YouTube birthing videos can, according to Ashley Mack, construct a narrative about mothering that functions to perpetuate the ideal of the good mother (62). As well, motherhood is a concept that may work to unite audience and speaker (Buchanan 6). For instance, Leslie Harris has examined the Liberty Bell gift books and found that motherhood was a significant rhetorical appeal used by male and female antislavery activists in the nineteenth century to unite women readers across race and class. Certainly, a rhetor can be a mother who may choose to bolster her identity as a mother through rhetorical means and, in so doing, encourage audience members to associate her with concepts such as "nurturance, empathy, and community" (Gibson and Heyse 253). As an example, in her 2008 address at the Republican National Convention, vice presidential candidate Sarah Palin employed the code of Mother as a rhetorical resource. However, she did it in such a way that her persuasive effort was simultaneously strengthened and harmed (Buchanan 5). This potential to move listeners—to persuade—is why the code of Mother is a rhetorical tool for all rhetors, including speakers, writers, and singers who are or are not mothers themselves.

To better understand the tension that exists between the Woman and Mother as cultural codes, Buchanan positions the constructs of Woman and Mother in opposition to each other. She uses Kenneth Burke's and Richard Weaver's concepts of devil and god terms to depict the tensions that exist between the two. Whereas the god term is pleasing, the devil term is repulsive. Some of the associations of Mother and Woman mentioned by Buchanan (9) are noted below:

Mother (God Term)	Woman (Devil Term)
Children	Childlessness
Home	Work
Empathy	Self-centeredness
Strength	Weakness
The Reproductive Body	The Sensual Body
The Private Sphere	The Public Sphere
Altruism	Irrationality

Buchanan's deconstructions of Mother and Woman each con-

tain both stereotypically masculine and feminine characteristics. For example, some of the terms associated with the devil term of Woman are often recognized as masculine concepts (for example, the "public sphere" and "work"), whereas other terms evoke stereotypically feminine traits (for example, "hysteria" and "extreme emotion"). Some of the terms associated with the god term of Mother are often associated with masculine traits (for example, "strength" and "protection"), whereas other terms are connected to stereotypically feminine traits (for example, "love," "nourishment," and "self-sacrifice"). The Mother-Woman binary, then, complicates traditional renderings of masculinity and femininity. The binary also functions to fracture women as a collective based on their motherhood status. Woman and Mother are symbolically constructed in an oppositional relationship with no apparent common ground other than their biological sex. Buchanan is curious about the rhetorical possibilities of the two binary terms but is also attentive to the space between. She asserts, "The Mother and Woman afford rhetors means for exalting or denigrating women, as does the terrain that falls between the extremes" (9).

MICHELLE SHOCKED: THE *SHORT SHARP SHOCKED* YEARS

Michelle Shocked was born in Texas as Michelle Johnston to a father who was a musician and a mother who was a devoted Mormon (Schindehette and Maier; Voland). According to Paul Robicheau, by the mid-1980s, she was travelling around the United States, often homeless ("Michelle Shocked" 10), while she honed her skills as a musician and adopted a punk sensibility. One of her first public appearances was in January 1985 when she performed her song "Anchorage" on Coca Crystal's Manhattan Cable Show. During this period, she travelled to Europe; however, after being raped and finding no place where she felt at home, she moved back to Texas (Schindehette and Maier 79). At the Kerrville Folk Festival in Texas, her performance at a late-night campfire was recorded on a handheld Sony Walkman by Pete Lawrence, who subsequently returned to England and released the compilation of recordings as *The Texas Campfire Tapes*. Her discovery was considered "Lana Turner-like" after the album reached number one on the indie charts in England (Gleason 28). It was impressive enough for some to consider it a "landmark record" and for a major record label to offer her a contract (Matthews 113; Robicheau 11).

Short Sharp Shocked was Shocked's first studio album, which was produced by Mercury/Polygram Records during a period of about four years in the 1980s, when other female musicians such as Tracy Chapman and Suzanne Vega were considered part of the "new folk revival" (Himes N15; "Walking the Line" 14). A 1988

"Picks and Pans Review" of the album in *People* magazine suggested her popularity was a fad; it noted that she was getting her "big break during a year when short-haired, iconoclastic female singers (Sinead O'Connor, Tracy Chapman) are the hot new thing." Shocked's decision to sign with a major record label was grounded in her hope that her audience would increase in size. In an interview in 1988, she stated, "I would've stayed on an independent if it was just a matter of getting recorded, but I'm playing with fire here. I want power, I want access" ("Walking the Line" 14). The album, which includes several songs based on her own life in Texas, is to date her most popular album—in large part due to the popularity of the song "Anchorage," which remains her signature song. In a 2009 interview she stated, "Anyone who knows my work, knows that song." It is, according to the interviewer, "a shared vocabulary and a point of contact that she enjoys" (qtd. in Kennedy).

A potentially significant component of a rhetor's efforts is the presentation and co-construction of his or her identity. Identity—defined as "physical and/or behavioral attributes that make a person recognizable as a member of a group"—is not politically neutral (Palczewski et al. 158). Catherine Palczewski and her colleagues note, "Rhetoric involves not only what people communicate (the words and the images), but also as whom they communicate—the identities they foreground" (158). Palczewski and her co-authors turn to scholarship about motherhood to illustrate how dimensions of one's identity (such as race and class) intersect with the identity of mother in significant ways. This illustrates that one's understanding of oneself and performance of oneself as mother (or non-mother) are influenced by and also influence the physical and behavioural elements of the self. Yet identities are not only foregrounded by the rhetor but are also foregrounded by audience members who talk and write about the rhetor and play a critical role in shaping the rhetor's image, which can be defined as "a verbal and visual representation, emphasizing particular qualities and characteristics, that creates a perception of the rhetor in the audience's mind" (Palczewski et al.167). To be sure, the rhetor has little control as to how his or her image develops in the public sphere.

At the time "Anchorage" was popular in the United States—when Shocked was being introduced to those outside of England—she was described as "skinny and pale, [wearing] the uniform of the defiant: close-cropped hair, black T-shirt and sweats, a British sailor's cap and black high tops" (Schindehette and Maier 79), and as angular and boyish (True 42). She dressed the part of the skateboard punk rocker she sings about in "Anchorage." The presentation of Shocked as a defiant rabble-rouser is most evident in a black and white photo of her being held in a chokehold by police at a protest of Diamond Shamrock, a company that manufactured Agent Orange. Shocked insisted that this photo be used as the cover of *Short Sharp Shocked* ("Walking the Line" 14). Audiences viewed and made sense of Shocked's physicality while through articles published in papers and magazines, they gained knowledge about her politically motivated, apparently rebellious activities—such as burning the American flag at the 1984 Republican National Convention (Voland) and moving to England because of disgust with the Reagan presidency (Gleason). She was cast as an unstable, manic musician by authors who noted her life as a squatter and her placement in mental health institutions (Voland H1). One journalist even questioned her "grip on reality" (Jennings 8).

Because of her appearance, her self-identification as a feminist (Waldman), and because her music was popular in lesbian and feminist communities, many inferred that she was a lesbian (Gremore; Gross 197; Aiges L6). Some writers unequivocally maintained that she was a lesbian (Mockus 523), and Shocked strongly implied she was a lesbian in 1989 when she was nominated for New Music Award for Folk Album of the Year along with Tracy Chapman, kd lang, and the Indigo Girls. She won the award, and stated, "The category should have been called the Lesbian Best Vocalist" (Russell 331). Some members of her fan base, including comedian and activist Margaret Cho, considered "Anchorage" a lesbian anthem (Cho).

In the late 1980s, Shocked's emerging identity was that of a politically, mentally, sexually, and interpersonally aberrant woman. Shocked was cognizant of how her identity was being shaped by her record label and the media, and she acknowledged "that she was originally marketed as some sort of authentically field-recorded noble savage, a combination of idiot-savant and feral child" ("Bio").

Shocked's identity was that of the socially conscious activist who questions and disrupts the status quo. Importantly, she was constructed as a dissident performer during a time when the female heretic in the music industry was profitable for record companies. Therefore, her music and behaviour functioned to simultaneously resist and support the status quo within the music industry. To some extent, she was what Pierre Bourdieu would call a "consecrated heretic": an individual with an "anti-institutional mood" who is given authority by those in power to critique the institution (qtd. in Paul Cohen 9). Those in power at her record label did not mind that she was vocal about motherhood or homelessness or problems within the economic or political systems. Any critique she made of the label or the industry actually reinforced her nonconformist identity. Shocked seemed to recognize this when after being nominated for a Grammy for Best Contemporary Folk Recording, she said "I've been pretty open about my motivation: basically to reclaim music to be made by people for people, and to destroy the system from within; now they're going to try to give me an award for it. It reminds me of that old cliché about capitalists throwing you the rope that you hang them with" (qtd. in Bream O1F). Unfortunately, her freedom to critique without backlash did not endure. By the 1990s her complaints about the restrictions placed on her musical endeavours rose to the level of a lawsuit in which she sued Mercury Records for violating the Thirteenth Amendment—"claiming that 'slavery' was unconstitutional—and the case was eventually settled in favor of Shock's contractual release and ownership of her songs" (qtd. in Torem).

"ANCHORAGE": FEMINIST SENSIBILITIES

Some reviewers recognized that the lyrics of "Anchorage" centred on the lives of women—particularly on the lives of two friends after one got married and had children, whereas the other developed into an active, travelling musician. Rodger Mullen, for instance, noted, "Shocked skillfully manages to express both the pain and joy of living with difficult decisions." Other writers noted that

"Shocked reads a letter from a former partner-in-crime who has settled down and given up" (Okamoto 2F) and that "Anchorage" expresses "the love retained by old friends who have shared strong experiences, as well as the confusion and awkwardness that lack of continued contact brings" (Pick 4F). Len Righi identifies motherhood as the discrepancy in the friends' lives:

> "Anchorage" sounds at first like a slightly nostalgic exchange between two friends who have gone separate career paths; one has become a housewife and mother isolated in Alaska, the other a singer living in New York City. But upon closer inspection, it's really about a woman who has been forced to shelve her dreams and follow her husband. (A62)

When interviewed by Righi, Shocked acknowledged that the song emerged from a letter written to her by an old friend: "We're supposed to have had the civil rights movement, then the equal rights movement ... 'You are my wife, Goodbye city life' ... that stuff doesn't happen anymore. But it does" (A62).

The lyrics of "Anchorage" do not just repeat the content of a letter; they present a reaction to the evaporation of a friendship (or, perhaps as some believed, the demise of a lesbian relationship). The lines "I took time out to write to my old friend / I walked across that burning bridge" convey the emotional courage to reconnect with her friend, for example. The song also presents a response to the persistence of patriarchal norms that encourage women to allow their husband's desires to trump their own. "Anchored down in Anchorage" may have appeared in the letter written by her friend, but Shocked opted to use it as the basis of the chorus, and it is repeated three times in the song. As such, Shocked emphasizes a consequence of her friend's choice to follow her husband—lack of freedom.

As noted earlier, in the late 1980s, Michelle Shocked labelled herself as a feminist (Waldman). In fact, she claimed in an interview that she was a "very strong feminist" (Rosen L3), and numerous articles noted her feminist leanings and influences (Bream O1F; Harrington B1; Okamota 2F). The song was a vehicle for Shocked to display her feminism, albeit in an understated fashion. In short,

Shocked did not overtly advocate feminism in the lyrics, which are infused in a text crafted in a feminine style.

"ANCHORAGE": FEMININE STYLE IN LYRIC AND SOUND

Karlyn Kohrs Campbell's influential *Man Cannot Speak for Her* introduced rhetorical critics and feminists to what Campbell refers to as the feminine style—a discursive style used by women in the suffrage movement, a historical period when speaking in the public sphere was deemed appropriate only for men. In the context of the suffrage movement, the feminine style grew out of women's lived experience; it was a strategic choice that allowed the female rhetors to "cope with the conflicting demands of the podium" (Campbell 12). Discourse that reflects the feminine style is, according to Campbell (13), "personal in tone," relies "heavily on personal experience," encourages "audience participation," and positions the audience and speaker as peers. "The goal of such rhetoric is empowerment" because it invites women to be agents of change or because it is consciousness-raising (Campbell 13). Campbell acknowledges that although the feminine style can be employed by male and female rhetors (as well as applauded by male and female audience members), it is labelled "feminine" because of the style's association with the nonaggressive manner of speech employed by female speakers in the nineteenth century (12).

Although Campbell identifies the feminine style as one that was evident in the nineteenth century, scholars have examined contemporary texts to discern the presence of the feminine style as well as to consider the implications of its use. For example, Bonnie Dow and Mary Boor Tonn argue that Governor Ann Richards's speech at the 1988 Democratic National Convention illustrates that "the characteristics of feminine style are part of a synthesis of form and substance that works to promote an alternative political philosophy reflecting traditional feminine values" (287). Dow and Tonn turn to the work of Rita Felski and, in particular, her discussion of the "feminist counterpublic sphere" in which common identity is affirmed and in which hegemonic ideologies may be opposed (Dow and Tonn 287). Palczewski and her colleagues characterize a counterpublic as a public that creates "safe spaces in which participants: 1) develop alternative norms for public argument and what counts as evidence; 2) regenerate their energy to engage in argument in the political and public spheres; 3) enact identities through new idioms and styles; 4) formulate oppositional interpretations of identities, interests, and needs" (243).

"Anchorage," through sound and lyrical content, illustrates the feminine style in musical form.

Feminine Style in Lyric

A characteristic of the feminine style is reliance on personal experience (Campbell 13). "Anchorage" was written by Shocked and is based on her friendship with a woman who moved to Alaska and is now "Anchored down in Anchorage." The song begins with "I took time out to write to my old friend / I walked across that burning bridge / Mailed my letter off to Dallas / But her reply came from Anchorage, Alaska." The lyrics then move to the content of the letter she received from her friend. The song suggests that the relationship between the two was once strong, but the lyric "I walked across the burning bridge" indicates the relationship had deteriorated. "Anchorage" is a memoir in musical form. Music reviewer Chris Woodstra writes the following: "The songs have a very personal, almost diary feel, but at the same time, they speak a universal language—none so poignant as the album's centerpiece, "Anchorage," a touching letter from an old friend." The old friend, Kelli Bingham, wrote the letter when she was feeling homesick. "I was feeling, you know, hohum blues," she once stated in an interview. "I was feeling like, I guess, a housewife" (qtd. in Rich E1).

As the author of the letter from "Anchorage," Kelli is the most prominent (although nameless) character in the narrative followed by Shocked and Kelli's husband, Leroy, and, to a lesser extent, Kelli's son Kevin and Kelli's daughter. The narrative indicates that Kelli is emotionally adrift while physically "anchored down in Anchorage" with her husband and children. There is a hint that Kelli is somewhat astounded by her current roles in life when she recognizes, "I think I'm a housewife. Hey, Shell. I think I'm a housewife." Her curiosity about, and perhaps veneration of, Michelle's lifestyle is addressed with the lyric "Hey Girl, what's it like to be in New York? New York City—imagine that! Tell me, what's it like to be a skateboard punk rocker?" Her wistfulness for her life premarriage and prechildren are illuminated by the lyric "Take me back to the days of the foreign telegrams and the all-night rock and rollin.'" Leroy is cast as a dominant husband. His name is featured in the song (repeated three times); he's the reason for the move to Anchorage, and his is the voice that interrupts Kelli's storytelling with "Send a picture," "Hello," and "Keep on rockin,' girl." It is evident that Shocked and Leroy have a relationship; the implication is that it is quite amicable. Yet his presence in the narrative is overbearing in comparison to the voice of the author of the letter.

The feminine style is also characterized by a personal tone (Campbell 13). Throughout the song, Michelle is referred to by her friend as "Shell" and greeted with "Hey, Girl." This language conveys familiarity and intimacy. The lyric, "Hey Shell, we was wild then" reveals a shared history as does "Hey Girl, I think the last time I saw you was on me and Leroy's wedding day," which, more specifically, evokes a shared milestone followed by the estrangement alluded to in the "burning bridge" lyric. Furthermore, within the narrative, the use of letters as the means of communication used to reunite these friends enhances the personal spirit of the lyrics. A personal tone, according to Dow and Tonn, emits "emotional support, nurturance, empathy" (287) and is "oriented toward relationship maintenance" (288). In the narrative, the letter from Michelle is construed as a way of salvaging a broken relationship and her friend—who has become a mother of two during their period of estrangement—reveals she is willing to revive what once was a significant relationship.

Another quality of the feminine style is that it encourages audience participation. For Campbell, audience participation does not necessarily mean that audience members participate in the performative moment and interact directly to and immediately with the rhetor. Rather, participation can involve a "process of testing generalizations or principles against the experiences of the audience" (13) by, for example, relying on the inductive reasoning skills of the audience. That is, the listener participates by adhering to the message and drawing conclusions based on the information presented. Such is the case with "Anchorage," in which there is no explicit assertion. The reasoning is inductive; Shocked encourages the audience to consider the evidence (the narrative) and determine on its own the assertion the evidence supports. After hearing "Anchorage," listeners may very well reach the conclusion that "life with a husband and children is confining." As well, audience members participate when they make personal connections to the text. To expand on this, Dow and Tonn contend, "Generalizations reached through validation of personal experiences lead to the realization that the 'personal is political,' a process which produces group cohesion" (289). Audience members who identify with the rhetor's narrative or with any characters in the narrative are incorporated into the meaning-making process and move into a relationship with the rhetor based on equality. Hence, the final characteristic of the feminine style—that the rhetor positions the audience and speaker as peers—is apparent in "Anchorage."

Feminine Style in Sound

Social scientific studies conducted as early as the 1970s have found that even children associate instruments with a gender; females are often associated with the violin, flute, and clarinet, and males are often associated with drums, trombone, and trumpet (Marshall and Shibazaki 495). It is not too surprising, then, that sounds instruments produce are also gendered. Because rhetorical critics have not articulated how the feminine style sounds, the work of scholars who understand the powerful role of sound as "an active participant in the shaping of cultural meaning and human subjectivities" is instructive (Monson 211). Desmond Sergeant and Evangelos Himonides highlight the role of the listeners in the meaning-making process: "Masculinity and femininity are mapped onto the music by the listener" (13). The sound of the bass guitar, for example, has been socially constructed as a masculine sound (Auslander 2). Timbre, too, is perceived as feminine or masculine (Shepherd 165). Sergeant and Himonides also found that the tempo of the music was the primary factor in listener's interpretation of music as feminine or masculine: "Faster tempi were associated with perception of the music as more stressed and dramatic, more assertive and masterful, more controlled and objective: slower tempi were associated with music perceived as more calm and reflective, mild, and submissive, sensitive and emotional" (7). Furthermore, not only are sounds gendered, they are also associated with sexual identity and sexuality (Sergeant and Himonides 13).

"Anchorage" is slow, soft, and folklike. One reviewer notes that Shocked's lyrics are set "against a melodic background of acoustic guitars and a Hammond organ right out of Bob Dylan's *Highway 61 Revisited*" (Okamoto 2F). Whereas the album's "If Love Was a Train" was played on hard-rock radio stations, "Anchorage" was the song from *Short Sharp Shocked* that was played on soft-rock radio stations (MacDonald T3). According to Shocked, it was the most highly produced song on the album ("Walking the Line" 14). Shocked was described as "more of a straightforward folkie than either Suzanne Vega or Tracy Chapman" who generated a sound with "a bluesiness ... a hint of country swing in some of it, and a strikingly contemporary sensibility that carries highlights such as 'Anchorage'" (McLeese 25).

In sum, Shocked presents a feminist text that is somewhat obscured by a feminine style. This approach of performing a feminist text in a feminine style was also used by women suffragists who "sometimes searched for ways to legitimate 'unwomanly' behavior and for ways to incorporate evidence of femininity into rhetorical action" (Campbell 12). Shocked's unwomanly (or masculine) presentation of self, along with her presence in the male-dominated music industry, is aesthetically and politically balanced by the feminine style discussed above. In this respect, Shocked is similar to suffragist Francis Willard who enacted a "feminine feminism" and embodied a number of paradoxes (Campbell 130).

PERSPECTIVES BY INCONGRUITY

Visually, acoustically, and lyrically, "Anchorage" produces and excavates tensions and is also embedded in the unique cultural landscape of the 1980s. Shocked's feminine lyrics and sound, for example, were in contrast to the image of Shocked in a chokehold on the album's cover. An intimate, private letter between friends was at odds with the very public recording and broadcasting of the letter's contents. A woman-centred song performed in a feminine style by a feminist in the late 1980s was oppositional to the "cock rock" produced within the music industry at that time (Frith and McRobbie 375). Because juxtaposed images, sounds, and ideas produce meaning (Aune 573), it is instructive to consider the juxtaposed textual elements creating and surrounding "Anchorage." Kenneth Burke's "perspectives by incongruity" is one theoretical tool that can help reveal the rhetorical value of these incommensurate textual elements that rub up against each other in "Anchorage."

When discussing perspective by incongruity, Burke notes that the world is full of incongruences that occur when two objects (or ideas, etc.) are positioned in close proximity to each other, but their "togetherness" is atypical. When an artist, for example, paints incongruous objects in her art, she does so purposefully. "The result," he says, "is a perspective with interpretive ingredients" (97). Burkean rhetorical scholars have noted that "incongruity can both elicit pleasure and shift perspective" (Anderson 165). It may induce pleasure if the incongruity is read as humorous or out of the ordinary. And it may function to shift perspectives because "it is through confronting moments of incongruity that people re-evaluate their experiences" (Dubriwny 398). There are three significant incongruities within "Anchorage" that centre on: 1) women's spheres of activity; 2) Shocked's identity; and 3) motherhood. Each incongruity is reflected in Buchanan's continuum in which Woman (the devil term) is juxtaposed with Mother (the god term) (9).

One meaningful incongruity in "Anchorage" centres on women's spheres of activity. The song lyrics contain quoted material from a letter written by one of Shocked's friends. When Shocked sang it during her live or televised performances and when the recording of it was distributed, replayed, and broadcasted, the letter—an intimate vehicle for communication—moved from the private to the public sphere. The public audience became privy to the content of what was originally generated as private communication. "Anchorage" was not the only text produced in the 1980s in which private communication was made visible to a large audience. In the same period that "Anchorage" was on the pop charts, *Designing Women* was in its third season. Bonnie Dow, writing about that popular television show, argues that the show is a "case study that illustrates the blurring of the demarcations between women's private talk and the public sphere ... this blurring occurs through the public performance of 'private talk' on television" (125). Before those boundaries were blurred, however, juxtaposing the activities connected to the private spheres (associated with femininity) and public spheres (associated with masculinity) made the usual tension between the two incongruent spheres more visible. In Buchanan's work, the private sphere is associated with the Mother (a god term) and the public with the Woman (a devil term) (9). Dow argues that such discourse "can work to create a definition of reality that contrasts with the dominant definitions offered by a patriarchal culture" (128). The subsequent heightening and releasing of the tension that occurs when the boundaries between public and private are blurred or juxtaposed may function to raise consciousness (Dow 125). Tasha Dubriwny, in fact, asserts that "Perspective by incongruity within the process of consciousness-raising can play a key role in reshaping of the meaning of individuals' experiences, for it is through confronting moments of incongruity that people re-evaluate their experiences" (398). Additionally, as a result of the consciousness-raising function, a feminist counterpublic sphere is plausible (Dow 125).

Another significant incongruity centres on identity. As noted earlier, Michelle Shocked's association with the folk genre was considered to be at odds with the feminist, punk, rabble-rousing image she (and her record company) constructed. In her review of *Short Sharp Shocked*, Deb Waldman notes that Shocked described herself as an ex-patriot and anarchist, "but you wouldn't know it from her new album on Polygram, *Short Sharp Shocked*." A reviewer from a 1988 People magazine's "Pics and Pans" notes, "musically Shocked doesn't sound at all like a typical punk rocker; she more closely resembles the protest-folk singers of the early '60s." And music reviewer Chris Woodstra similarly states, "The cover photo, which shows Shocked restrained by police officers during a protest, indicates little about the music found within."

Although her radical image may not have been attractive to a large audience, the folk aesthetic of "Anchorage" proved to be very popular. Importantly, although female pop musicians have steered away from integrating the topic of motherhood into their music, female country and folk musicians such as Dolly Parton, 1960s folk revival performers such as Peggy Seeger and Joni Mitchell, and musicians associated with "new country" such as Bonnie Rait and Mary Chapin Carpenter have integrated the topic of motherhood into their music (Grieg 173). Despite the fact that motherhood is not widely addressed even in the country-folk genre, the folk genre is more generally affiliated with motherhood than are other genres. Shocked might have understood this association when she articulated her strategy in interviews: "Sure, the songs could be all nice and sweet, but put that shot on the cover, and I knew I'd get a chance to talk about something that mattered" ("Walking the Line" 14) and "I feel that what I've done by keeping the record fairly subtle is to make people curious enough to come see me live" (qtd. in Harrington B12). The tension that exists between her image as a radical, black-clothed punk rocker and her folksy, country sound (arguably connected to the god term of Mother) may lead some to consider Shocked as nonsensical, which, per Buchanan, is a characteristic associated with the devil term of "Woman" (9). However, it is a tension Shocked may have not minded if it functioned to heighten the curiosity of listeners and get them to her performances.

The most salient incongruity in "Anchorage" centres on mother-hood. It is a tension that was apparent to listeners who described the song as a "contrast between Shocked's rambling life and the stable married world of a childhood friend" ("Picks and Pans"). In the song (and in their lives), Shocked and her friend's primary commonality is now a history of their youth when they shared common ground (literally and metaphorically). As well, discourses that address the Woman and the Mother "provide speakers with immediately recognizable (and culturally resonant) stereotypes" (Buchanan 8). The shift from a woman's voice to a mother's voice in one text highlights the dissimilarities in the lives of the mother and the nonmother. Within a single text, listeners are confronted with the Mother (the godly) and the Woman (the godless)—two characters that are part of a woman-mother dichotomy. According to Buchanan, the "mother stood at the apex and was followed (in order of significance) by the maiden, eagerly awaiting marriage and family, the mother and the maiden were, in turn, trailed by the spinster, a pitiful figure lacking the home, husband, and children required for social consequence" (18-19). There is no hint in the lyrics that Shocked has the same degree of interest in her friend's life as her friend has in her life. There is no indication that Shocked envies her friend in Alaska or that she hopes to someday be a mother. Therefore, Shocked is more likely to be constructed as a spinster than a maiden. Shocked's transient life (as identified in her lyrics as well as in discourse about her) when paired with the absence of any lyric that speaks to a longing for parenthood reinforces her spinster status. Furthermore, in the late 1980s, Shocked was emerging as a favourite of lesbians and was believed to be homosexual. This aspect of her identity adds complexity to the song because of the assumed incommensurability of "lesbian" and "mother"—a tension that is the result of the widely held belief that mothers must be heterosexual. Homosexuals are considered sexually "explicit and perverse" and "sexuality is emphatically *not* an attribute of the mother" (emphasis in original, Buchanan 20).

To review, Michelle Shocked's country-folk sound is generally associated with femininity and the maternal. This maternal sound, however, is in contrast to the aesthetically harsh photo of a short-haired Michelle Shocked in a chokehold at a protest. As well, when Shocked shares the contents of a letter between friends in "Anchorage," she exposes the private sphere in a very public manner. Like country-folk music, the private sphere is also identified with the mother. Combined, the folk sound, revelation of the private sphere, and the lyrics that showcase the voice of the friend extol the Mother. As such, the god term does its rhetorical work. On the other hand, the visual aspects of the album (along with Shocked's appearance), the reliance on the public sphere, and the lyrics focusing on Michelle magnify the woman (specifically, the spinster). So, too, is the devil term doing its rhetorical work.

FINAL THOUGHTS

Buchanan declares that the "Mother and Woman afford rhetors means for exalting or denigrating women, as does the terrain that falls between the two extremes" (9). She asserts that the "middle ground" on the Woman-Mother continuum is a space that is rhetorically rich because of its ambiguity. Texts that "combine elements of the Woman and Mother" fall in this middle ground (9). "Anchorage" is such a text. "Anchorage" contains paradoxical elements, yet through music and lyrics, the codes of Mother and Woman are brought into relief.

Michelle Shocked's popularity in the late 1980s may have been accelerated, in part, by the popularity of other female songwriters. "Anchorage," in particular, may have appealed to listeners attracted to its feminine style—exemplified by its reference to personal experience, its personal tone, the inclusion of the audience, and its subdued and folksy sound. Yet other songs on *Short Sharp Shocked*, such as "When I Grow Up," and "Memories of East Texas," could arguably illustrate this feminine style. It was "Anchorage," not any other song on *Short Sharp Shocked,* that appealed to the largest audience, gracing the top the charts during a period in which pop musicians were not singing about mothers or motherhood (Grieg 169).

"Anchorage" presented disparate listeners with the familiar characters of the Mother and the Woman (Spinster). The character of the Mother, as has already been discussed, is an influential symbolic construct that "is easy to evoke but difficult to resist" (Buchanan 7). Any reference to Mother "discourages critical distance, in effect shutting down analysis, discussion, deliberation, reflection, and nuance" (Buchanan 7). "Anchorage" relies on the god term of Mother. Shocked's friend, Kelli, is presented as having a stable home, a satisfied (potentially domineering) husband, and children whom she protects. She is concerned about others (for example, by revealing interest in Shocked's life and sharing information about her children), and she certainly has sacrificed for her family by leaving the familiar Texas landscape and her friends for Anchorage, Alaska. In all of these respects, Kelli is a fine representative of the Mother. Yet, significantly, the Mother is not idealized in the song. The strength of the Mother as god term is weakened when the Mother is juxtaposed with the Woman who, in "Anchorage," is not vilified. Although Shocked is presented as a childless woman (a spinster and possibly a lesbian) who is focused on her work as a musician in the public sphere, she is also presented as a woman who is taking the risk of walking "across the burning bridge" to rekindle a once-significant relationship. As such, Shocked displays some characteristics associated with the code of Mother—namely love and strength. Thus, by way of the lyrics, the Woman is softened. Furthermore, the feminine style noted above augments the mothering of the spinster.

Shocked assisted audience members in gaining perspectives about the constructs of Mother and Woman through the narrative presented in the song—particularly via the conversation between Kelli and Michelle Shocked featured in "Anchorage." "Anchorage" invited audiences to consume the music without resistance while subtly presenting a feminist sensibility in which motherhood's cultural hegemony within a patriarchal system is recognized and, perhaps, questioned. Furthermore, the song's feminist bent, largely displayed by the juxtaposition of the incongruous Mother and Woman, is tempered by a feminine style—a strategy for introducing unorthodox or unpopular content to an audience.

As a text, "Anchorage" had rhetorical force, a characteristic of music Shocked appreciated. It was noted earlier that Shocked believed that her music—particularly the music that was played on radio stations and distributed to a wide audience (as was "Anchorage")—was the means to realize her goal of sharing her political viewpoints with live audiences. For political and artistic reasons, Shocked also hoped to unite diverse audiences (Jennings 8; True 42). In 1988, the appeal of "Anchorage" to a large audience helped her in those efforts.

ENDNOTE

[1] This chapter focuses on Shocked's early years in the music industry and, in particular, her song "Anchorage" as it functioned within the context of the late 1980s. Another analysis would be necessary to address the homophobic rhetoric she espoused at performances in 2011 and 2013 (Rawls; Schneider).

WORKS CITED

Adorno, Theodore. "Music and Language: A Fragment." 1956. *Quasi Una Fantasia: Essays on Modern Music.* Translated by

Rodney Livingstone, edited by Theodore Adorno, pp. Verso, 1998, pp. 1-6.

Aiges, Scott. "Michelle Shocked Bares her Wit." *The Times-Picayune* [New Orleans], 6 Apr. 1990, p. L6.

Anderson, Karrin Vasby. "Deflowering the Voting Virgin: Piety, Political Advertising, and the Pleasure Prerogative." *Quarterly Journal of Speech*, vol. 103, no. 1-2, 2017, pp. 160-181.

Attali, Jacques. *Noise: The Political Economy of Music.* Translated by Brian Massumi. University of Minnesota, 1985.

Aune, James Arnt. "Perspectives by Incongruity." *Encyclopedia of Rhetoric*, edited by Thomas Sloane, Oxford, 2001, pp. 572-75.

Auslander, Philip. "I Wanna Be Your Man: Suzi Quatro's Musical Androgyny." *Popular Music*, vol. 23, no. 1, 2004, pp. 1-16.

"Bio." *Shellshocked.* 1997. www.shellshocked.com.

Blacking, John. "The Music of Politics." *Music, Culture, & Experience: Selected Papers of John Blacking*, edited by Reginald Byron, University of Chicago, 1995, pp. 198-222.

Bowers, Jane and Judith Tick, editors. *Women Making Music: The Western Art Tradition, 1150-1950.* University of Illinois, 1987.

Bream, Jon. "Michelle Shocked is Rebel with a Cause: To Reclaim Pop Music." *Star Tribune: Newspaper of the Twin Cities*, 5 Mar. 1989, O1F.

Buchanen, Lindal. *Rhetorics of Motherhood.* Southern Illinois University, 2013.

Buerkle, C. Wesley. "From Women's Liberation to Their Obligation: The Tensions between Sexuality and Maternity in Early Birth Control Rhetoric." *Women & Language* vol. 31, no. 1, 2008, pp. 27-34.

Burke, Kenneth. *Perspectives by Incongruity*, edited by Stanley Edgar Hyman. Indiana University,1964.

Campbell, Karlyn Kohrs. *Man Cannot Speak for Her: A Critical Study of Early Feminist Rhetoric.* Vol. 1. Praeger. 1989.

Cho, Margaret. "Michelle Shocked Me." *Huffington Post*, 3 Mar. 2013, www.huffingtonpost.com/margaret-cho/michelle-shocked-me_b_2918927.html. Accessed Nov. 16 2017.

Citron, Marcia J. *Gender and the Musical Canon.* Cambridge, 1993.

Cohen, Paul M. *Freedom's Moment: An Essay on the French Idea of Liberty from Rousseau to Foucault.* University of Chicago, 1997.

Cohen, Sara. *Rock Culture in Liverpool: Popular Music in the Making*. Clarendon, 1991.

Dow, Bonnie. "Performance of Feminine Discourse in *Designing Women*." *Text and Performance Quarterly*, vol. 12, no. 2, 1992, pp. 125-45.

Dow, Bonnie and Mary Boor Tonn. "'Feminine Style and Political Judgement in the Rhetoric of Ann Richards." *Quarterly Journal of Speech*, vol. 79, 1993, pp. 286-302.

Drinker, Sophie. *Music and Women: The Story of Women in Their Relationship to Music*. 1948. Feminist Press at the City University of New York, 1995.

Dubrinwy, Tasha. "Consciousness-Raising as Collective Rhetoric: The Articulation of Experience in the Redstockings' Abortion Speak-Out of 1969." *Quarterly Journal of Speech*, vol. 91, no. 4, 2005, pp. 395-422.

Edwards, Janis L., and Amanda Leigh Brozana. "Gendering Anti-War Rhetoric: Cindy Sheehan's Symbolic Motherhood." *Journal of the Northwest Communication Association*, vol. 37, 2008, pp. 78-102.

Frith, Simon. "The Industrialization of Popular Music." *Popular Music and Communication*. 2nd ed. Edited by James Lull, Sage, 1992, pp. 14-24.

Frith, Simon, and Angela McRobbie. "Rock and Sexuality." *On Record: Rock, Pop, and the Written Word*, edited by Simon Frith and Andrew Goodwin, Routledge, 1990, pp. 317-32.

Gibson, Katie L. and Amy L. Heyse. "'The Difference Between a Hockey Mom and a Pit Bull': Sarah Palin's Faux Maternal Persona and Performance of Hegemonic Masculinity at the 2008 Republican National Convention." *Communication Quarterly*, vol. 58, no. 3, 2010, pp. 235-56.

Gleason, Holly. "Short, Sharp, Talented." *Rolling Stone*, 3 Nov. 1988, p. 28.

Gremore, Graham. "Folk-Rocker Turned Gay-Hater, Michelle Shocked Blames *Queerty*, 'Lynch Mob' For Her Fall From Grace." *Queerty*. 29 June 2013, www.queerty.com/folk-rocker-turned-gay-hater-michelle-shocked-blames-queerty-lynch-mob-for-her-fall-from-grace-20130629. Accessed Nov. 16 2017.

Gross, Larry. *Up from Invisibility: Lesbians, Gay Men, and the*

Media in America.: Columbia University, 2012.

Harrington, Richard. "Michelle Shocked, Taking Stock." *Washington Post*, 15 Mar. 1989, pp. B1; B12.

Harris, Leslie J. "Motherhood, Race, and Gender: The Rhetoric of Women's Antislavery Activism in the Liberty Bell Gift-books." *Women's Studies in Communication*, vol. 32, no. 3, 2009, pp. 293-319.

Hasian Jr., Marouf, and Lisa A. Flores. "Mass Mediated Representations of the Susan Smith Trial." *The Howard Journal of Communication*, vol. 11, no. 3, 2000, pp. 163-78.

Himes, Geoffrey. "Women on Verge of a Musical Break." *Washington Post*, 15 May 1992, p. N15.

Jennings, Dave. "Michelle Shocked: Cause Celebres." *Melody Maker*, 4 Mar. 1989, pp. 8-9.

Katz, Steven B. *The Epistemic Music of Rhetoric: Toward the Temporal Dimension of Affect in Reader Response and Writing.* Southern Illinois University, 1996.

Kennedy, Sharon. "Michelle Shocked on Life, Love and Not Talking to Your Mother." *ABC South West WA.* 26 Feb. 2009, www.abc.net.au/local/stories/2009/02/26/2502460.htm. Accessed 16 Nov. 2017.

Knudson, Laura. "Cindy Sheehan and the Rhetoric of Motherhood: A Textual Analysis." *Peace & Change*, vol. 34, no. 2, 2009, pp. 164-83.

Langer, Susanne K. *Philosophy in a New Key: A Study in the Symbolism of Reason, Rite, and Art.* Harvard University, 1957.

MacDonald, Patrick. "Shocked Treatment - Songs of Angry Politics, Tart Humor Defy Classification." *Seattle Times*, 24 Feb. 1989, p. T3.

Mack, Ashley Noel. "The Self-Made Mom: Neoliberalism and Masochistic Motherhood in Home-Birth Videos on YouTube." *Women's Studies in Communication*, vol. 39, no. 1, 2016, pp. 47-68.

Marshall, Nigel, and Kagari Shibazaki. "Gender Associations for Musical Instruments in Nursery Children: The Effect of Sound and Image." *Music Education Research*, vol. 15, no. 4, 2013, pp. 406-20.

Matthews, J. "Short Sharp Shocked" *Rolling Stone*, 3 Nov. 1988, pp. 112-13.

McClary, Susan. *Feminine Endings: Music, Gender, and Sexuality*. University of Minnesota, 1991.

McLeese, Don. "Bryan Ferry Proves Where There's Smoke, There's Fire." *Chicago Sun-Times*, 29 Aug. 1988, p. 25.

Mockus, Martha. "Women's Music." *Lesbian Histories and Cultures: An Encyclopedia*, edited by Bonnie Zimmerman, Taylor & Francis, 2000, pp. 521-24.

Monson, Ingrid. *Saying Something: Jazz Improvisation and Interaction*. University of Chicago, 1996.

Mullen, Rodger. "Michelle Shocked's Second Album is Nearly Perfect." *Fayetteville Observer,* 15 Jan. 1989.

Neuls-Bates, Carol. *Women in Music: An Anthology of Source Readings From the Middle Ages to the Present*. Northeastern University, 1996.

O'Brien, Lucy. *She Bop: The Definitive History of Women in Rock, Pop, and Soul*. Penguin, 1995.

Okamoto, David. "Acoustic Stew with a Hearty Dash of Spice." *St. Petersburg Times*. 11 Sept. 1988, p. 2F.

Palczewski, Catherine Helen, et al. *Rhetoric in Civic Life*. Strata, 2012.

Peeples, Jennifer A., and Kevin M. DeLuca. "The Truth of the Matter: Motherhood, Community and Environmental Justice." *Women's Studies in Communication*, vol. 29, no. 1, 2006, pp. 59-87.

Pick, Steve. "With Second Album, Shocked Has Arrived." *St. Louis Post-Dispatch*. 2 Sept. 1988, p. 4F.

"Picks and Pans Review: Short Sharp Shocked." Rev. of *Short Sharp Shocked, People Weekly,* 12 Dec. 1988, people.com/ archive/picks-and-pans-review-short-sharp-shocked-vol-30-no-24/. Accessed 16 Nov. 2017.

Poulakos, John, and Takis Poulakos. *Classical Rhetorical Theory*. Houghton Mifflin, 1999.

Rawls, Kristin. "Wild Goose Festival's (Mostly) Welcoming Spirit for LGBT Christians." *Religion Dispatches*, 3 Aug. 2011, religiondispatches.org/wild-goose-festivals-mostly-welcoming-spirit-for-lgbt-christians/. Accessed 16 Nov. 2017.

Rich, Kim. "The Boundaries of Friendship." *Anchorage Daily*

News, 14 Dec. 1988, p. E1.

Righi, Len. "Michelle Shocked Jolts the Star Making Machinery." *Morning Call*, 11 Mar. 1989, p. A62.

Robicheau, Paul. "Michelle Shocked" *Boston Globe*, 25 Mar. 1989, pp. 10-11.

Rosen, Craig. "Campfire Still Burns for Feminist Folk Singer Shocked." *Daily News of Los Angeles*, 30 Sept. 1988, p. L3.

Russell, Paul. *The Gay 100: A Ranking of the Most Influential Gay Men and Lesbians, Past and Present*. Kensington. 2002.

Sergeant, Desmond C, and Evangelos Himonides. "Gender and Music Composition: A Study of Music, and the Gendering of Meanings." *Frontiers in Psychology*, vol. 7, 2016, doi: 10.3389/fpsyg.2016.00411. Accessed 16 Nov. 2017.

Schindette, Susan, and Ann Maier. "World Woes and Texas Terrors Give Balladeer Michelle Shocked Her Name, Game, and (Unwanted) Fame." *People Weekly*, 1988, pp. 79-80.

Schneider, Marc. "Michelle Shocked Speaks Out as Full Audio of Meltdown Emerges." 20 Mar. 2013, *Billboard*, www.billboard.com/articles/news/1553842/michelle-shocked-speaks-out-as-full-audio-of-meltdown-emerges. Accessed 16 Nov. 2017.

Shepherd, John. *Music as Social Text*. Polity. 2001.

Shocked, Michelle. "Anchorage." *Short Sharp Shocked*, Mercury, 1988.

Stearney, Lynn M. "Feminism, Ecofeminism, and the Maternal Archetype: Motherhood as a Feminine Universal." *Communication Quarterly*, vol. 42, no. 2, 1994, pp. 145-59.

Torem, Lisa. "Reinventing the Deal: An Interview with Michelle Shocked." *Popmatters*, 16 July 2009, www.popmatters.com/93693-re-inventing-the-deal-an-interview-with-michelle-shocked2-2496024093.html. Accessed 16 Nov. 2017.

True, Everett. "Michelle Shocked: The Rites of Swing." *Melody Maker*, 4 Nov. 1989, pp. 42-3.

Upton, George P. *Women in Music*. McClurg. 1899.

Voland, J. "She's Shocked." *Houston Post*, 19 Mar. 1989, p. H1.

Waldman, Deb. "Shocked's Sharpness Cuts Deep." *New Haven Register (CT)*, 21 Oct. 1988.

"Walking the Line" *Melody Maker*, 3 Sept. 1988, p. 14.

Walters-Kramer, Lori A. *Performing Emancipatory Rhetorics:*

The Possibilities of Michelle Shocked's Musics, Discourses, and Movements. Proquest Information and Learning Company, 2001.

Winn, James Anderson. *Unsuspected Eloquence: A History of the Relations between Poetry and Music.* Yale University, 1981. Print.

Wood, Elizabeth. "Preface." *Music & Women,* edited by Sophie Drinker. Feminist Press 1995, pp. vii-ix.

Woodstra, Chris. "AllMusic Review. Rev. of *Short Sharp Shocked.*" *Allmusic Review,* 1988, www.allmusic.com/album/short-sharp-shocked-mw0000652371. Accessed 16 Nov. 2017.

12.
Electric Mommyland

Writing a Sociological History through
Autoethnographical Art and Music Performance
toward a Deeper Understanding of Everything Mom

MARTHA JOY ROSE

Historically, music has been a force for change. In *The Sounds of Resistance: The Role of Music in Multicultural Activism*, Lindsay Michie and Eunice Rojas outline the ways "overt and implied messages of resistance from slave songs to rap" have challenged the status quo and paved a path to a "Truer World" (1). As anyone who has attended a protest rally accompanied by great music can attest, the heart beats faster, the body rallies, and the mind leaps. My chapter examines some of the ways music has confronted stereotypes and challenged mainstream ideology within the world of mother culture. Throughout the chapter, I identify the mom rock movement of the late twentieth and early twenty-first century, and trace the efforts of mom rockers as they played instruments, wrote songs, and created community. It was this newly formed community that contributed to a metamorphosis of "everything mom," which is recognized today in the context of "mommy bloggers;" the literary series *Listen to Your Mother*; such Hollywood shows as *Desperate Housewives*, *The Housewives of Beverly Hills*, *Rita Rocks*, and the rumoured, soon-to-be-made feature film based on Judy Davids's book, *Rock Star Mommy*; and other creative venues.

The mom rock movement formed organically as a source of empowerment and connection. What started as a single concert in New York City in 2002 quickly grew to include four countries, twenty-five cities, and hundreds of performers ("About," *Mamapalooza*). There was a struggle to attempt to name and label many of the issues mothers faced. We searched for a solid platform to stand on, songs like "Fuzzy Slippers," "It's Only Life," and "Eat Your Damn Spaghetti" insinuated rebellion. But in retrospect, a clear identification of exactly what we were rebelling against posed challenges. Were we engaging in effective protest or groping for dissent? As recently as 2017, the *Journal of the Motherhood Initiative for Research and Community Involvement* issued a call for papers on the topics of "the social devaluation of motherwork, the endless tasks of privatized mothering, and the incompatibility of waged work and care work, and the impossible standards of idealized motherhood." These salient points have not changed much during the last twenty years. Challenges remain. Though in some cases, bands such as the Oakland-based group Placenta were able to confront contemporary social issues like poverty and queer mothering, others sought to examine the lived mother experience and establish a cultural repository where none existed. Consensus on a shared agenda for mom rockers was elusive. Some mothers were simply looking to get out of the kitchen for the night. In her book *Rock Star Mommy*, Judy Davids writes, "[Joy, the founder of Mamapalooza] was on a mission to empower, encourage, and enlighten all women to find their voice, whereas the Mydols were just looking for an excuse to get out of the house" (169).

Despite massive amounts of dialogue, media, and press attempting to "transform [motherhood] into a label that includes creativity and independence" (Sharon Hayes, qtd. in Della Cava), the platform for an organized and united voice crumbled. Within a few years, an assimilation process began. By 2006, motherhood was being used to sell everything from sex, to diapers, to dishwashers. The mom rock, Mamapalooza initiative was ultimately subsumed by a consumer society that translates such terms as "action" and "agency" into the economic imperatives within a mainstream ideology. It is often within this ideology that a new "mommy identity" continues to thrive.

In the first portion of this chapter, I demonstrate not only how the mom rock movement of the early twenty-first century awakened mothers to their individuality and creativity, but also how the embedded mother identity posed ongoing challenges to the narrative. Throughout this chapter, I use an autoethnographic approach to the subject as both a performer and the founder of a large-scale international festival featuring mother artists. I couple my analysis with relevant work by such contemporary scholars as Andrea O'Reilly, Amber Kinser, and Patricia Hill Collins. Importantly, I turn back the clock to examine some of the second-wave women's movement theory by Dorothy Smith, and even go back over one hundred years to look at the music and writing of suffragettes like Charlotte Perkins Gilman. This is to make a point about the persistent nature of many women's issues.

In the second section, I explore mother's marginalization and make an argument for electric music as a medium for expression. The marginalization of women is not an original idea, nor is the argument for music as a medium for expression. Its newness is in the manner in which music has been employed, specifically within the realm of motherhood and activism. The third section looks at creating a mother culture; here, I review a very brief history of some of the cross-cultural identification of a category known as "mother identity labelling" in business, politics, scholarship, art, and literature in order to better lay a general framework for mapping this emerging area of investigation. The final section looks specifically at activism and art in a consumer society, and highlights the work of Hester Eisenstein (*Feminism Seduced*) and David Suisman (*Selling Sounds*). This portion of the chapter focuses on how urges for lasting change are often usurped by the same systems they attempt to confront. In these ways, I summarize some of the successes and failures of the contemporary mother's movement.

Throughout this chapter, I embrace an interdisciplinary approach and draw from sociology, gender, and media studies, American studies, feminist texts, as well as from consumer culture. Both hegemony and the ideology to which I refer throughout the chapterr represent patriarchal constructions of power in which maleness or men themselves have held primary positions. Because this is autoethnographic, I will also draw on some of my experiences. By exploring this sociological history, I aim to facilitate a better understanding of current evolutions (or deevolutions) of a modern American mothers' movement as well as to create a backdrop for those wishing to do future research on this topic. I also aim to secure a position of legitimacy for the art and culture of mom rock within the great body of work that constitutes women's and gender studies, and, more specifically, mother studies.

ELECTRIC MOMMYLAND AND THE MOM ROCK MOVEMENT

"Electric Mommyland" represents a period in time (1997 to 2008) well documented through music, video, and photographs, as well as through media interviews, featuring a number of artists who were also mothers. Just as Dorothy Smith invited women to "grasp their own authority to speak" (34) within a feminist sociology in the 1980s, women began staking claim to the relatively uninhabited space of mother articulations within an area of the performing arts. The energy of this initiative was a spirited revolution against the tyranny of subsumed identity within the role of the mother-housewife. The original mother rocker did her best to draw up a rallying cry against the hard labour and banality of raising children and the constraints of the physical body, the imperatives of hegemony; she wanted to challenge the stereotypes that permeated mother culture. Likewise, many of the women past the age of thirty challenged gender constraints as well as ageism. All of these intentions resulted from a subconscious understanding rather than one particular activist agenda.

As the leader, organizer, and songwriter of the first self-identified mom rock band, named Housewives on Prozac and founded in 1997, I relied on this platform because performance art had framed my life. As a university-trained actor, and then as a New York City-based artist, I had been performing in a variety of projects since the 1970s. It was not until I became a mother that I saw the need for supporting other artists who were disenfranchised artistically, spiritually, culturally, and practically because of their motherhood experience. For many of us, once the transition to motherhood happened, we found ourselves out of opportunities, searching for community as well as for a voice. My goal became focused on amplifying the lived experience of the woman performing motherhood, declaring or dis-claring the mother identity, and on claiming motherness as a legitimate point of artistic expression within popular culture. The goals as they became clearer over the years from 1997 to 2005 included sharing mothers' lived experience, framed by social imperatives, in order to increase agency for those performing motherwork. Likewise, and particular to my story, making music was absolutely essential to my emotional and creative survival. Long understood to be a vehicle for healing as well as change, music corroborated the essential truth that I was "singing and performing to maintain [my] own existence" as Lindsay Mitchie and Eunice Rojas identify in *Sounds of Resistance* (xv). The results of these efforts have no doubt furthered an international mother discourse but have still left many issues unresolved.

In the late 1990s and early 2000s, our planning sessions, song writing, and art making were an attempt to articulate a state of being, but they were not framed by any theoretical justification. We were very much unlike other organized social justice movements, including the first- and second-wave women's movements, which initially advocated for women's suffrage and the abolishment of slavery, and then in the second wave tackled workforce equality and reproductive freedom, among other things. More closely aligned with third-wave feminists, we were more concerned with disassembling social structures and expectations. These grumblings were frustrated, angry, and longed for change. But other than clearly wanting to make art and music and to be recognized for that, we tried and failed to articulate an agenda, despite many roundtable meetings held in both my home and in New York City.

A number of organizations that curated information to better support mothers were on the horizon. The Mothers Movement Online was founded in 2003 out of the original work of J. Brundage, dating back to 1987, and which served as a clearinghouse for reporting and resources for mothers. The National Association of Mothers Centers advocated for paid leave, affordable childcare, and support for mothers through community and connection ("Action Alerts"). It was not until 2006 that a clear political agenda took shape within this mother sphere with the founding of Moms Rising by Kristin Finkbinder and Joan Blade. Their group focused on maternity and paternity leave, flexible work and wages, and healthcare for all ("Our Issues").

Our project originated and remained focused on voice and identity within the music-art performance spectrum. We wanted to deal with the issues at hand, identify our positions, turn those perspectives into art, and ultimately have opportunities for performance and community. The media attention my Housewives project garnished enabled me to leverage the notion of a mother-artist into a music festival series called Mamapalooza in 2002. The series was flanked by women-made, mother-branded art, comedy, theatre, literature, poetry, music, and commerce. This fugacious annual endeavour was noisy, but it proved difficult to track. Each May for a week or a month, exhibits, performances, poetry slams, theatrical events, and rock concerts exploded onto the scene at multiple venues throughout New York City and across the U.S. Despite extensive media attention, copious monthly conference calls, an expanded legion of Mamapalooza event planners, thousands of concertgoers, and sponsorships, accompanied by rapid expansion between the years 2002 and 2005, our events happened but then dissipated. Performances took place in underground nightclubs and church basements, public parks and schools. But individual identities changed often, sometimes quickly, which resulted from events such as a divorce, a move, a child's birthday, or a band breakup. Circumstances were also beyond institutional regulation: unmeasured, unrecorded, untrained as well as fiscally unsupported. Just as the arts activist group the Guerilla Girls suggest, many women in the arts continue to face difficulties, and their art continues to be a subset of mainstream culture. The Guerilla Girls' statistical updates about women in the arts are posted and shared on the National Museum of Women in the Arts website in Washington:

51% of visual artists today are women; on average, they earn 81¢ for every dollar made by male artists.

Work by women artists makes up only 3–5% of major permanent collections in the U.S. and Europe, and 34% in Australian state museums.

Of 590 major exhibitions by nearly 70 institutions in the U.S. from 2007–2013, only 27% were devoted to women artists. ("Get the Facts")

Art made by mothers, as well as art about motherhood, is a minute fractional subset of any projections about women-made art and music. The fact of reduced visibility as well as the absence of women and mother-made art cannot be emphasized enough. There are multiple explanations and accounts of this. One particularly salient perspective regarding dominant culture versus subordinate culture is offered by Carlo Ginsburg in his book about the sixteenth century, as his gaze backward, toward the early foundations of Western culture, offers insight. He establishes in his exploration of dominant culture that "the culture of the subordinate class is largely oral" (xv). By their ephemeral nature, oral traditions easily dissipate. It is the written word that most often prevails. Patricia Hill Collins also makes this claim in her book *Black Feminist Thought*. Regarding the "subjugated knowledge" of black women in particular, in which ideas and consciousness are constructed out of music, literature, daily conversations, and everyday behavior" (251), she argues that even as visibility increases (in academia, for example), it becomes "differently subjugated" (252). Although our movement was a stride in the direction of articulating our lived experiences, the volume, duration, and effect did not offer the kind of residual for which I hoped. For a variety of reasons, the assimilation process that both controlled activities within the home and commercialized them outside co-opted successes as quickly as agendas and expectations were articulated.

In addition to the temporal nature of our musical and other artistic creations, formidable cultural expectations dogged our platform. The role of the woman in American households is specific and constrained. The general social mandate keeps mothers in their place, doing what they are supposed to, at least in many heteronormative socioeconomic circles. As Johanna Brenner asserts in *Women and the Politics of Class*, managing a family-household system "in which the class-structured capitalist system of production incorporates the biological facts of reproduction" (25) is very much a reality. A system like this leaves women either working the second shift or the whole shift as a virtual "slave."[1] In the long view our rallying cry, while noisy, was defenseless against what I have come to recognize as a unified

American ideology. Good mothers take care of their children, and are pleasant to each other, their husbands, and their communities. For the most part, participants in the Mom Rock arena of Mamapalooza adhered to this code. Whereas alt-mothers, queer mothers, and single mothers participated in Mamapalooza, the ethos of many of the mom rockers was dominated by a white, heteronormative, and middle-class ideology.

Music and art defined our rebellion. This was our challenge to the status quo, the "good mother" stereotype, and the tyranny of expectations. However, in reality, we were much too connected to our children to demand real liberation from the job of mothering. This was despite the fact that some of us harboured a great deal of ambivalence about our roles. We continually vacillated between caregiving imperatives and a desire to actualize the lived experiences of the woman at the centre of the caregiving responsibility. In other words, our identity and our lived experience involved our children, so we were not willing to leave them very far behind, even as we sought to define ourselves as individuals with our own wants, needs, and agency. For those of us who were married and were living in heteronormative households, our loyalty to our husbands was greater than any compulsion to dismantle the system that in many cases kept us subsumed. Many of us had a history of volunteerism, so equitable pay for performance or the idea of monetizing our projects proved to be challenging. This lack of monetization also complicated things. Whereas professional musicians were mercenary, many of us just wanted to "do good things." With no pay structure in the home, how were women accustomed to working for nothing going to suddenly transform themselves into artists and businesswomen demanding payment for talent rendered? Whatever progress we did make was so rapidly assimilated into consumer culture that it became impossible to identify how exactly the lifestyle and music message was identified and then co-opted throughout the mom rock timeline. Despite this fact, the economics of those participating in the project varied greatly. Branding was employed at the project's inception, albeit somewhat haphazardly, but it was quickly co-opted by more powerful corporate structures, which I explain more in this chapter's final section.

Patricia Hill Collins argues in *Black Feminist Thought* that a "highly effective system of social control [was] designed to keep African-American women in an assigned, subordinate place" (5). I would add that this was true for both black and white women involved in the original mother arts movement who were also actively engaged in mothering. For the most part, we struggled against some invisible force that we could not put our fingers on, which kept us in our place except for the nights we donned guitars. Like peasants during the medieval festivals of the past who were allowed participation in the excellent revelry of the season, we believed we were actual queens breaking ground on some reimagined vision of motherhood. Alas, in the morning we returned to our kitchens, cubicles, and carpools, buoyed up but with the world around us relatively unchanged. Our communal experience viewed through the festival lens, were, in the words of Alessandro Falassi, celebrations of "time out of time" (7). We were not, in fact, focused on defining the ways in which the institution of motherhood needed to change as much as we were interested in expressing our frustrations and making art about them. The songs, reviews, and films that ensued remind me now that we were saying something. It was amplified, and it did get a lot of attention, There were interesting things happening, but the terms of the revolution were unresolved.

The preamble was interminable. As the leader of Mamapalooza as well as the Housewives band, I traversed the offices and studios of Hollywood where a variety of animated reality producers tried to set the stage for a mom rock competition or a mom makeover show. From there, I attended national women's conferences, groping a path through the subject of motherhood. The subject animated the entirety of my intellectual and material labour, yet I was unable to precisely put my finger on this thing called motherhood. Its theory and practice, and the "art of" of motherhood, is something scholars, it turns out, had written about. However, I had no such exposure, and it was not until 2005 that I began to envision a path through the academy that might elicit some kind of lasting change. Until that time, I continued to strum my guitar and howl through performances, such as "Shut Up and Drive" and "The Housewife's Lament."[2]

WOMEN'S MARGINALIZATION AND AN ARGUMENT FOR
ELECTRIC MUSIC AS A MEDIUM FOR EXPRESSION

In their insightful and thorough work *The Women Founders: Sociology and Social Theory 1830–1930*, Patricia Madoo Lengermann and Gillian Niebrugge, question why women's contributions have been obliterated from the history of sociological thought. They find that on each count—the first count being social control and the second being legitimacy within the social order—women have been marginalized from positions of authority. The authors contend that women's voices were systematically erased from the canons. They give examples of female sociologists theorizing in the nineteenth and early twentieth century who, unlike their male counterparts, were purposefully omitted because of at least two major factors: "the politics of gender" and "the politics of knowledge" (11-14). According to these authors, the accounting is situated within a patriarchal framework; women were not considered as important as men. Sociology's contributions to humankind's understanding of the nature and causes of the complicated interpersonal interactions in the 1800s and 1900s led to the legitimization of the field and to the "scientization" of sociology as a practice (15). Finally, the emergence of the university as a stable source of income was a "move that was part of a quest for professional authority, social status, and job and salary security" (15). These power arrangements proliferated for sociologists. *The Women Founders* focuses on women who lived a hundred years ago. Since that time, the first and second wave of feminism have come and gone.

Some of the legal and political problems associated with those movements have resolved themselves—the abolition of slavery, voting rights for women, to name a few—whereas others continue to be debated, including, for example, reproductive justice and equality in the workplace. Similarly, feminist articulations remain removed from the domestic sphere where motherhood is enacted. There are many reasons for this, including the fact that mothering labour in America is performed within the home, a privatized zone. If being mother were a real job in the public, it would require education and training. But because motherhood is not generally considered a social issue, but rather a private one, the system is difficult to penetrate. Amber Kinser, author of *Motherhood and Feminism*, describes yet another reason for the divide. She argues that the "Cartesian divide" began to assign the role of the body to women and the role of the mind to men as early as the seventeenth century. This divide was enacted philosophically, as it positioned women as intellectually inferior and also left them materially in the "private world," whereas men claimed the "public world" (11). Unfortunately, many of the texts, such Kinser's, which could be instrumental for liberation, do not find their way into the mainstream. They remain relegated to the privilege of the very few who embark on a rigorous academic journey. From the front lines of the kiddie parks of New York City to the playgrounds of suburbia, these women—my friends—did not know such books existed. If they did know, then I would have heard of them.

Women's marginalization, or more specifically their silencing, is a two-way street enacted by both men and women, according to Dorothy E. Smith. In *The Everyday World as Problematic*, she directs the reader to look at the idea of silencing in the following ways: male authority is not a conspiracy among men simply imposed on women; it is a complimentary social process between women and men—one in which women are complicit in their silencing. Because of the authority of their male voice, "men have authority in the world as members of a social category" (29). This category of authority serves as a form of power allowing men to get things done. Likewise women—and I argue, especially women who have children—are susceptible to the general social ideology of the good and obedient "silently suffering" mother, and those in partnerships are likewise bound by their husband's or partner's compliance (42). Such was the case with me. Although I was financially protected from the harshness that might result from a lack of food or shelter, I was a fulltime mother of four children. Even with help, of which I had much, the task of domesticity was real and tangible. As I described in the opening to this chapter, our little mom rock movement was hampered on several counts, not the least of which was that mothers do what needs to be done. If the children's noses were runny, we wiped them. I offer up a lyric from one of Housewives on Prozac's most well-quoted songs called "Fuzzy Slippers." The opening goes as follows: "I wipe my baby's chin with my college diploma and wonder how did I ever get here? I take the gold record off the wall, from 1983. Crack open the plexiglass and declare an emergency." Had I known of Smith's writing and been educated in the idea of "grasping our own authority to speak" (Smith 34) by recognizing a deprivation of authority and my own training to facilitate male-controlled topics, I might have written an academic paper instead of a song. But, then the question arises, would that have been better?

Just as I was scribbling on napkins and recipe cards, Andrea O'Reilly and Sharon Abbey were hard at work in Canada editing *Re-defining Motherhood: Changing Identities and Patterns*, which was published the year after I started the Housewives project. They write of their goals in the introduction to the edited collection:

> These authors move beyond myths and stereotypes of mothering to explore differences among women and within individual women in order to challenge the existence of a universal meaning of motherhood.... Mothers are never only mothers. Simultaneously they are lovers, workers, activists, daughters, partners, sisters, neighbors, aunts, friends, and so on. (14)

I am fairly certain that as a feminist scholar, O'Reilly had read Dorothy E. Smith, and was addressing directly issues cited in the opening chapter of Smith's *Everyday as Problematic*. Those issues posit that as of the 1980s, we are deprived of developing among ourselves the thoughts and images that express the situations we share; it is only when women treat one another as those who count that we can break free of silence. In November 1997, my singing partner and I were interviewed for a *New York Times* article called "Band Sings What It's like To Raise a Family in the Nineties." Part of that interview reads as follows: "The two women, whose stage banter is part of their performances, regard themselves as foot soldiers for meaningful lives within the family. When such women have fierce creative energy and a tendency to break the mold, that plight becomes even more complex" (Hershenson). The song "I Am Not a Barbie Doll" released on Housewives first album, titled "No Prescription," chants, "Just because I'm beautiful, just because I'm sweet. Just because my eyes are blue, doesn't mean—I am not a Barbie doll." What was I saying when I wrote that? Was I not grasping my own authority to speak? And where were all the women of the 1970s in the 1990s? Why did I not know these things? Why did I have to go deep into the cave of my own subconscious to draw out these truths?

"I am not a Barbie doll" was one of many anthems intended to vocalize the unseen forces that were constraining and controlling my life. What of the "violence done to women?"—"and there is violence done," as Dorothy Smith says (25). The lyrics demonstrate "the ideological practices of our society provide us with forms of thought and knowledge that constrain us to treat ourselves as objects" (Smith 36). The marginalization of women is established (and continues today in our culture) through the evidence presented in feminist texts, gender studies classes, statistical evidence on equity between men and women in America, and through the general atmosphere of which anyone with a sensitive nature can palpably intuit. Music and voice, however, can be a method of amplification, if not an antidote to this condition.

Over 120 years ago, mother, writer, and sociologist Charlotte Perkins Gilman used music and poetry to awaken women to their position in society. The year was 1898. Her booklet *Suffrage Songs and Verses* admonishes women to seek their place in the world. The activist-minded song "Women of To-day" sought to challenge obstacles to women's rights. Ironically, for the women of Mamaplooza, it retained relevance:

> And still the wailing babies come and go,
> And homes are waste, and husband's hearts fly far;
> There is no hope until you dare to know
> The thing you are! (Perkins 5)

Although much has changed for women and families since Gilman's day, significant barriers remain. Women in the United States can vote; they have rights to their property and children, and they enjoy the same opportunities to work outside the home that men do. But other hurdles—including policy slights, access to affordable childcare, a ratified equal rights amendment, equal pay for equal work, reproductive justice, and issues of gender parity—continue to permeate social structures. According to biographer Cynthia Davis, Charlotte Perkins Gilman was an activist with a broad set of goals. Davis describes Gilman as setting "her sights on women's domestic, maternal, and wifely duties whenever she believed they uniquely restricted women to the home and hence prevented them from pursuing fulfilling work in the public sphere" (xii). Gilman used music, literature, and the arts to express her position and influence community support.

In much the same way, standpoint theorists like Dorothy Smith and intersectional theorists like Patricia Hill Collins call for feminists to develop knowledge based on women's experiences and then do what feminists do: write, form coalitions, march, and sing out. Using one's voice to speak truth—whether about theory, or calls for action, for uprising against violence, or for emancipation—is a primal act. For those not suffering from a physical condition that prevents them from moving their mouth or blowing through a voice box, it is one of the most essential features of the human expression. When my daughter was three, I taught her to roar, literally to throw back her head and roar.

Music as a form of worship, celebration, and activism has a long history, and thought-leaders like Smith, Collins, and Gilman are inspirational on multiple counts. Their work covers a broad scope regarding what they view as some of the core causes of inequality. Patriarchal properties of acquisition and possession as well as dominance thread through their works. Why more inroads have not been forthcoming from within the home is truly stunning. Gilman was writing in the 1800s. Her interest in "promoting progress and fairness" (125), and her theories about the sexuo-economic relation resonate (117). The latter theory, in which sex is leveraged (often unknowingly) as an economic stabilizer, deserves more mention but must be left for another time. However, sexual leverage is something very much at work in relationships even today. Despite its presence within relationships, there are still many layers of things passing as socially acceptable that disguise it. Presented here are examples of the same topics the mom rock movement aimed to articulate through a variety of songs, events, interviews, and an independently produced feature film called Momz Hot Rocks by Kate Perotti (2008).

Music can be a notable appendage to any endeavour and need not be practised as a sole source of meaning or money, but as a way in which to promote an agenda. This is a good thing, since being an artist in the U.S. is a nearly impossible way to survive unless the ascension to the elite realm of stardom has been established. In the U.S., elite music stars are inducted into The Rock & Roll Hall of Fame. But the Hall of Fame's mandate may serve the message of this chapter regarding music being employed as an activist platform. Located in Cleveland, Ohio, the Hall of Fame museum website claims that it "exists to educate visitors, fans and scholars from around the world about the history and continuing significance of rock and roll music" ("Learn"). The museum does this through exhibits, classes, as well as teaching plans it offers to those who wish to use music education in their classroom. A lesson plan for junior high students called "Fight the Power: Music as a Social Force" is posted online at the museum website. This course description acknowledges that music has historically been used as a force for change:

> In many times and places, people have used music as a powerful tool for social change. The story of rock and roll overlaps with some of the most turbulent times in U.S. history. In the 1960s alone, American society was being torn apart by debates over the Cold War, the Civil Rights Movement, the Women's Liberation movement, and the Vietnam War. Since that time and well into the present, musicians have entered such debates by spreading messages of revolution, protest, and empowerment through musical styles as diverse as folk, rock, and soul. ("Learn")

The Hall of Fame is in the business of educating students about the intersection of music and social change. Sheila Whiteley, in her book *Women and Popular Music: Sexuality, Identity and Subjectivity*, examines "sexuality, gender, freedom, and repression constructed and rooted in the lived experience and then related to ways in which art, music, and popular culture provide a focus for challenging established representations of femininity" (11). She confirms that the employment of music for self-identification purposes is substantiated, something I will elaborate on next. The use of amplification, necessary in the making of electric music, is a tool that requires only brief mention. Its purposes and practicalities are self-evident. Amplification makes things louder. Instruments and songs plugged into equipment can result in a clamouring dispatch of messaging and music that resound more than those levied from acoustic accompaniments.

CREATING A MOTHER CULTURE

A cross-pollination of literature, popular culture, and identity politics shaped by the feminist movement(s) of the sixties, seventies, and eighties has informed subsequent generations of procreators. In this section, I review a very brief history of some of the cross-cultural identification of a category known as "mother identity labelling" in business, politics, scholarship, art, and literature to better lay a general framework for understanding this emergent area of investigation. Largely without fanfare, mother labelling transpired organically. Academics wrote about it, and journalists labelled it, much like radical feminism, Marxist feminism, and queer feminism. Before there could be a concept of a woman, who was specifically a mother acting out her motherhood within the public sphere, there needed to be an identification of this state of being. This state could be conceived of from multiple perspectives and through many lenses. The capitalist explanation for the rise of the mother identity could be called branding. The philosophical point of view could include a desire toward a particular political bent, such as is the case of Sara Ruddick's, *Maternal Thinking; Towards a Politics of Peace*. Within the academy, feminist mothers may find themselves examining ways to elaborate on theoretical questions. Just as music has been used to break down boundaries and create dissent, inventing identities like "mom rocker" could assist in creating conversations about good mom and bad mom stereotypes among other things.

Literature, music, business, and art bring a message to the masses, and although they may not solve problems, they certainly can capture the essence of what is wrong with something. Solutions are not always the primary concern. It is sometimes first necessary to take the thing out of the box (or in this case the house, or uterus, or consciousness) and examine it. This topic alone could comprise an entire body of work. I suggest a brief overview to better demonstrate the way in which the concept of "mother"—specifically "working mother," "maternal philosopher," "maternal theorist," and "mom rocker"—are embodied in the public sphere. These concepts of mother have paved the way to coursework found in today's universities, in art exhibits like Natalie Loveless's "New Maternalisms," and in interdisciplinary forums like mother studies.[3]

Perhaps one of the clearest attempts at forming a mother identity emerged immediately following the mainstream second-wave feminist movement. *Working Mother Magazine* (WMM) was founded in 1979 and incorporated the concept of mother as a worker outside the home. The magazine focused on such issues as equal pay, flexible work schedules, and childcare. Primarily a how-to advocacy magazine for corporations and their female employees, the WMM media kit claims it is a mentor and advocate for America's 17 million moms and that its media and print readership has grown to readership of 200,000 ("2017 Online Media Kit"). The working mother identity helps to prioritize women's labour in the American workforce and to balance the feminist agenda of followers of Betty Friedan in the sense that the housewife has left her home. The magazine makes an appeal on issues of diversity and best work practices. These ideas continue to perpetuate themselves through books like my friend, the former president of WMM, Carol Evan's, *This Is How We Do It* as well as corporatized movements like Sheryl Sandberg's *Lean In*. It makes sense, given Americans' proclivity toward capitalism that the idea of the working mother, as a purely economic construct, is perhaps the most widespread, marketable concept among the manifold identities.

Two years prior to WMM's founding, Adrienne Rich leveraged feminist theory to examine the institution of motherhood, and ten years after WMM got its start, Beacon Press published Sara Ruddick's ground-breaking *Maternal Thinking*. Ruddick introduces the concept of mothering itself as a form of labour (and thought) able to be performed by men as well as women. Largely philosophical in its approach, Ruddick also argues for a "politics of peace" from those engaged in the raising of the next generation of human beings. Rich's and Ruddick's inspiration lead to the self-identification of "feminist others." Spearheading the charge in Canada in 1998, Andrea O'Reilly pioneered the concept of "feminist mothers" in her classes at York University, and went on to found organizations like ARM (Association for Research on Mothering) at York University, now renamed MIRCI (The Motherhood Initiative for Research and Community Involvement). The aim of these organizations is to support scholarship and activism on and about motherhood. Meanwhile, American mothers were articulating motherhood in rock bands like Housewives on Prozac (1997), the Mydols (2002), and FRUMP (2003). In 2004, *The Wall Street Journal* reported on the rise of mom bands in an article called "Mommy Loudest," which connects bands from New York to Chicago and San Francisco (Keates). By 2005, over 250 bands, comics, poets, actors, and singer-songwriters were playing on national Mamapalooza stages at twenty-two different locations, and the festival had spread to four different countries with media imprints in the millions. Coinciding with these events and the rise of mother culture, Demeter Press was founded in 2006, with an interdisciplinary focus on feminist motherhood. The nature of all these activities lends itself to identifying a collective of mom rockers, and mother feminist academics. The purpose of illustrating this parallel is to identify the interconnectedness of these economic, philosophical, political, academic, artistic, and popular creations that were forming themselves as mothers engaged in the shaping of their identities.

A recognition of the failure of much of the second-wave feminist movement to address LGBQT, non-white, black, Latina, Arab, and other(s) emerged throughout the 1990s and continues in some way through the thread of women's discussions today—these women who are in the continual process of making and unmaking themselves, and their concepts about themselves as well as their children. This is at the forefront of what any motherhood movement is—the constant expanding and microscoping of identity, action, theory, and its ongoing creations. I had been speaking, singing, writing, and talking gender, class, power, and motherhood since 1989. But for the person engaged in mothering—with only a general reference to feminist theory, who was living outside of the academy and exposure to its methods for research and discourse, looking for concepts and connectivity was implausible—I was in the position of most American mothers who lack the rarified position of illuminated connection. Our rallying cry was a yelp in the dark, not a clearly articulated vision for change.

In tandem to many general issues being explored within the culturally dominant forces of 2003 America, *The Bitch in the House: 26 Women Tell the Truth About Sex, Solitude, Work, Motherhood, and Marriage* (edited by Cathi Hanauer) was released as a collection of essays by mother authors. According to reviewers, the authors of *Bitch in the House* recognize their post-second-wave feminist status; however, they do not necessarily identify as feminists. The women in the book are not really brave enough to actually take a stand, "Housework without a fierce feminist underpinning make for dull reading. Back in the 70s, the utopian demands for 24-hour nurseries and wages for housework at least had drama, passion and intensity. These girls are not bad enough to be bitches" (McRobbie).

Despite the women's frustrations, "the equality that they can just about expect at work finds no equivalent at home" (McRobbie). Without taking a specific political stand, the authors confirm a general outcry regarding the competing burdens of career and motherhood. Though not registering on the academic or theoretical landscape, this book does register regarding cultural conversations about motherhood. The book itself represents the writings of twenty-six creative authors and journalists sharing their experiences since becoming mothers, which enforces the collective nature of the articulation as well as confirms a general confusion regarding exactly how to create change for women within the home.

Throughout the third-wave movement and beyond, feminists diversified into more and more specialized manifestations of themselves, whereas some women who thought of themselves as feminists continued the process of interpreting their feminism within the context of motherhood. These mothers were largely expressing ambivalence and confusion, according to Amber Kinser in her book *Mothering in the Third Wave*. Confusion and an inability to adequately describe solutions to problems is a common theme. Although these young feminist mothers expressed uncertainty about how to claim a place in the "mothersphere," one breakthrough attempt emerged ten years after the first chord was struck on an American stage. Andrea O'Reilly's edited academic collection *Maternal Theory* was published in 2007. In this text, O'Reilly consolidates a maternal feminist theory into one place and promotes a scholarly approach that is both inclusive and far reaching, including Native American, Hispanic, and black authors. In 2010, Amber Kinser published *Motherhood and Feminism*, which ties together the history of the first-, second-, and third-wave feminist movements.

General theorizing (or attempts to theorize) continued to arise on a national level, as multiple activist, arts-based, and intellectual groups sprung up. A more complete list of these organizations can be found within the three-volume *Encyclopedia of Motherhood* (edited by Andrea O'Reilly) and *The 21st Century Motherhood Movement* (also edited by O'Reilly), both published in 2011. Through the interwoven, interconnectedness of corporate culture, high literature, academe, popular fads, and literary texts, feminist mothers began the attempt to identify themselves in the private and public sphere. They looked to form their identity about themselves and their children within their new roles as wife (sometimes), birther (adopter, fosterer, surrogate), and caregiver, just as feminist identities continue to split, expand, reform, and rename.

Why mother identities emerged to include the popular and the theoretical at this exact point in herstory is unclear. But, as noted earlier, the original inspiration was organic, and it appears to have come from several different sectors simultaneously (within a ten-year period). It could be argued that mother theory is the original daughter of feminism's insistence for equal pay and equal rights, except this was not the original theme. It is more likely that many motherists in the mainstream did not want to make trouble, and even denied their feminist tendencies. In popular culture the thread seems to follow an unnamed problem, one that cannot be precisely articulated. In the working mother identity, the struggle is perhaps the most obviously feminist, but many would not call themselves that. This is a specific brand of corporatized feminism that Hester Eisenstein would label "feminism seduced"—the title of her book. It situates itself firmly within the corporate capitalist framework. For example, with conferences, awards, and tangible financial gains, *Working Mother Magazine* concerns itself with numerous initiatives that champion the rights of the working woman within the corporate structure. Its initiative the Working Mother Institute conducts research on "disabilities in the workplace, multicultural moms, and Working Mother 100 Best Companies ("Research"). All of these concerns are within the corporatized framework, whose institutional pull cannot be ignored as being pivotal in American consciousness. It is also worth mentioning that any of the previously mentioned shifts from 2000 on have been largely empowered by an expanded use of the Internet.

Likewise, "maternal philosophers," "maternal theorists," and "mom rockers," as well as contemporary "mom-authors," float through the national consciousness and across our computer screens. The website Ephemera.com carries buttons and magnets that say "moms rock," whereas the characters on "Housewives of Beverly Hills" make trouble on TV and sip martinis. Mother-hood is here, as identity and theory. Unfortunately, while there is growth, we are making and unmaking ourselves at the same time.

ACTIVISM AND ART IN A CONSUMER SOCIETY

It was not far into my scholarly investigations when I realized that in order to exhume a feminist maternal perspective, it was para-mount to examine notions of economics, class, and consumerism. One simply cannot understand motherhood in America without becoming versed in its economic imperatives. Bethany Moreton opens her book *To Serve God and Walmart: The Making of Christian Free Enterprise* with a nod to Walmart Moms, who according to Moreton represented a demographic of one in five mothers in 1995 (1). In 1997, I was oblivious to the "Walmart Mom" (unless you count my friend Sue Fabish's song Walmart Woman), mostly because there were no box stores near me in New York City, but at the same time, I was irrefutably cognizant of being buoyed up by a financially stable marriage that allowed me not to shop at Walmart. I pursed music with zeal and passion. I again acknowledge my privilege because this marriage allowed me to have the means to pursue my art. But in this tenuous melding of material culture there is an ever-present consumer capitalist hierarchy that hungrily devours everything in its path, and it eventually devoured my marriage too. I echo the sentiment of Charlotte Perkins Gilman who regarded marriage as being built on the "sexuo-economic relation [which historically] places the man in position of master [and] the woman in position of subordinate" (128). Although much progress has been made since Gilman's time, echoes of these theoretical realities persist. They are evidenced in far-right politics and rhetoric as well as in ongoing resistance to issues regarding women's equality.

The third wave brought LGBQT issues to the fore, and changed legislation leading to more equal standing. Where legislation lags, there is still an eye towards change. But what of the mothers? Is this true for them? What legislative action can we take that will end domestic violence, or the severe poverty of older and divorced mothers, or the unpaid labour provided within the home by mothers, or the psychological shame of women who do not conform to the American motherhood ideal? Gilman's position on an androcentric culture resonates despite her inadequate treatment of difference, which I believe can stand theoretically in alliance with Patricia Hill Collins and Smith if we simply expand our theory to include them. Drawing a broad connective stroke such as this, while linking the long-standing history of women's struggles for equality, is essential within the context of women and mother's contemporary issues.

In personal terms, I was "socialized as a servant" to the household (Gilman 290). Despite very visual, prominent, and loud performances outside the home, my experience within the home was one of service for sexuo-economic security. In modern terms, I was compromised because of my lifestyle. This is the only way I can account for the gross imbalance of power relations within my family and the lack of equitable ownership I had within my own so-called partnership. But let me not stand alone in this. In my experience, American suburbs are filled with women who have left their Mac-mansions behind for tiny apartments and the serenity that comes with not being subjected to domination or violence and the prosperity that accompanies the vague notion of one's own integrity. It is clear that forms of social imbalance are still at work in the domestic sphere. Looking at the larger economic picture can help us to understand how music, motherhood, and feminism fit together.

Music and money go way back. According to David Suisman, the ephemeral nature of the parlor piano was tidily replaced in the late 1800s and transformed into a commodification by the wily likes of the early sheet music tradesman of Tin Pan Alley. Ironically the period from 1880 to 1930 coincides with the first wave of American feminism (the original suffragettes) and the Hollywood star system (Suisman 128). It is not a stretch to observe the ways in which the artist becomes much less important than his or her ability to sell and promote the product. Suisman acknowledges how "the contours of American consumer society became clear in the early twentieth century" and that "access to goods could be equated with the expansion of American democracy" (123). Suisman's treatment of Black Swan Records closely parallels my own experience with the music industry and Mamapalooza. Black Swan engaged in a "radical attempt to confront, challenge, and disrupt the invisibility of the modern music industry" (205). The label was the first label formed by African Americans making black music and selling to black audiences. It was a political statement as much as an artistic one and it was focused on calling on Americans to think about their consumerism. Harry Pace, the founder of Black Swan, understood "social relations and the distribution of power in society" (qtd. in Suisman 238), and Suisman points to Pace's use of branding, music, and activism in the following way: "the meaning of music depended not just on what was recorded but also which messages were associated with those recordings" (238). Pace was experimenting with complex interdependencies that constitute the human economy, not just the financial economy. He was unsuccessful. The story of Black Swan Records is one of a small company, with a vision, getting swallowed by its own attempts at integrity. The bigger labels won the business, and Black Swan folded.

I saw music as a vehicle for questioning the status quo, and as with Pace, I believed that by establishing mother-made, mother-organized, mother-branded music, women would find ownership and empowerment outside an industry that marginalized them. We would make the product. We would produce the venues. We would buy the product from each other. We would claim empowerment. What I did not understand was how quickly appearances on TV and meetings in Hollywood enticing me to become the next reality star would become co-opted into the existing entertainment system. A book by A.M. Collins and Chad Henry called *The Angry Housewives* was produced at the Minetta Lane Theatre in New York City on 7 September 1986. So the theme of housewives was not revolutionary, but the concept of women self-identifying as a mom rocker was. The meetings in Hollywood that ensued with Freemantle Media, Spielberg Offices, and Nickelodeon, and the countless lunches with independent producer and writers resulted in *The Real Housewives* (franchise) and *Rita Rocks* (the ill-fated, ill-conceived TV show). Next was *Motherhood* the movie, starring Uma Thurman (2009). The film leveraged my Mamapalooza festival brand. Uma's character participates in the Mamapalooza contest to become a writer. The producers did not contact me, consult me, or pay me. Corporate capitalism won. It swallowed my mom-movement whole, and is still putting it to use today to make money using the mom brand to sell everything from diapers to sex (just Google "sexy mommies" if you dare).

Hester Eisenstein's book *Feminism Seduced* and Barbara Katz Rothman's book *Recreating Motherhood* further substantiate the capitalist consumer narrative in two primary ways. First, Eisenstein identifies the permeating qualities of neo-liberal capitalism and illustrates the ways in which the feminist movement has more or less been duped into adopting lifestyles within the same system they fought against; and second, Rothman connects patriarchy and capitalism to a universal view of women as disposable producers within a society that fundamentally commodifies life (20). In both these scenarios, some truly new and revolutionary advocacy is required. As Eisenstein asks, "is there a way to decouple modernity from capitalism" (201)? The democratizing features of capitalism—at least as it was first presented in the discussions of Westernizing the world and the "modernization of women, linked to having economic independence, getting married later, and changing attitudes about sex" (Eisenstein 20)—still leaves open the question of how women who are mothers and are engaged in performing motherhood affected, moved, and ultimately changed by these developments. I posit that perhaps this happens through a slow shift. But the deep and abiding connection of the woman to her role and to her child complicates all of these issues in ways that remain largely outside, or more accurately inside, a larger worldview.

From a sociological perspective, motherhood was invented and continues to serve the society in which it exists. In plain terms, we do not really care very much about empowering mothers. But, from a consumer perspective, we care a great deal. Mothers are important as shoppers and as products to be consumed by others, including children and fathers. The ways in which notions of activism and agency have been co-opted by brands confuse people into the symbiotic interplay of shopping for a cause. How can it be that a contemporary "Gap Mom" finds agency by wearing rock star jeans, or how are "Wal-Mart employees and customers attain[ing] an experience of national belonging simply by shopping and working in the store" (Moreton 3)?

The consumer culture in which we live pervades all aspects of our daily lives. Along with the rise of the mother identity, there also arose more and more marketing agencies specifically targeting mothers. The prevalence of leveraging the motherhood identity for the purposes of marketing, consumerism, and capital is evidenced in three examples presented here: the case of BSM Media, the Marketing 2 Moms Conference, and contemporary marketing research.

The marketing and media firm BSM Media headed by Maria Bailey has developed multiple media properties, such as Mom Talk Radio, Mommy Parties, Moms Nite, which collect data on mothers as consumers and exploits the relationship between brands and mothers as consumers. According to BSM, selling to millennial mothers is a $750 billion industry per year ("About," BSMMedia).

The annual Marketing 2 Moms Conference, founded by PME Enterprises, connects Fortune 500 companies with advertising agencies that target mothers. PME has been in the business of events focused on advertising for thirty years but got into the business of motherhood with the M2Moms conference in 2005. The Marketing 2 Moms website claims that the organization is intensively and aggressively engaged in activities that leverage the mother identity into marketing strategies: "Highlights include case studies and how-to sessions on topics such as media, creative, research, packaging, purchasing habits and point-of-sale interaction" ("About," M2Moms.).

As for market research, a white paper report issued by the business analytics magazine *Advertising Age* and sponsored by the Meredith Corporation details how marketing to women is nothing new (Mack and Miley), but the point is the ways in which "empowerment" is sold through products:

> In 1968, Philip Morris introduced a new product line to the market: Virginia Slims, the slender "cigarette for women only." To promote the line, Philip Morris built on the energy of second-wave feminism and cleverly co-opted much of the movement's language. The result: "You've come a long way, baby," a powerful and long lasting advertising campaign that juxtaposed photographic images of the inhibited, unhappy women of yesteryear with the liberated, empowered women of the day. More than 40 years later, American women have come an even longer way. They are highly educated in greater numbers than ever before; they are working professionals climbing the ranks; they are the privileged product of generations of women who have fought for equality in and outside the home. Yet as much as they have changed, in many ways they are the same. Today's woman is still the designated chief operating officer of the home. (Mack and Miley)

The insidious ways in which progressive identities continue to evolve and become bonded with consumer culture can be difficult to discern. While at the helm of a mom rock revolution, I too was complicit in helping to promote identity through consumerism before I clearly understood the direction in which these initiatives were leading.

Between 2004 and 2006, I worked with Dove on their campaign for "real beauty" as part of both the Mamapalooza Festival and *Mamazina Magazine*. I appeared in eBay ads touting "Life is Good" and Dixie Campaigns that confused my personal story with the paper product. In my own way, I became part of the system that I was railing against because I lacked the kind of critical thinking and sociological understanding necessary to separate myself from the American construct of which I was a participant. Although I was able to draw the line at McDonald's giving product samples away at Mamapalooza family festivals, other things were not so clear. What was clear, and is still clear to me today, is the ways that consumer culture imposes itself on every facet of American life, including creativity, activism, and identity.

Throughout this chapter I have searched for ways to position mom rockers within the cultural landscape to interpret their contributions. My argument poses their legacy as instrumental. They were a visible presence in the national consciousness and paved the way toward new constructions of mother identities. These mother identities contributed to the field of mother studies as a multidisciplinary approach to understanding the human motherhood experience as well as the issues mothers face. This still stands, but the metamorphosis is ongoing.

I have traced the co-option of the mother identity in corporate, capitalist terms, and used such books as Hester Eisenstein's *Feminism Seduced* to tease out an explanation for what happened to mom rock. I have also highlighted germane aspects of mother identity today—either situated in the academy or in its position within the greater landscape of our consumer society. Some mother-identified groups continue the good work of a noncorporatized ideology and are making inroads in the academy and beyond. Moms Rising continues its national grass roots activism working toward political change. Advocating for paid parental leave, improved family health care, and advancing the cause for equal pay, the group's platform is significant. Publications that challenge the status quo include the following: *Brainchild Magazine*, *Mutha Magazine*, and *Literary Mama*. However, questions remain about the financial viability of these endeavours.

What is important to emphasize is the notion of how unaware

many of us are to the forces acting upon us. Every person, especially every woman and certainly every mother, should have access to tools that open her eyes to the issues of class, race, gender, and consumerism so that she can raise her children accordingly. My original attraction to music and its ephemeral qualities is longstanding. In larger philosophical terms, I have been comfortable with qualities of performance, festivals, and human interactions regarding a lifelong career in music. However, I now understand the significance of legitimized, academic works resulting in language and text that gives access to those wishing to explore the history, sociology, psychology, art, and cultural significance of motherhood. Therefore, I have transitioned from a career in music to a career on the page. It is in this place that I consider a hopeful future, buoyed up by the academy, its resources, and its potential to impact young minds. By way of a postscript, it is important for me to share what I have learned. I currently see the most promising outcome for a modern motherhood movement within the sphere of education. Advocating for mother studies within the academy is a practical way to change attitudes as well as influence young women's and men's preconceptions: the goal of which is a more enhanced, better-educated life experience. In addition to that, I remain committed to holding a physical space where mother arts, books, and history can be archived. Therefore, the Museum of Motherhood remains at the forefront of my personal ensuing practical activity alongside writings, such as the one contained in this edited collection for Demeter Press.

ENDNOTES

[1]Slavery can be perpetuated through emotional and physical violence within the domestic sphere. In the 1800s, Harriet Martineau describes the indulgences of women by men as a "substitute for justice" (qtd. in Lengermann and Niebrugge 38).

[2]*Shut Up and Drive* was a rock musical written by Martha Joy Rose and performed by Martha Joy Rose with Housewives on Prozac throughout New York City. It premiered at The School House Theater in Croton Falls, NY and opened their 1998 season. *The Housewife's Lament* was written and performed by Martha

Joy Rose and Housewives on Prozac intermittently throughout New York City from 2001 to 2005 and debuted at the Duplex in Greenwich Village.

[3]For much of the vocabulary of this section, including the crucial term "mother studies," I draw on my earlier work presented in Rose, *The Journal of Mother Studies*, where I argue for the use of this vocabulary against alternatives that have been proposed.

WORKS CITED

"About." *BSM Media*. 2016, www.bsmmedia.com/about/. Accessed 17 Nov. 2017.

"About." *Mamapalooza*. mamapalooza.wordpress.com/about/. Accessed 17 Nov. 2017.

"About." *m2moms*. 2016, www.m2moms.com/about/. Accessed 17 Nov. 2017.

"Action Alerts." *mom-mentum*. 2016, action.mom-mentum.org/. Accessed 17 Nov. 2017.

Brenner, Johanna. *Women and the Politics of Class*. New York: Monthly Review Press, 2000.

Collins, A.M., and Chad Henry. *The Angry Housewives*. Samuel French, 1983.

Collins, Patricia Hill. *Black Feminist Thought: Knowledge, Consciousness, and the Politics of Empowerment*. Routledge, 2000.

Davids, Judy. *Rock Star Mommy: Motherhood, Music and Life as a Rocker Mom*. Citadel Press, 2008.

Davis, Cynthia J. *Charlotte Perkins Gilman: A Biography*. Stanford University Press, 2010.

Della Cava, Marco R. "The Bands That Rock the Cradle." *USA Today*, 31 Jan. 2005, www.usatoday.com/staff/1005/marco-della-cava/. Accessed 17 Nov. 2017.

Eisenstein, Hester. *Feminism Seduced: How Global Elites Use Women's Labor and Ideas to Exploit the World*. Paradigm Publishers, 2009.

Evans, Carol. *This Is How We Do It: The Working Mothers' Manifesto*. London Penguin Group, 2006. Print.

Fabisch, Sue. "Walmart Woman." *Music 4 Mommies Vol. 1, Songs to Make You Laugh*. Mommy Music Inc., 2007.

Falassi, Alessandro. "Festival: Definition and Morphology." *Time out of Time: Essays on the Festival*, edited by Alessandro Falassi, University of New Mexico Press, 1987.

"Get the Facts." *National Museum of Women in the Arts*, nmwa. org/advocate/get-facts. Accessed 17 Nov. 2017.

Gilman, Charlotte Perkins. *Suffrage Songs and Verses*. The Charlton Company, 1911.

Gilman, Charlotte Perkins. *Women and Economics: A Study of the Economic Relation netween Men and Women*. Small, Maynard & Co., 1898.

Ginsburg, Carlo. *The Cheese and the Worms: The Cosmos of a Sixteenth-Century Miller*. Translated by Anne C. Tedeschi, Johns Hopkins University Press, 1992.

Hanauer, Cathi, editor. *The Bitch in the House: 26 Women Tell the Truth About Sex, Solitude, Work, Motherhood, and Marriage*. W.W. Norton, 2003.

Hershenson, Roberta. "Band Sings What It's Like to Raise a Family in the Nineties." *New York Times*, 9 Nov. 1997, www.nytimes. com/1997/11/09/nyregion/band-sings-about-what-it-s-like-to-raise-a-family-in-the-90-s.html. Accessed 17 Nov. 2017.

Keates, Nancy. "Mommie Loudest-Now Rocking: It's Your Mother, Singing of Suburban Angst; An Ode to Uneaten Spaghetti." *Wall Street Journal*, 25 June 2004.

Kinser, Amber E. *Motherhood and Feminism*. Seal Press, 2010.

Kinser, Amber E. *Mothering in the Third Wave*. Demeter Press, 2008.

"Learn." *The Rock & Roll Hall of Fame*, www.rockhall.com/learn. Accessed 17 Nov. 2017.

Lengermann, Patricia Madoo, and Gillian Niebrugge. *The Women Founders: Sociology and Social Theory 1830-1930, A Text/Reader*. Waveland Press, 2007.

Mack, Ann, and Marissa Miley. "The New Female Consumer: The Rise of the Real Mom." Advertising Age, 2017, adage.com/trend-reports/report.php?id=10. Accessed 17 Nov. 2017.

McRobbie, Angela. "Smug Shots." *The Guardian*, 29 Mar. 2003, www.theguardian.com/books/2003/mar/29/highereducation. news1. Accessed 17 Nov. 2017.

Moreton, Bethany. *To Serve God and Wal-Mart: The Making of*

Christian Free Enterprise. Harvard University Press, 2010.

Motherhood: New York. Directed by Katherine Dieckmann, John Wells Productions, 2009.

O'Reilly, Andrea, editor. *Encyclopedia of Motherhood.* Sage, 2011.

O'Reilly, Andrea, editor. *Maternal Theory: Essential Readings.*: Demeter Press, 2007.

O'Reilly, Andrea, editor. *The 21st Century Motherhood Movement: Mothers Speak Out on Why We Need to Change the World and How to Do It.* Demeter Press, 2011.

O'Reilly, Andrea, and Sharon Abbey, editors. *Redefining Motherhood Changing: Identities and Patterns.* Toronto: Second Story Press, 1998.

"Research." *Working Mother,* 2017, www.workingmother.com/about-us. Accessed 17 Nov. 2017.

Rojas, Eunice, and Lindsay Michie, editors. *Sounds of Resistance: The Role of Music in Multicultural Activism.* ABC-CLIO, 2013.

Rose, Martha Joy. *The Journal of Mother Studies: A Peer Reviewed, International, Interdisciplinary, Open-Access, Digital Humanities Hybrid Project.* MA thesis, the CUNY Graduate Center, *2015.*

Rose, Martha Joy. *No Prescription Required.* Housewives on Prozac, CD Baby, 1998.

Rothman, Barbara Katz. *Recreating Motherhood.* Penguin Books, 1989.

Ruddick, Sara. *Maternal Thinking: Toward a Politics of Peace.* Beacon Press, 1989.

Sandberg, Sheryl. *Lean In: Women, Work, and the Will to Lead.* Alfred A. Knopf, 2013.

Smith, Dorothy E. *The Everyday World as Problematic: A Feminist Sociology.* Northeastern University Press, 1987.

Suisman, David. *Selling Sounds: The Commercial Revolution in American Music.* Harvard University Press, 2009.

Whiteley, Sheila. *Women and Popular Music: Sexuality, Identity and Subjectivity.* Routledge, 2000.

"2017 Online Media Kit." *Working Mother,* www.workingmother.com/working-mother-media-kit-2016. Accessed 17 Nov. 2017.

13.
Closing Reflections

LYNDA ROSS AND JENNIFER HARTMANN

The co-editors opened this collection with Jennifer Hartmann's personal reflections about the ways in which music and dance profoundly impacted her pregnancy and labour experiences. Hartmann's practices as a mother who bellydanced through pregnancy and labour in concert with her background as a professional musician, music manager, and ethnomusicologist, coincided in a fascination with the ways in which mothering and motherhood can be deeply related to music and how "musicking" can affect one's identity and practice as a mother, and vice versa. Martha Joy Rose—president and founder of Mamapalooza Inc., founding director of the Museum of Motherhood, and award-winning artist, performer, activist, scholar—and mother has long realized that music not only "feed[s] her soul" but also that struggles surrounding what it means to mother and "musick" can only be resolved through "expressing them—in popular culture, the arts and in academia, which lays the foundation through research and legitimizes the discussion" (Gordon). Lynda Ross—a women's and gender studies professor with research interests grounded in motherhood studies, a mother of two creative children, and a founding volunteer member of the Rose City Roots Music Society in Alberta—came into this project as a listener with only a vague appreciation of the critical role music may play in relation to mothering. In short, all three co-editors were fascinated by the topic and this fascination, we hope, is reflected for the readers in the *Music of Motherhood* collection. It might have appeared to some of our readers that the ideas expressed by the contributors to this collection seemed disparate, coming from a group of authors with diverse and varied backgrounds. Although each of the authors approached the relationships between music and motherhood in different ways, we trust that upon finishing the text that you reached conclusions similar to ours. The ideas presented in these chapters can be drawn together with one common thread—music matters in the lives of children and mothers and it matters in so many different and complex ways. Some of the ways in which music matters are captured by the three broad content areas we outlined in the opening chapter for this collection: first, it matters in terms of transmission and what music contributes to the everyday lives of mothers and children; second, the therapeutic value of music promotes the physical and mental wellbeing of mothers and their children; and third, music has the capability to incite positive social change for mothers. Through juxtaposing music with mothering in these ways, this collection adds to a growing body of literature informing the practice of mothering and theory surrounding mother studies. It does so through the unique lens of music in ways that both confirm our understandings of the complexities that surround mothering in contemporary societies and through insights into the ways in which music and mothering co-exist.

The overwhelming presence of music in our day-to-day lives verifies philosopher Friedrich Nietzche's statement that "Without music, life would be a mistake" (qtd. in Jaupi). Music surrounds us—as we work, shop, play, relax, and parent. At times, we are its passive recipient, and at other times, we actively seek out music through electronic sources, live performances, and in musical performance of our own (Wann). Many of us spend countless hours discussing music with others, and sharing our favourite songs and melodies with loved ones and friends and sometimes even with strangers. We use music for many different reasons: sometimes to calm ourselves and at other times to arouse our senses. For those of us old enough to remember, in the mid-1960s, there was in many households a Sunday evening tradition of family members gathering together to watch the Ed Sullivan Show. For young teenagers, this was an event that sometimes resulted in putting up with parental criticism, as such groups as the Doors, the Beatles, and the Rolling Stones made their debut on black and white screens across North America. We were exhilarated by the "live" performances, although not all parents shared the same excitement with listening to our music. And for many of us whose musical preferences were awakened during those years and who became mothers a decade or so later, and perhaps as a consequence of our experience with parental derision, were more tolerant of our own children's musical choices. Nonetheless, we were often delighted when our prodigy announced with excitement their discovery of "new" bands: the Beatles, the Doors, or the Rolling Stones! There was, and remains today, a joy in the mutual sharing of our music with our children as well as sharing theirs with us.

MOTHERING WITH MUSIC

Clearly, there can be great enjoyment in the sharing of music between mothers and children. Beyond the delights of a common bond formed between mother and child in sharing musical preferences, something much larger transpires from these experiences. Interactions, musical, or otherwise, between parents and children play a critical role in relation to developing children's higher order functions (Pitt and Hargreaves). Music, specifically, promotes the development of these skills through enhancing spatial-temporal reasoning, encouraging early word use, increasing socioemotional development, aiding achievements in fundamental motor skills, benefitting attentional control, and contributing to general improvements in IQ scores (Bond; Hallberg, Martin, and McClure; Pitt and Hargreaves). Although some research has shed light on the outcomes of shared musical interactions in terms of child development, there is little published work assessing the mechanisms surrounding the transmission of musical tastes from one generation to another. Jillian Bracken (chapter two in this collection) examines the ways in which intergenerational transmission actually occurs in families and the specific roles filled by each family member. Adding to the body of literature assessing the benefits of musical mothering, Bracken finds that "music listening and talk about music are vital components of each family's music script." Discourse surrounding music is used as a mechanism to transmit not only values about music but family values more generally. Through her study of the ways in which families engage with music, Bracken moves the discussion forward by identifying the specific processes facilitating the intergenerational transmission of knowledge and values. Parents use music as part of their spectrum of care and socialization strategies to scaffold learning activities as well as to mother (Bond; Bracken). As such, great benefit comes to both children and mothers through their individual and collaborative musicking efforts, formal and informal, from infancy through to adulthood.

In looking at other factors associated with the musicking practice that transpires between the generations, Rena Upitis et al., in contrast to the informal "moments" described by Bracken, have examined the ways in which parents involve themselves in their children's formal, studio musical education. Parents were deeply invested in their children's musical education. But Upitas and colleagues also highlight how "this dedication is reflected in years of commitment they make to supporting music learning, the active and thoughtful roles they take in supporting their children's evolution as self-regulating musicians, and the respect they hold for the teachers of their children" (84). Although support behaviour changes as children mature, for many parents, support over the years "remain[s] stable throughout their children's musical studies" (Upitas et al. 85).

Sally Savage and Clare Hall (chapter three in this collection) provide further detail, through the voices of mothers engaged with their children's formal music education, about the ways in which participating in their children's early years music classes enriches family life, advantages children educationally, and also contributes to mothers' wellbeing and the fulfillment of their desires as individuals. Given the level of involvement of mothers in their children's formal music education, Hall and Savage's study of musical mothering "complicates the construction of intensive mothering." While much has been written about the costs to women of adopting intensive mothering ideologies (Green and Groves; Liss et al., Warner), Savage and Hall confound this discussion with their findings that involvement in children's music education provides mothers with many benefits, despite the huge investment in mothers' time and energy.

Children are encouraged by parents to participate in musical programs and to play musical instruments for a variety of reasons, including forging family cohesion and fostering family identities (Reeves). Whereas Bracken highlights the mechanisms of transmission and Savage and Hall interrogate a theoretical conflict between intensive mothering as a general ideology and intensive mothering as it applies specifically to musical mothering, Lydia Bringerud (chapter four in this collection) through her ethnographic writing about her observations of the St. John's Ukulele Club brings another perspective to the discussion of musical mothering and the transmission of musical values. As Bringerud highlights, reflections about potentially complex relationships between mothers and music can arise out of unusual circumstances. She talks about the conscious decision she made not to follow in her mother's footsteps as a professional musician because of the "emotional baggage" she carried that originated from her family of origin. Contrasting her sometimes fraught musical experiences in childhood—in which perfection was idealized—with the joyful, inviting, and spontaneous experiences offered by the St. John's Ukulele Club, she concludes her reflective journey with a deeper understanding of what becoming involved with a group that shares both music and laughter means. Whereas other authors in this collection (Bracken; Savage and Hall) and outside of this collection (Liss et al.) have focused largely on the positive aspects of mothers' involvement with early childhood music listening and practice, both for themselves and for their children, Bringerud adds a sombre insider perspective. It is also important to acknowledge that while mothers may desire to use music as a mechanism to cultivate shared musicality in their children (Reeves), the outcome may not always be the one that is desired or intended.

THERAPEUTIC VALUE OF MUSIC IN PREGNANCY, BIRTHING, AND POSTPARTUM

There are many examples in the literature showing the benefits of music in relation to mothering. The chapters in this section of the collection both highlight some of the published research findings as well as provide fresh perspectives on the benefits of music and singing during pregnancy, childbirth, and postpartum. Cara-Leigh Battaglia (chapter five in this collection) acknowledges how "science is beginning to verify that music has a healing effect on medical and emotional damage to body, mind, and heart [whereas] mothers have instinctively been using it to foster social and emotional healing." She goes on to describe the therapeutic value of music in the lives of adoptive mothers who use music as an effective tool for the healing the emotional and social trauma foster children have been subjected to.

In looking at music in relation to childbearing, like other researchers, Caroline Martin concludes that "music has immutable capacity to influence how childbearing women and neonates feel and has the capacity to improve their physical well-being" (265). Some of the specific areas related to pregnancy and childbirth where music has been shown to promote wellbeing includes the reducing of maternal stress and anxiety, enhancing the mood of childbearing and postnatal women, and reducing the pain women experience during labour. In an experimental study, Hsing-Chi Chang et al. find significantly lower levels of psychosocial stress in their experimental group (those listening to music and receiving prenatal care) as compared to the control group (those receiving prenatal care only), particularly in relation to stresses surrounding baby care, changing family relationships, and maternal role identification. Serap Simavli et al. similarly find that women assigned to a music therapy group—listening to self-selected music during labour—experienced lower levels of postpartum pain and less anxiety during labour than did the group who did not listen to music during labour.

Ilona Demecs, et al. also find that participation in a music group not only provides women with social support but enhances their perceptions of emotional wellbeing during pregnancy. They highlight the fact that singing was identified by some participants because "it facilitated the most obvious communication with the baby" (115). Amanda Mehl West (chapter six in this collection) also looks at the ways in which singing eases women's transition in motherhood. In examining the origins of the practice and benefits of "prenatal singing" and at the current growing trend of professionals incorporating song into their work with prenatal, birthing, and postpartum women, West notes how "it is obvious that song and singing connect mind, body, and spirit, which helps to ease the sometimes painful, sometimes terrifying, and always incredible, transition into motherhood." West's work, like others summarized in this section, shows the power of music in women's transition to motherhood. Elena Skoko (chapter seven in this collection) discusses the ways in which "voice is a powerful tool during childbirth." She talks about the intimate connections between "voice" and "yoni." Both West and Skoko celebrate the freedom that this knowledge provides women and those involved with the birthing experience. As Skoko notes at the outset of her chapter "singing during childbirth has still to be addressed properly as a beneficial and powerful practice used by women and by traditionally and medically trained midwives and obstetrician-gynecologists who provide maternity assistance today." Both West and Skoko acknowledge the potential for a deeper understanding of the relationship between song and birthing to foster women's empowerment and to allow women to reclaim their birthing experience.

MOTHERS MAKING MUSIC

The first two sections of this collection highlight what music contributes to the everyday lives of mothers and children and the therapeutic value of music in promoting the physical and mental wellbeing of mothers and their children. Exploring relationships between mothering and music takes another turn in the final section of this collection, which looks specifically at musical mothers and how they use feminist ideologies to actively inform and promote social change. In 1991, the Feminist Theory and Music Conference held their first biannual meeting opening up "popular music as a recognized and even desirable area of expertise" (McClary 89). The 1990s onward saw an increase in the number of award-winning female singer songwriters. Since that time, "feminist music studies have made astonishing progress" (McClary 88). Popular music become legitimate terrain for scholarly research, as many factors contributed to its legitimization, the influence of Christopher Small's notion of "musicking," which allowed a "swerve toward sociological models" (McClary 90) and the increasing importance of interdisciplinarity as a focus in academic disciplines. These two aspects are present inside this collection. Rachelle Louise Barlow's discussion of Clara Novello Davies (chapter eight in this collection) begins with an acknowledgment that "although women in Welsh history have received increasing attention in recent decades, the participation of women in music remains underexplored." Barlow challenges the paternal perspective that is often used to represent Wales through her examination of Novello Davies and the success she brought to the Royal Welsh Ladies Choir. She documents the life of Novello Davies, noting that despite her pioneering leadership as a musician and choir master, her "longstanding musical career is often overshadowed by her son, composer Ivor Novello." Barlow interrogates paternalism and by doing so helps to restore women's place in history by displacing sole notions of "land of my fathers." She highlightes the relevance of women and women's contributions, and describes Wales appropriately as "land of my mothers."

There are other ways in which music and musicians become instrumental in shifting paradigms. Damris Parsitau, for example, interrogates the role of gospel music and dance as a medium for sociopolitical change and reform in Kenya. Because both music and dance play powerful communicative roles in invoking emotion, songs have historically provided support for democratization. Parsitau argues that "music, whether gospel or secular is a dynamic and highly charged force that affects other aspects of life such as democracy, economic growth, empowerment" (55). Similar to Parsitau's analysis, David Eichert (chapter nine in this collection) looks at the important role of the creation of a Chicano and Chicana identity. He looks specifically at the songs and lyrics of Las Cafeteras and the ways the group uses its music to address the violence and discrimination faced by mothers on both sides of the Mexican-American border. Music, in this instance, serves as a site of resistance and as a mechanism to "praise and honour the sacrifices made by mothers on both sides of the border." In a similar way Elizabeth Keenan highlights the band Sublime's "Date Rape" as a song that "plays out over a catchy, major-key, ska-punk rhythm that emphasizes the upbeat and lacks a sense of foreboding" (108). The song tells following story:

A blond-haired, blue-eyed man with a double chin [who] approaches a woman in a bar and, after a few drinks, convinces her to leave with him. When she tries to escape, he rapes her. Nowell [band's singer] sings, quoting the rapist, "If it wasn't for date rape, I'd never get laid." From there, the tale becomes one of retribution: the woman goes to the police, who believe her; the rapist is prosecuted and convicted; finally, he's sentenced to twenty-five years in prison and, in the song's punchline, he becomes a victim of rape himself. (108)

Keenan credits, in part, such music's influence on moving conversations about sexual assault forward. "Understanding that the history of these debates was deeply enmeshed with popular music serves as a reminder that musical texts form an important element of the public sphere" (Keenan 115).

Karen Dubinksy describes Telmary Diaz as "among the many women who have pushed against the formidable patriarchal walls of Cuban music" (221). Diaz sees her music as a continuation of the work of her mother, a journalist, who died tragically when Telmary was eight years old. In her own words, Diaz describes the intense relationship she had with her mother: "Between husbands she was a single mom and I had to go with her everywhere. And even when she remarried, wherever she went I went with her. I say this because, of course, there is something about writing that is close to me. I remember my mom being at her old typewriter, writing, writing, writing throughout the night. She would kiss me goodnight and then I'd listen to the tic tic tic of her typing as I was falling asleep" (qtd. in Dubinsky 224).

Jackie Weissman (chapter ten in this collection) challenges stereotypical images of "sex- and drug-fuelled rock stars" as being diametrically opposed to stereotypical images of the good mother. She examined the lives of three rockers—Ms. Su'ad, Kristin Hersh, and Zia McCabe—and their struggles to balance children with their art. Although each musician's path in moving toward balance was different, Weissman learns that regardless of their musical styles, career paths, and economic circumstances, each woman was both a dedicated mother and musician.

Unlike the musicians studied by Weissman, who were both musicians and mothers, Lori Walters-Kramer (chapter eleven in this collection) explores motherhood through the music of Michelle Shocked, who was not a mother, but imbedded mothering and motherhood into her writing. Walters-Kramer highlights in her chapter the ways in which lyrics can be a vehicle for maternal discourses, regardless of the maternal status of the musician, and to share political views. Martha Joy Rose (chapter twelve in this collection) also interrogates the ways in which the mom rock movement awakened mothers to their individuality and creativity. Rose's work addresses the persistent nature of many women's issues, including the continued marginalization of mothers. She makes a strong argument for electric music as a medium for expression and for the creation of a mother culture. Regardless of the social, political, or economic cause being addressed, all of these authors in this collection and in the literature more broadly show the ways in which musicians and music are powerful tools for informing change.

POLITICS, MOTHERING, AND MUSICKING

There is no doubt that when music and mothering combine the benefits afforded to both mothers and their children are multifaceted. At a broader level, music serves as a way to bind movements and to support social and political change. Throughout the collection, we have seen the positive role that music can play in the lives of mothers and children as well as the concrete benefits that result from participation in musical mothering. In one sense, music is free: regardless of social and economic positioning, all mothers can listen, can sing, can share, and can reap the benefits of music for themselves and for their children. In another sense, however, freedom is informed by knowledge and by access; in this sense, many women and their children will be denied the benefits of music as a mode for sharing family values, as a primary source of children's education, as a way to unite mothers, and to give rise to social change. It is a fact that women form the overwhelming majority of the world's poor. So it should not be surprising that poverty also affects huge numbers of children every year, not only

in nonindustrialized nations but in some of the wealthiest industrialized nations in the world. For example, one in five children in
the U.S. face poverty in any given year; in Canada, close to one in
ten children under the age of eighteen live in low-income families
(Ross 81). Furthermore, single mothers and women from racial
minorities in the U.S. and Indigenous populations in Canada are
disproportionately represented among the poorest citizens of these
wealthy countries. The effects of poverty are intensified for those
living in nations where income disparities between the rich and the
poor are at their greatest. Wealth inequality in the U.S. remains
at a historic high, "with some estimates suggesting that the top
1% of Americans hold nearly 50% of the wealth" (Norton and
Ariely 9). Poverty for mothers manifests itself in a reduction in
quality of life—exemplified by food and housing insecurity, higher
morbidity rates, increases in mental and physical health issues, and
vulnerability to violence (Ross). Although poverty imposes itself
on persons, poverty is not a personal issue.

Social, economic, and political structures inform and define
poverty in Western industrialized nations; the structural nature of
poverty calls for socially responsible, government-funded solutions
to the elimination of poverty for all. Middle-class parents spend
a great deal of time, energy, and money in cultivating children's
artistic talents and their cognitive and social skills often through
leisure activities, including music lessons. For many working-class
and poor families the focus is often not on music but on feeding
and clothing children, where "sustaining children's natural growth
is viewed as an accomplishment" (Lareau 5). As a starting point
in examining equity in arts education in American schools, Ariana
Stokas has reviewed the 2012 National Center for Education Statistics report, which reports "a statistical equity-divide in access
to the arts" (140). Ironically, schools appeared to be forced into
choosing food to feed the soul or food to sustain the body; the report
shows that "the higher the percentage of students receiving free
and reduced lunch, the lower the percentage of students receiving
arts instruction" (Stokas 140). In light of this relationship "nearly
20% of the lowest income children in the United States receive no
education in music" (Stokas 140). Although in comparison to the
magnitude of the consequences of food and housing insecurity that

face mothers and children living in poverty, it may seem trivial to bring up discussions about the impact of cultural disparities between the middle class and the poor. But these inequities further lead to the transmission of differential advantages to children based on parental socioeconomic status (Lareau).

Depriving some children of music and education and providing it to others is yet another way to ensure the cycle of poverty will continue. Exposure to and participation in the arts have been shown to improve the wellbeing of individuals, unify communities, improve academic performance, strengthen economies, spark creativity, improve healthcare, and foster healing (Cohen). We have seen in the works of this collection the many important roles that music plays in the lives of mothers and children. Engaging in music in one form or another—dancing, singing, listening, or participating in any other passive or active act of "musicking"—can improve social understanding and appreciation of what motherhood is, and can build upon mothering strategies from conception through adulthood. Given the many benefits of music education, univer-sal delivery should be the only choice for governments to make. However, funding cuts threaten the integrity of arts and music programs (Livingstone). The remarkable correlation between music and motherhood suggests that although it may be easy to dismiss the funding of arts education because it could be seen as unnecessary, the reality is that by dismissing the value of arts and music education and by restricting national funding, the government is denying the fact that, in the words of President Johnson, "an advanced civilization needs to foster arts and culture with public support" (qtd. in Livingstone).

WORKS CITED

Bond, Vanessa. "Music's Representation in Early Childhood Edu-cation Journals: A Literature Review." *Update: Applications of Research in Music Education*, vol. 31, no. 1, 2012, pp. 34-43.

Chang, Hsing-Chi, et al. "The Effects of Music Listening on Psy-chosocial Stress and Maternal-Fetal Attachment during Preg-nancy." *Complementary Therapies in Medicine*, vol. 23, no. 4, 2015, pp. 509-15.

Cohen, Randy. "Top 10 Reasons to Support the Arts in 2017." *Arts-blog*, 14 Feb. 2017, blog.americansforthearts.org/2017/02/14/top-10-reasons-to-support-the-arts-in-2017. Accessed 17 Nov. 2017.

Demecs, Ilona, et al. "Women's Experiences of Attending a Creative Arts Program during Their Pregnancy." *Women and Birth*, vol. 24, no.3, 2011, pp. 112-21.

Dubinsky, Karen. "'Music is my Weapon': An Interview with Tel-mary Díaz." *Canadian Journal of Latin American and Caribbean Studies*, vol. 42, no. 2, 2017, pp. 221-41.

Gordon, Andrea. "What Motherhood Means and Why It Matters." *Toronto Star*, 5 May 2010, www.thestar.com/life/parent/2010/05/05/what_motherhood_means_and_why_it_matters.html. Accessed 17 Nov. 2017.

Green, Katherine, and Melissa Groves. "Attachment Parenting: An Exploration of Demographics and Practices." *Early Child Development and Care*, vol. 178, no. 5, 2008, pp. 513-25.

Hallberg, Karin, et al. "The Impact of Music Instruction on Attention in Kindergarten Children." *Psychomusicology: Music, Mind, and Brain*, vol. 27, no. 2, 2017, pp. 113-21.

Horowitz, Andy. "Who Should Pay for the Arts in America?" *The Atlantic*, 31 Jan. 2017, www.theatlantic.com/entertainment/archive/2016/01/the-state-of-public-funding-for-the-arts-in-america/424056/. Accessed 17 Nov. 2017.

Jaupi, Eriona. "Going into All That Treble: A Parent's Guide to Starting their Children on Music Lessons." *Open Music Library*, 2016, openmusiclibrary.org/article/52839/. Accessed 17 Nov. 2017.

Keenan, Elizabeth. "Asking for it: Rape, Postfeminism, and Alternative Music in the 1990s." *Women and Music: A Journal of Gender and Culture* 19 (2015): 108-15.

Lareau, Annette. *Unequal Childhoods: Class, Race, and Family Life*. University of California Press, 2003.

Liss, Miriam, et al. "Development and Validation of a Quantitative Measure of Intensive Parenting Attitudes." *Journal of Child and Family Studies*, vol. 22, no. 5, 2013, pp. 621-36.

Livingstone, Josephine. "Why Are Americans So Hostile to State-Funded Art?" *New Republic*, 26 May 2017, newrepublic.

com/article/142925/americans-hostile-state-funded-art. Accessed 17 Nov. 2017.

Martin, Caroline. "A Narrative Literature Review of the Therapeutic Effects of Music Upon Childbearing Women and Neonates." *Complementary Therapies in Clinical Practice*, vol. 20, 2014, pp. 262-67.

McClary, Susan. "Making Waves: Opening Keynote Twentieth Anniversary of the Feminist Theory and Music Conference." *Women and Music: A Journal of Gender and Culture*, vol. 16, 2012, pp. 86-96.

Norton, Michael, and Dan Ariely. "Building a Better America—One Wealth Quintile at a Time." *Perspectives on Psychological Science*, vol. 61, no. 1, 2011, pp. 9-12.

Parsitau, Damaris. "Sounds of Change and Reform: The Appropriation of Gospel Music and Dance in Political Discourses in Kenya." *Studies in World Christianity*, vol. 14, no. 1, 2008, pp. 55-72.

Pitt, Jessica, and David Hargreaves. "Attitudes Towards and Perceptions of the Rationale for Parent-Child Group Music Making with Young Children." *Music Education Research*, vol. 19, no. 3, 2017, pp. 292-308.

Reeves, Aaron. "'Music's a Family Thing': Cultural Socialisation and Parental Transference." *Cultural Sociology*, vol. 9, no. 4, 2015, pp. 493-514.

Ross, Lynda. *Interrogating Motherhood*. Athabasca University Press, 2016.

Simavli, Serap, et al. "Effect of Music Therapy during Vaginal Delivery on Postpartum Pain Relief and Mental Health." *Journal of Affective Disorders*, vol. 156, 2014, pp. 194-99.

Small, Christopher. *Musicking: The Meanings of Performing and Listening*. Wesleyan University Press, 1998.

Stokas, Ariana. "Letting All Lives Speak: Inequality in Art Education and Baumgarten's Felix Aestheticus." *Studies in Art Education: A Journal of Issues and Research*, vol. 57, no. 2, 2016, pp. 139-48.

Upitis, Rena, et al. "Parental Involvement in Children's Independent Music Lessons." *Music Education Research*, vol. 19, no. 1, 2017, pp. 74-98.

Wann, Jey. "Without Music, Life Would be a Mistake: What Oregon Library Employees Listen to at Work." *Outside the Lines: Creativity in Libraries*, vol. 20, no. 2, 2014, pp. 15-17.

Warner, Judith. "Is Too Much Mothering Bad For You? A Look at the New Social Science." *Virginia Quarterly Review*, vol. 88, no. 4, 2012, pp. 48-53.

About the Contributors

Rachelle Barlow received her PhD in ethnomusicology from Cardiff University (Wales, UK) in 2016. Her thesis examined constructions of gender and identity in relation to the development of the Welsh choral tradition in the late nineteenth century. In 2016, she was awarded a postdoctoral Cultural Engagement Fellowship from the Arts and Humanities Research Council (UK) to lead a multidisciplinary project at Cardiff University on conflict, creativity, and commemorations of the First World War, involving Welsh National Opera, National Museum Wales, and Somme100Film. Her current work explores the First World War efforts of Welsh musicians Clara Novello Davies and Ivor Novello, and music for healing in times of conflict.

Cara-Leigh Battaglia holds an MS in English/Composition from Radford University and a BA in English/Writing from Nazareth College. She is currently executive director of the National Math Foundation, Inc. in the U.S., and is a writer and consultant with thirty-two years of senior business administration experience. She has worked as an educator, executive, and therapeutic foster parent, and adopted a son who is the light of her life.

Jillian Bracken has aPhD in music education from the University of Western Ontario. She also holds an MM (ethnomusicology) and MS (education) from Florida State University, and a BM (honours, music education) from the University of Western Ontario. Her research interests include music listening in families and community music.

Lydia Bringerud is an American PhD candidate at Memorial University of Newfoundland in the Department of Folklore. Her dissertation addresses issues of authenticity, ethnicity, gender, and globalization in two Eastern Orthodox churches in the U.S. and Canada—one a majority-convert church and the other a majority of Orthodox-born immigrants.

David Eichert is a graduate student at New York University's Center for European and Mediterranean Studies, where he is specializing in the politics of gender and sexuality. He is a graduate of Brigham Young University and has also contributed a chapter to the Demeter Press book *Mothers in Conflict* (2015).

Clare Hall is lecturer in performing arts in the Faculty of Education at Monash University, Australia and leader of the Arts, Creativity, Education Faculty Research Group. Her research is located in the sociology of education and the creative arts, with a focus on music and intersectionality (gender, class, ethnicity, age). She brings together over twenty years of experience as a musician and music educator in her research and teaching. Her first book, *Masculinity, Class and Music Education*, is published by Palgrave (2017).

Jennifer Hartmann is an ethnomusicologist, violist, and liturgical vocalist who holds a BMus (history and literature) from Dalhousie University and a MA (musicology) from McGill University. She is currently a PhD candidate at Memorial University of Newfoundland, where her primary research involves the cultural study of wedding string quartets, with a focus on the occupational folklife of gigging musicians. She has also conducted research on the use of bellydance as a coping strategy during pregnancy and labour, inspired by her own experience as an amateur dancer. She lives in Iowa with her husband and two young daughters.

Lori Walters-Kramer is an assistant professor of communication studies at Monmouth College in Monmouth, Illinois. She earned her PhD from Bowling Green State University where her focus on feminist rhetoric, transformational pedagogies, and women's studies culminated in the dissertation *Performing Emancipatory*

Rhetorics: The Possibilities of Michelle Shocked's Musics, Discourses & Movements.

Martha Joy Rose is a musician, concert promoter, museum founder, and fine artist. Her work has been published across blogs and academic journals, and she has performed with her band Housewives On Prozac on Good Morning America, on CNN, and at the Oakland Art & Soul Festival to name a few. She is the NOW-NYC recipient of the Susan B. Anthony Award. Her Mamapalooza Festival Series has been recognized as "Best in Girl-Power Events" in New York, and her music has appeared on the Billboard Top 100 Dance Charts. She founded the Museum of Motherhood in 2003, created the Motherhood Foundation 501c3 nonprofit in 2005, and saw it flourish in NYC from 2011 to 2014. Her current live-work space in Kenwood St. Petersburg, Florida is devoted to the exploration of mother labour as performance art.

Lynda Ross is a professor of women's and gender studies in the Centre for Interdisciplinary Studies at Athabasca University in Alberta. She graduated with a doctoral degree in psychology from the University of New Brunswick in 1998. Lynda's research interests focus on the social construction of theory and psychological "disorder," attachment, and motherhood. Tying together these interests, her first book on the subject, *Interrogating Motherhood*, was published by the Athabasca University Press in December 2016.

Sally Savage is a PhD candidate at Monash University, Australia, completing her studies in the Faculty of Education. Her research interests centre on parental practices in relation to early years music. She is an early childhood educator who has worked in a range of educational settings in Australia and the UK. She has performed in musical theatre and opera, and for the last fifteen years, she has combined her teaching and musical expertise to facilitate early-years music classes.

Elena Skoko is a mother, singer, and advocate for human rights in childbirth. As founder of Singing Birth Workshops (www.singingbirth.com), she teaches the use of voice and creative power in childbirth and motherhood, empowering women in their inner ability to enjoy and give birth with a smile. She is a songwriter and front woman in Bluebird & Skoko blues band.

Jackie Weissman is an award-winning documentarian living in Portland, Oregon. She is a founding member and past president of Women in Film, Portland (2012 to 2014), and executive director of Oregon Doc Camp (2013)—a documentary retreat for seasoned filmmakers embarking on its fifth year. Her most recent film, *Rock N Roll Mamas* (2013), has screened worldwide.

Amanda Mehl West is an award-winning singer-songwriter, recording artist, music teacher, and mother. She is co-founder of Womb Song U.S., an organization that offers singing circles for pregnant women as well as labor and postpartum support through song. She holds a BA in cultural anthropology from the University of California, Santa Cruz, and understands music to be a part of our universal human birthright, and plays an essential role in our experience of being alive. She has trained with DONA (Doulas of North America) and lives her life at the intersection of music and motherhood.